W9-AKC-479

WITHDRAWN

down in houston

NUMBER EIGHT

Jack and Doris Smothers Series in Texas History, Life, and Culture

down in houston bayou city blues

BY ROGER WOOD   PHOTOGRAPHY BY JAMES FRAHER

University of Texas Press   Austin

library of congress cataloging-in-publication data

Wood, Charles Roger, 1956–
    Down in Houston : Bayou City Blues / by Roger Wood ; photogra-
phy by James Fraher.
       p.   cm. — (Jack and Doris Smothers series in Texas history,
life, and culture ; no. 8)
    Includes bibliographical references (p.   ) and indexes.
    ISBN 0-292-79159-3 (alk. paper)
     1. Blues (Music)—Texas—Houston—History and criticism.
2. Blues musicians—Texas—Houston.   I. Fraher, James.   II. Title.
III. Series.
    ML3521 .W66   2003
    781.643'09764'1411—dc21   2002010526

contents

acknowledgments

the writing of this book was supported by an Individual Artist Grant Award provided by the City of Houston through the Cultural Arts Council of Houston/Harris County.

Research and preliminary writing for this book were supported by a Sabbatical Leave Award provided by the Houston Community College System.

Portions of Chapters 2 through 6 incorporate passages excerpted from interviews or profiles previously published by the writer in *Arkansas Review, Houston Press, The Journal of Texas Music History,* and *Living Blues.*

A portion of profits realized by the writer from the sale of this book will be donated to two nonprofit organizations based in Houston: the Conrad Johnson Music and Fine Arts Foundation and the Musicians Benevolent Society of Houston.

Roger Wood and James Fraher wish to extend their special gratitude to the following people and institutions: Marla Bergquist Wood and Connie Scanlon for granting us time, space, and immeasurable support to pursue writing, photography, and music (and for letting James make Houston his second home); David Nelson, Scott Barretta, and *Living Blues* magazine for encouraging our collaboration; Dick Shurman and David Vest for invaluable advice on revision of the final manuscript; Central College of the Houston Community College System, especially Dean of Academics Cheryl Peters and other personnel who helped in the on-campus production of the reunion portrait event (and additional sessions), as well as colleagues in the English Department, particularly Alan Ainsworth, Linda Daigle, and Edwin Gallaher; Project Row Houses, especially Rick Lowe, Deborah Grotfeldt, and Andrew Malveaux; Reg Burns and the Cultural Arts Council of Houston/Harris County; Steve Sucher and the Musicians Benevolent Society of Houston; past and present members of the Houston Blues Society, especially Ed Berry, Diunna Greenleaf, Sandy Francis, Sheryl Liskow, Travis Peoples, and Russ and Cathy Setzekorn; KPFT Radio program hosts Kathleen Kern, Jo and James Vaughn (with Nancy McAfee), Nuri Nuri, Joe Montez, James Nagel, and Rick Mitchell; William Clements and the Delta Studies Symposium at Arkansas State University (the conference where we initially met in 1995); Carl Lindahl for insight and advice on collecting oral histories; Mack McCormick for inspiration; Chris Strachwitz for coming to Houston years ago with open eyes and ears and for sharing his memories; Eric LeBlanc for his encyclopedic command of dates; Bob Eagle for Lightnin' Hopkins data; Andrew Brown and Stephen Schneider for advice on recordings; *Houston Press* music editors, especially John Nova Lomax; Jim O'Neal and Cary Wolfson for bibliographic data; numerous business proprietors, but particularly Steve and Mike Butera of Butera's on Montrose (for hosting exhibitions and opening-night parties highlighting photographs from this project), Alfred and Curley Cormier of the Silver Slipper, Clarence and Wayne Davis of C. Davis Bar-B-Q, Bobby Lewis of Miss Ann's Playpen, Tom McLendon of the Big Easy, and Maxine Williams of El Nedo Cafe; and, of course, the many Bayou City blues people we interviewed and photographed, for sharing their songs, stories, and smiles—with extra special thanks to Kinney Abair, Johnny Brown, Eugene Carrier, Gloria Edwards, Grady Gaines, Earl Gilliam, I. J. Gosey, Clarence Green, John Green, Henry Hayes, Joe Hughes, Conrad Johnson, Evelyn Johnson, Jerry Lightfoot, Trudy Lynn, Pete Mayes, Eugene Moody, Robert Murphy, Jimmy Nelson, Calvin Owens, Teddy Reynolds, Sherman Robertson, and Robert Smith for providing us with many additional leads, uncommonly generous friendships, and uniquely helpful history lessons.

introduction

in an era in which some musicologists have perpetuated the generalization that blacks don't make blues music for black audiences anymore, there *are* exceptions. The Texas city of Houston has long maintained a tradition of blues performance as an African American community event—especially in the near-southeast area known as Third Ward, as well as in the near-northeast location called Fifth Ward and other places.

For the latter half of the twentieth century, Houston has been home to what the sociologist Robert D. Bullard has identified as perhaps "the largest black community in the South." More to the point, as David Nelson says in an editorial in *Living Blues* magazine, the city is also the birthplace for "some of the most significant developments in modern blues." What follows is an account, based on over 150 hours of tape-recorded oral histories and various other types of fieldwork and research, of what I have learned over the past two decades about the relationship between these two facts. At the start of the twenty-first century, the indigenous blues culture of Houston is still alive. This book seeks to explain, to some degree, how and why.

Especially in the twenty-five years or so following the end of World War II, Houston was a place where African American musicians created some of the most influential blues-based music ever played, ranging from the down-home sounds of Lightnin' Hopkins to the more refined orchestrations of the Duke-Peacock recording empire and beyond. In more recent times, the local blues community has had somewhat less impact on the rest of the world than before, but it has remained vital despite—or maybe because of—being largely self-contained. Now the fourth largest city in America, Houston today is one of the few places anywhere in which a person can regularly, practically any night of the week, find venues where blues is performed by talented practitioners who grew up with the music and call it their own.

The text that follows introduces you to people and places I have come to know, mainly during the 1990s, while researching the roots of Houston blues culture in black communities. These individuals and their old neighborhoods have graciously helped me to understand some of the past and present realities of the Bayou City blues tradition. I have made countless friends, and I have really enjoyed the live music. To paraphrase Huddie Ledbetter (aka Leadbelly), if you ever go to Houston, you'd better do right—and hear some of it for yourself. Meanwhile, let me tell you what I've come to understand—and how my life-enriching experience with local blues people all began.

down in houston

Lightnin' Hopkins, 1970.

learning about lightnin'

The Soil beneath My Feet

the videotape opens with his face staring straight into the camera, with some type of urban street scene reflected in both lenses of his dark glasses. He sings about how he hates to travel on "this lonesome road." He's seated on a chair at a dirt-worn sidewalk interchange in a fairly ragged-looking neighborhood. He's got a folded hand towel draped over his right shoulder and an acoustic guitar perched on his pulsing right thigh. Using thumb and fingers, he's picking out a country blues tune. The black-and-white footage shifts as he continues to play. An indoor scene: Four middle-aged to elderly black men huddle around a square wooden table as others look on. Taking their turns, they slap down rectangular domino slabs and score. The camera dwells momentarily on a twenty-dollar bill and a stogie butt resting at table's edge. All the while, Lightnin's guitar can be heard as he fingerpicks solos, that heavy bass thumb-work never missing a beat. The video cuts back to the solitary musician out on the street. His voice conveying a world of weariness, he intones the final lines of an improvised song: a vow, repeated, to keep on traveling till he

3

finds some place to go, followed by the simple observation that it's lonesome when you go down such a road by yourself. He drags the thumb across the strings to provide a final flourish, dominant chord resonating as the film cuts to another scene.

Now he's inside, maybe in the same cafe where the domino players congregated in the earlier footage. There's still not a female to be seen. Men sit and stand, drinking from long-necked bottles, and stare at the lone guitarist. Lightnin's on a chair in front of some old venetian blinds, rocking gently as his knees flex in and out. This time he's not singing but just playing the same guitar— really working it, making it moan and cry, with measured bursts of boogie bass connecting the viciously precise solo passages. As his left hand runs the frets while the right deftly plucks separate strings, I see with my own eyes what previously I had only heard on records.

And as the imagery lingers beyond the *click* to stop the videotape, I more fully understand some things I had read or been told. For instance, this wiry fellow in the porkpie hat may well have been (as Wolfgang Saxon asserted in the *New York Times*) "the greatest single influence on rock guitar players," the eccentric master of a blues idiom all his own. And as Robert Palmer put it (in another article for that same newspaper), this man "was a blues poet, if there ever was one."

I also intuitively grasped something else: Though Lightnin' Hopkins might sing convincingly of a need to travel, that gritty street corner and that little cafe sure looked like places where he felt right at home.

like thousands of other people from elsewhere, I immigrated to the city of Houston in 1981, drawn here by job prospects and the region's booming economy. The sprawling metropolis an overwhelming unknown, I first did the same as many newcomers: moved into a suburban condo, learned by trial and error which freeway ramps and back streets offered the best bets against predictably jammed daily commutes, and absorbed an image of the city based mainly on its depiction in local and national media.

My direct observations and experiences were then limited, for the most part, to those areas immediately surrounding the Southwest Freeway, that massive strip of concrete connecting Point A, my residence, and Point B, my workplace. If Houston initially suggested to me some sense of place, it was that freeway. Daily I negotiated its lanes, driving over and through a city that seemed only an ever expanding amalgam of similar shopping centers and malls, apartment complexes and subdivisions, office parks and skyscrapers. To my naive perception, local culture defined itself mainly via stereotypes generated by two dominant industries, petroleum and NASA, while perpetuating some conspiracy of pretense regarding the mediated image of the urban cowboy.

Anchored in Houston, nevertheless, by a satisfying professional position and the regularity of my paychecks, I sought refuge in my lifelong habit of listening to recorded music as a form of strategic retreat. Given my feelings of estrangement from the new environs, what I needed most was something real to provide solace and escape. Sampling previously collected LPs and making regular forays to local record stores, I began to find that solace mainly in blues and gospel music, most of which was performed not by twenty-something males like myself (at that time) but by African Americans my father's age or older. As has been the case with countless other fans before me, the more of the good stuff I heard on records, the more I had to hear: T-Bone Walker, Leadbelly, Muddy Waters, The Five Blind Boys of Alabama, The Dixie Hummingbirds. Each discovery satisfied a need—and made me want more

This music, I increasingly realized, was the honest source of so many of the classic rock-and-roll and soul tunes with which I had come of age in the 1960s and 1970s. It formed the primal headwaters of a cultural river I had been swimming in for years—only I had started out farther downstream, where some contamination and dilution were now evident to me. So, as if craving the mythic purity of the springs of origin, I gradually immersed myself in classic blues, fairly oblivious to the antithetical current of 1980s mainstream music culture. And being a newcomer to this huge and hustling city, I found that immersion to be particularly satisfying. As the singer-songwriter and former resident Townes Van Zandt (1944–1997) once told the author Kathleen Hudson, "If you can't catch the blues in Houston, man, you can't catch them anywhere."

Granted, my knowledge of the music remained limited mainly to what I could glean from various liner notes and LPs. But at the time, that was enough. I figured that as long as I had my job, my stereo, and my blues records, I could survive down in Houston.

Then something happened that would eventually change my life. On the first day of February 1982, I read an article in the *Houston Chronicle* announcing the death of, and local memorial service for, Sam "Lightnin'" Hopkins. As it recounted the life of "one of the most extensively recorded blues artists" (the man the musicologist Samuel Charters was quoted as describing as "the last singer in the grand style"), I was struck by one simple sentence: "Yet, he remained Houston's own."

Remained Houston's own? I couldn't fathom the notion. What did this postmodern city—which seemed to me a huge, heartless network of concrete, glass, and steel—really have to do with the earthy poetry and acoustic guitar of Lightnin' Hopkins? What neighborhood here could still legitimately claim Lightnin' as its own?

I had earlier been aware that this legendary Texas bluesman was somehow historically associated with Houston, but to me it was abstract knowledge, only a bit of trivia from some ancient past. And it had never occurred to me, during my previous eight months holed up at home listening to blues records, that he was still here, that the great Lightnin' and I were actually fellow citizens of the same city for a short while.

Just as I had previously known in my head that blues was the fundamental American roots

Lightnin' Hopkins, 1970.

music but had only just begun to understand it on a deeper level, I was now struck by a fact I had vaguely stored in my brain but had never before fully confronted: Lightnin' Hopkins, the epitome of the real-deal blues man, was a Houstonian. Reading that newspaper account, I now understood that following his birth in Centerville, Texas (on a date given in the *Chronicle* and elsewhere—including Hopkins' tombstone—as 1912, but which the researcher Bob Eagle has determined to be 1911, based on his scrutiny of the 1920 census records and the Social Security Death Index), he had first come to the Bayou City in the 1920s and had been here for most of his sixty-nine (or seventy) years. His art, his blues were part of Houston history—a part that suddenly intrigued me, as it seemed so distant from my daily reality here.

I had two immediate impulses: first, to go buy another Lightnin' Hopkins record, and second, to learn more about the connection between this artist and this city. Where had he lived? Why was he here, of all places? And more broadly, what blues did this city still have to offer that I hadn't yet discovered in my limited observations from the freeway (or been informed of, until now, by the local media)?

Returning to that newspaper article, I copied down the information about the memorial service for Lightnin' Hopkins: "8 P.M. Tuesday in Johnson's Funeral Chapel, 2301 McGowen." Then, after fetching the city map from the glove compartment of my car, I searched the index for the name of the street. To my intense surprise, I located the 2300 block of McGowen just southeast of downtown, about a mile from the main campus of Houston Community College, where I served as a rookie faculty member.

Still an outsider to the area then, I had no sense of that campus being part of any neighborhood, in the traditional sense. It was just a freeway exit-ramp destination, a cluster of buildings where I parked my car, entered, and did my job before departing each afternoon for the suburbs. Now I was jolted to imagine what kind of community might lie just beyond my classroom walls, a place that Lightnin' Hopkins (I would later learn) had long called home.

The following evening I somehow lacked the energy or the nerve to drive back into that unknown neighborhood and attend the service for Lightnin' Hopkins. I immediately regretted that missed opportunity, and the passage of years has only made my passive mistake more apparent. It would have been an honor to bid farewell to such a distinguished musician. And who knows what I might have learned had I been there when people who knew enough to care gathered to say good-bye to a true blues genius?

But the news of Lightnin's death had already suggested something valuable to me—two concepts that I would gradually come to understand much more fully over the years: First, the city I now called home, and more particularly the neighborhood where I worked, had a specific blues heritage about which I was largely ignorant, despite my supposed affinity for the genre of recorded music called blues. Second, blues reality was perhaps accessible as something other than historical performance removed in time and place and captured on record, something other than the larger-than-life status of a few major stars such as B.B. King, whose massive touring productions I had witnessed. Blues reality, even in the 1980s, still encompassed people like Lightnin', who had lived in what the newspaper called "his tiny apartment" in the working-class community just east of my school.

One afternoon about a week later, motivated by curiosity, I drove past the funeral chapel on the corner of McGowen and Dowling and on into the heart of a neighborhood I would later come to know as Third Ward. Surveying the rows of simple wood-frame houses, decaying storefronts, and abandoned buildings, I thought, "This is not the kind of place where one would hope to find an artist who had graced the stage of Carnegie Hall." I struggled to reconcile two contrasting images, one of this "master" whose virtuosity had been celebrated at the nation's finest performance venues and the other of some scruffy fellow who reportedly had regularly walked these humble streets.

I wondered about this place and the people who lived here. How many of them had known Lightnin' personally? What did they think of him? Did they still embrace his blues? Did his legacy survive among them? I had an urge to stop the next old "bluesy-looking" guy I spotted coming down the street and ask him about Lightnin' Hopkins, but I dared not.

It would be years later, following additional formal education and the gradual digestion of more records, books, and magazines, before I would finally begin to talk purposefully and directly to the people of Third Ward about their blues.

My decision to pursue doctoral studies at the University of Houston both postponed and enhanced any fieldwork I would ultimately do. The delay was necessary during the seven years I carried the dual responsibilities of both a full-time teacher and a graduate student. My opportunities for extracurricular pursuits were somewhat limited, to say the least, as a result of that load. However, it was also during that same time period that I was first exposed to the formal study of folklore, which made clear to me the value of conducting historical inquiry via tape-recorded interviews with everyday people. This introduction to folkloristic methodology was an essential prerequisite, I now realize, for the serious blues research I would eventually undertake.

After completing my dissertation (which focused on, among other issues, the transformation of historical reality into written text), I graduated and decided to apply my skills to a subject that appealed as much to my heart as to my head: the blues. Inspired especially by the notion of collecting oral histories from real people, from living texts as it were, I began to seek out and interview members of the African American blues community of Houston. This independent work has proven to be as fulfilling as any course of study I could ever pursue at a university.

Now, years later, I find deep satisfaction also in the numerous personal friendships with blues artists (and their families)—relationships that often have evolved past a common interest in the music history to include other elements of human experience. In addition to club gigs and jams,

recording sessions, television studio performances, music festivals, radio interviews, special programs, and major concerts, I have attended birthday parties, church services, dental appointments, weddings, hospital visitations, funerals, and burials with many of these dear friends. From them I have learned much about Houston, about blues, about life and death.

The writing in this book is intended not only to document the experiences of these individual Houston blues artists, most of whom first came of age as performers in the 1940s, 1950s, or 1960s, but also to achieve some synthesis of disparate elements to reach a viable definition of Houston blues. What are its dominant characteristics, especially in relation to those of other centers of blues culture such as Chicago or Memphis? Why is Houston blues—despite the depth of its legacy, past and present—generally not as widely recognized as that from these other cities? Where does it come from? Why is it still here at the start of the twenty-first century? Where is it going?

A lot has changed for me since I first moved to Houston in 1981, not the least of which is some enlightenment regarding local culture. Now proudly at home here, I have learned my way around some of the fascinating, predominantly African American neighborhoods that remain largely obscure to those who speed past on the ubiquitous freeways. More importantly, I have learned directly about the lives of some of the most creative and historically significant folks to come from these neighborhoods and beyond: the true blues people of Houston.

Let me tell you more about where they come from, who they are, and how and why they're still holding on to the blues. And for some of them, as it did for me, it all seems to begin with Lightnin' Hopkins.

remembering lightnin': a sampler

JOE "GUITAR" HUGHES, LOCAL MUSICIAN:

Lightnin' was a very good friend of mine. I was aware of him really way before I met him because my stepfather loved Lightnin', you know. My stepfather, he'd sit by the Victrola and play Lightnin' Hopkins tunes and drink his bourbon. And a lot of times I'd see him sitting there crying. But I don't think it was tears of sadness. He just liked the music—and the stories that Lightnin' was telling. More or less, he was living it as he listened. Yeah, Lightnin' really was a storyteller.

Most of his stories came from people around him, the things that were happening around the neighborhood. He didn't write his songs; he made them up as he recorded them, or as he sang them in a club, on the street, wherever.

When I first saw him, it was on the bandstand at a little place called McDaniel's Lounge, off the Gulf Freeway. He was playing by himself, you know. It was just him and a chair onstage, and a bottle

Joe "Guitar" Hughes, 1998.

Milton Hopkins, Reddi Room, 1996.

of wine on the floor next to the chair. He had an acoustic guitar, with one of those old pickups on it—the way they used to amplify the guitars in those days.

I just sat and listened. I was interested in the guitar and well aware of his presence and a lot of his songs. Matter of fact, later on I would get up on the bandstand and give him a break every now and then. And I would play some of his songs—because I knew most of them then because my stepfather would listen to Lightnin' all the time.

I don't think Lightnin' knew how big he was. And the way he carried himself, he was just like the old guy next door. But actually, at the time, I didn't know how big Lightnin' was. He carried himself just like one of the fellows, so that was the way we dealt with him, you know. I found out later just how important Lightnin' Hopkins really is to blues music.

ANONYMOUS WOMAN, THIRD WARD RESIDENT:

When I was little, Lightnin' Hopkins would sit on the front porch and play his guitar in the afternoons, here in the neighborhood. Once he made up a song about my aunt. She was a real short lady—she wasn't even five feet tall. And he made up a funny song about her. He could do that like it was just natural.

MILTON HOPKINS, LOCAL MUSICIAN:

Lightnin' was my cousin. I knew him but never played with him. He was much older than me and doing a different style of blues from me.

Now I started out playing like Lightnin', you know, the country-style blues. But it didn't last long. I always wanted an electric guitar, way before I got one. I enjoyed hearing all the different orchestrations and stuff that was going on. . . . I liked this style over here that had more flair to it, had more class. So I went for that. That's how I got to be where I am now—knowing all these different parts, playing various kinds of songs. I never was a blues purist, I don't think. I think of it all as just music. But blues is the only thing I ever had any success with, right on down to today. . . . That guitar hanging up on my daddy's back porch—which he didn't want me to touch—was my only way.

CHRIS STRACHWITZ, CALIFORNIA-BASED PRODUCER:

After I came to this country from Europe and was first turned on by New Orleans jazz, I fell in love with blues. And the record that knocked me out more than any other was by a man named Lightnin' Hopkins. When his voice came at me over a radio station in Los Angeles, it just took me away from this planet. I had to meet this man named Lightnin'.

My friends at school back then were listening to people like Doris Day or The Four Freshmen. . . . Saccharine slop was all over the radio. Then all of a sudden, here was a guy, Hunter Hancock in L.A., who was broadcasting a program called Harlem Matinee every afternoon. And I got totally addicted to it. He would play low-down blues. . . . This was before rock and roll. This was powerful stuff to me.

Here was a man with just his guitar singing in this lazy, relaxed style. To somebody like me—who could barely speak English—I felt terribly inferior. But I said, I've got to meet this man Lightnin' Hopkins. That was really the reason I started the [Arhoolie] record label.

I finally got to Houston in 1959, after my friend Sam Charters sent me a card saying "I found Lightnin' Hopkins. He lives in Houston, Texas." You see, we didn't have any sense of where he might be, even if he was still alive. This was totally out of our realm of romanticism or whatever. Even the magazines in France were discussing: Where is Lightnin' Hopkins from? Is he a Mississippi singer? Or is he from Georgia, or Alabama? Anyway, this was like holding the Holy Grail for me, when Sam Charters sent me this postcard.

So I went there that summer in 1959, because my sister needed her car driven to Albuquerque. I said, "Hell, that must be almost halfway there." When I got there, I took a bus the rest of the way. I remember staying at the YMCA in Houston, and then meeting this fellow Mack McCormick who introduced me to him.

We went to visit Lightnin' Hopkins that afternoon. He was cool as could be, smoking his cigar. Said, "Oh you're from California? Well, come and listen to me. I'll be at Pop's Place tonight." So we went out there to Pop's Place, and he saw us walking in. He was singing a low-down blues about how his shoulder was aching, and how he could hardly get to the job that night—but he rhymes it up all perfectly! About the chuckholes in the street all covered by water, and his car hardly made it and all. Then he sings, "Whoa man, this man come all the way from California"—pointing his finger at me— "just to see Po' Lightnin' sing."

He would just improvise constantly, that whole evening. There were only a few people in the place. It was like what I would now imagine is the role of a griot in Africa. He was simply the community poet who would tell people what they like to hear. And he would argue with the woman in front of him, "Whoa, woman, you in the red dress!" And then he would just go into this musical tirade about her, and she would yell back at him! It was a real two-way communication. It was like a church service in a totally nonchurch atmosphere.

I just felt that somebody had to document this man in those beer joints. . . . I was simply a fan. I just liked certain sounds. I was absolutely enamored of Lightnin' Hopkins. I thought, "This is the nastiest down-home blues I ever heard." And that's all I wanted to hear.

ROBERT "SKIN MAN" MURPHY, LOCAL MUSICIAN:
That was the summer of '61 that I was on tour with both Lightnin' and Clifton Chenier. But until Lightnin' died, off and on Lightnin' would come on little jobs that we'd have like on Sunday afternoons and things. He'd come by and sit in. Whenever we played out in Third Ward, they had a little

Robert "Skin Man" Murphy, at home, 1997.

club there, was made from a two-story house. I've forgotten the name of it, but it was right around the corner from where Lightnin' used to live in Third Ward. And Lightnin' would come around, and the three of us would have a ball! Me and Clifton and Lightnin'.

I think I was one of the very few drummers who could get along halfway decent with Lightnin'. Lightnin', he didn't like too many drummers. Uh-uh. . . . People wouldn't dance for Lightnin'. They'd just crowd around, get all up on the tops of things, and sometimes he'd even make up songs right there.

Do you know I "traded fours" with Lightnin' Hopkins? Fours—you know what I'm talking about? Solos, four measures, yeah. He'd play something: dee-da-dee-da-dee. And then I'd do: ba-bomp-pa-doo-ba. We worked out a little thing like that. I know I'm one of the very few drummers could do that with him.

RAYFIELD JACKSON
(AKA HOUSTON'S "GUITAR SLIM"), LOCAL MUSICIAN:

I first met Lightnin' in 1953. I was about seventeen. We eventually played together on some gigs. He taught me a lot and always called me his little cousin, which we ain't no kin. He taught me very much about the guitar and old blues, and I was a youngster. I was living in Third Ward, and he was living in Third Ward at the time. And I used to go over to his house when I'd get out of high school, and we'd play on his guitar and laugh and talk. He would show me all he knowed, and a lot of times on the weekend, I'd go on a gig with him and sit in, play right along with him.

He lived on—we used to call it "Short Gray"—right off of Gray and Live Oak. He used to live in a little shotgun house. And when I'd get out of high school I would go over to his house, before I would even go home, and he'd say, "C'mon in, little cuz. I know why you're coming here. C'mon in." And we'd start playing them guitars. I'd play there for about an hour or so, and then I'd go on home. Mama knowed where I'd be going, when I'd get out of school, so she didn't fuss at me.

I played some gigs with him, sure did. Right here in Sunnyside, up and down Cullen [Blvd.]—back when Cullen was a shell street. It was called Chocolate Bayou Road then, wasn't no Cullen. And it was a shell street, wasn't no pave. And we was playing in little old joints with about three or four tables in them, and when you got five or six people in there, you had a crowd. That's right.

And we played a little gig here in Third Ward, on Live Oak and McGowen. I can't remember the name of the place, but it was a small joint. And we played on Live Oak and Delano, another little joint. That would be on the weekends, when I'd be out of school. And I'd go in there and play a little while, sit up there and back him up with the guitar, what he taught me how to do. And it wouldn't be anyone but him and I. Wouldn't have no drummer, just two guitars—and Lightnin' stomping his feet. That's it. He'd have them big old shoes on and one of them Big Apple hats, big old wide hats with a feather stuck up in it—looked like a peacock.

Houston's "Guitar Slim," Rayfield Jackson, 1997.

His guitar playing was his own style of the blues. And his songwriting was the same thing. . . . I would say Lightnin' is important to American music because of the era he came up in, for black America, the style that reaches back to the old days while being modern too.

Houston, and Third Ward, recognized Lightnin's music, very much so. The younger people don't know anything about him—no more than what they hear the older people talk about. But the older folks, they'll never forget Lightnin'. He played for the Queen of England! And at Carnegie Hall! So he was well recognized.

Young people should be taught about the roots of the blues and where it came from. And one of the main rooters was Mr. Lightnin', Sam Hopkins. . . . He had a very nice personality—always had a smile on his face, with all that pretty gold in his mouth.

STEVE EARLE, SINGER-SONGWRITER, FORMER HOUSTON RESIDENT:

Lightnin' had a lot of gold in his mouth. He figured it was a good investment.

KINNEY ABAIR, LOCAL MUSICIAN:

He'd make up songs and never play them again, at least not exactly the same words. . . . And Lightnin' was a comic, a real joker, onstage too—always cracking wise.

ROY GAINES, LOS ANGELES–BASED (HOUSTON-RAISED) MUSICIAN:

My mother played Lightnin' Hopkins religiously when Christmas came, from like late November, when they would start fixing food for Thanksgiving and playing records that they liked. Sometimes it might be gospel, if it would get close to Sunday. But most of the time it was Lightnin' Hopkins.

TEXAS JOHNNY BROWN, LOCAL MUSICIAN:

I had some times with Lightnin'. As a matter of fact, we did a couple of things together. They had a little recording studio out Washington Avenue called ACA. . . . And we used to go out there, and he'd sit and play. Wouldn't be nobody, just he—and I'd be there with him. Sometime I'd play with him, and sometime I wouldn't. And I remember Lightnin' used to take a board, put a board down underneath his feet. And if he didn't have a drum, he'd just pat his feet real hard—on that board—and play right along with it. It always amazed me how he did it, because his timing was his own timing as far as rhythm is concerned.

He was a wonderful person to know, kind of easy spoken. Despite what some folks say, he really wasn't a mean person. He was a person who didn't talk a heck of a lot—till he got to making a song, you know.

Later on, when I came back off the road, he was working at a little club at the corner of Dowling and Cleburne. And I used to get off of gigs, or some nights when I didn't have a gig, and I'd go by there

Texas Johnny Brown, 1995.

Lightnin' Hopkins' grave, 2001.

and we'd sit down and laugh and talk about different things. He'd ask about some of the places I'd been, 'cause I'd been on the road then for awhile. Lightnin' himself really didn't like the road that much. He liked to stay home.

And we spoke about Mrs. [Lola Anne] Cullum [Houston talent scout for Los Angeles–based Aladdin Records] a few times, because back in the forties and early fifties she worked with both of us, when I was with [singer and pianist] Amos Milburn and right after.

I remember a time when Mrs. Cullum used to take her husband's shirts, his white shirts, and give them to us so we'd have some shirts to go on the gig, you know. Her husband was a dentist—and had good shirts. And I remember one time Lightnin' was putting this song together, and they had a time arguing. I can't remember exactly the title of the song, but anyway, there's a part in there where he says, "The woman was lit up like a neon sign," you know. But he always said, "lit up like a Nehi sign," and he and Mrs. Cullum used to argue back and forth about that.

I knew about him even before I started professionally because I'd heard some of his records. Couldn't miss him on the jukebox. He was pretty heavy on the jukebox around Houston—and all over. And when I finally came to Houston myself, I met him, finally ran up on him.

Lightnin's style of music, the feeling is different. You might say that the environment was different. He told his stories just as he lived them, and just as the way he was, the way he saw things. And these were the things he ran upon, the things that happened to him, so that's what he wrote about. It's the same with me, but it's different in the terms of music, the tonality and the theory. It's a little more progressive, the blues-type thing that I did. He was more old style. The type of guitar that he played was like from my dad's era more than from mine. . . . He played that finger guitar, and played it in the natural keys, like the E-natural, A-natural, or D-natural. You know, where they could play that finger guitar and could carry a melody right along with the bass line.

He was a person that mainly did it solo, everything he did. I can't remember a time that he really had a full band together. He enjoyed doing it himself because his way was his way. And his timing— if his timing was off, he didn't have to worry about nobody saying nothing about his timing being off or however it was. He just played it on his own terms. And that's the way it was with Lightnin'.

Melvin Newman, Miss Ann's Playpen, Third Ward, 1999.

CHAPTER 2

digging the roots
A Cultural Context

it's somewhere between five and six on a Monday afternoon on Dowling Street, early May 1998. In a small brick-front establishment, inconspicuous but for the royal blue awning over its entrance, neighborhood patrons, both male and female, crowd onto barstools or find chairs among sixteen blue-cloth-covered tables. The walls are decorated with artwork depicting figures from black history, photographs of musicians, and plastic facsimiles of various musical instruments, as well as a large framed corkboard covered with snapshots of happy participants at previous gatherings. In a corner against the front wall, where men in work clothes stand next to a glowing jukebox, the slightly raised stage is crowded with five musicians spontaneously coalescing into a sweaty Gulf Coast groove. In a weekly ritual that attracts amateurs and seasoned veterans alike, these players perform only for love of the blues.

The bassist is a retired career military man, a former trumpet player who later in life picked up his current instrument just so he could more readily cultivate opportunities to make music with others in Houston clubs. The drummer, a middle-aged bus driver by occupation, hasn't really ever played professionally, despite his impeccably funky sense of timing. Since giving up drinking, he just likes to keep busy doing something constructive, and in this environment, he's most at ease tucked in the corner behind the drum kit, a pair of drumsticks in hand. The saxophonist, a relatively young college graduate, would love to make a full-time living performing music but can't find steady gigs that pay enough, so he maintains a stable day job behind a computer in a downtown office. The guy on the keyboard once toured the United States playing behind his former neighbor and childhood friend, blues star Albert Collins, back during some vague time in the late 1970s or 1980s. These days he's mostly hustling in fits and starts to maintain a series of gigs around the region, with this band or that, doing his own thing or backing others on request, whenever the phone calls come. On electric guitar, there's an internationally famous recording artist, just home from a festival appearance in Europe. During the breaks between songs, he trades joking insults with two old high-school buddies, who tease him relentlessly about the photograph on his latest CD cover. Most of the clientele, however, recognize him only as an intermittently familiar hometown face at the Blue Monday jam, oblivious to his status in the global blues industry.

Yet, following a lengthy pause in the music (while the bass player steps out to move his car from the impossibly congested sidewalk area, where too many people have tried to pull off Dowling Street and park, blocking each other in), the five men regroup. The guitarist plugs his Strat back into the amp, nods to the grinning drummer, and the mood of the just previously rowdy room is suddenly hushed and focused. The regulars, some of whom first witnessed this six-string wizard perform decades ago as a teen prodigy, know what to expect. And by the time he starts the second verse of a classic Albert King shuffle, his graceful prowess on fretboard and vocals have confirmed it once again: This man is gifted at creating the music that everyone here calls his or her own.

But as the set continues and the players trade turns singing the lead or soloing, something else becomes clear: It's a shared gift that goes both ways, one that draws strength from and in turn inspires the others onstage and in the audience. The vocal encouragement and enthusiastic outbursts shouted by patrons, like the roomful of applause that caps each number, are directed equally to all members of this makeshift band, though at any given moment any one of the individuals might be singled out for special comment.

"Come on with it, Pops!" one large woman in lime green short pants yells as the bass player holds a vocal note to end a song.

"Blow that horn, boy!" a satisfied gentleman exhorts from the bar, nodding his head all the while.

And this hearty interchange among participants continues all night, triggered by the dozens of different performers who will grace the stage before closing. At one point, when a young woman in blue jeans and a T-shirt cuts loose like a spirit-filled preacher to interpret Aretha Franklin's

Sherman Robertson, Miss Ann's Playpen, Third Ward, 1997.

Joe Halliburton, Miss Ann's Playpen, Third Ward, 1997.

classic soul number "Dr. Feelgood," the audience goes wild, shouting the singer's name well after she's returned to her chair at a table crowded with friends and eventually forcing her to come back to the front of the room to "do another." She responds with a lengthy version of "Down Home Blues," including an impromptu midsong monologue explaining why she needs the blues, an impassioned speech punctuated by the musicians playing softly behind her as well as by cries of approval and confirmation from people throughout the packed-to-capacity room.

"Tell it, sister, for true! That's right!"

Meanwhile, the owner and his wife hurry to set out a full-course soul-food buffet, always served free of charge. Later, as he rapidly hands bottles to thirsty people at the L-shaped bar, the owner knows it's Monday, inevitably a good night for his business. He just hopes it's not so good that he won't have time to join the folks onstage himself.

Later in the evening the six-foot-four-inch proprietor, a former would-be professional football player, finally takes the microphone. As a new assortment of musicians (only the bassist remains the same) kick off the opening measures, he steps out into the audience, raises a large hand, shuts his eyes, leans back, and sings—undeniably in his bluesy element as he walks between tables, taking offered hands and working the patrons into a satisfying frenzy. For this combination entrepreneur-performer, the Blue Monday jam-session tradition he revived after opening the club in 1996 is surely a double blessing.

For him, it's also a tradition inspired especially by memories of an earlier Dowling Street club called Nola's. Seeking to do it "like they used to do in the old days," he initiated his own late-Monday-afternoon gatherings by first promoting the idea among barbers, beauticians, and other folks who typically had the day off. But the success of the weekly ritual, which draws almost as many musicians as fans, now reaches deep into the community—drawing employed and unemployed, old and young, to make blues together till quitting time a few hours before midnight.

numerous small African American–owned-and-operated venues, in the old wards and scattered elsewhere in Houston, still regularly feature live music that its performers and audience mutually define as "blues." Of course, the precise implications of that generic label evolved significantly during the twentieth century, both in the United States and all over the world. So what does it mean when a black Houstonian uses the word to refer to locally performed music in the 1990s (and beyond)? What are the roots and current realities of the original Houston blues culture?

In most cases today, that label is best understood—by folks in the old neighborhoods, at least—in terms of the electric, relatively polished (and sometimes orchestrated) sound first associated with recordings popularized by T-Bone Walker (1910–1975), who cut his initial sides for Columbia Records in 1929 but mainly emerged to stardom after waxing a single ("T-Bone Blues") for New

York's Varsity label in 1940. An equally apt and more versatile analogue is found in Fifth Ward's hugely influential Duke-Peacock Records, which existed from 1949 until 1973—and through the fifties reigned as one of the most successful African American–owned record labels in the world (i.e., before the rise of Berry Gordy Jr.'s Motown empire). Its sound is personified by the most well known artists in its impressive catalogue, stars such as Clarence "Gatemouth" Brown (b. 1924), Willie Mae "Big Mama" Thornton (1926–1984), Bobby "Blue" Bland (b. 1930), Junior Parker (1932–1971), and so on—all of whom were based in Houston during key phases of their careers. Despite its capacity for earnest earthiness or folksy metaphor (consider Thornton's original Peacock recording of "Hound Dog"—released well before anyone had ever heard of Elvis Presley—as just one example), most of this band-based, often horn-accompanied, tightly produced music differs significantly from the predominantly solo ramblings of a country-style minstrel such as Lightnin' Hopkins. Some people might more precisely define this relatively progressive urban sound as early rhythm and blues, with its lineage traced to the upscale artistry pioneered by Walker. And they'd be right. Depending on artist and venue in Houston today, this music may also display large elements of jazz or swing—following in the rich local tradition of horn-playing bandleaders such as Milt Larkin (1910–1996) or Arnett Cobb (1918–1989). In other cases, it may veer into territory better defined as zydeco, soul, or funk. And whatever the classification, it's often flavored by distinctively gospelesque flourishes. But its foundation draws heavily from the classic Walker repertoire and incorporates direct influence from well-known blues artists such as Jimmy Reed (1925–1976), Freddie King (1934–1976), and B.B. King (b. 1925), to name a few. And to many of the people who grew up with it and still play it, as well as to those who still gather to hear it and respond to it at Blue Monday jams and elsewhere, it's mostly just called "blues."

Like other southern cities (such as New Orleans, Memphis, and Dallas), Houston first experienced blues as an early-twentieth-century folk music originating in the ever expanding community of black immigrants from surrounding rural areas. The sociological roots of this rapidly metamorphosing form lay deep in the post-emancipation world of sharecropping and fieldhand work. Searching for better jobs and improved living conditions, thousands of African Americans relocated to the Bayou City from regional farms or ranches, a trend that began in earnest following the "Juneteenth" declaration ending slavery in Texas (June 19, 1865). This rural-to-urban migration pattern continued, in Houston as elsewhere, throughout much of the twentieth century. But it was particularly accelerated locally by the city's emerging status as the boomtown center of the global petrochemical industry. Just as thousands of black workers gladly left the impoverished Mississippi Delta region of the Deep South and journeyed to the industrialized north (especially to "Sweet Home Chicago," as Robert Johnson [1911–1938] immortalized it), many others—especially those from the Piney Woods of East Texas and the Gulf Coast region west of the Mississippi River—came to the factory-filled port city of Houston.

Howard Beeth and Cary D. Wintz, in *Black Dixie: Afro-Texan History and Culture in Houston*, point out that the city's black population officially registered only 3,691 in 1870, but had risen to 23,929 by 1910, and then to 86,302 by 1940. The burgeoning numbers of new arrivals included (and continue to do so to this day) many black Creoles from the prairies and bayous of nearby southwestern Louisiana, a cultural presence that has strongly flavored the development of African American music in Houston, especially blues-based forms. (In fact, this city also played a crucial role in the midcentury evolution of the old-style French acoustic music known as *la-la* into the now widely popular modern form called *zydeco*.)

Regardless of where the black immigrants may have originated from, upon settling here they typically discovered Houston to offer a significantly different living environment than they might have found in the major industrial centers up north—mainly because of its relatively low density of population, as well as "the fact that blacks were not concentrated in a single concrete ghetto," as Beeth and Wintz put it. However, these scholars also note that institutionalized resistance to racial integration was a sad fact of life in mainstream Houston well into the second half of the twentieth century, adding that various barriers of social and educational segregation also, and ironically, encouraged a positive sense of self-containment for black Houstonians:

> *Most blacks responded to segregation by turning inward, relying on their own families and communities, creating their own institutions, and avoiding, as much as possible, contact with the outside white world. There were black restaurants, saloons, theaters, and movie houses. Blacks celebrated their own holiday, Juneteenth, and round the turn of the century they established their own fall festival, De-Ro-Loc ("colored" in reverse), a black version of the historic No-Tsu-Oh carnival ("Houston" spelled backward). In one sense segregation thus stimulated the black community.*

It was in such an isolated social context that black life and popular black music (gospel, blues, R&B, jazz, and zydeco) evolved in Houston, especially from the turn of the century till around the year 1963, when wide-scale public integration first began in this city (a historical moment superbly documented in David Berman's 1998 film, *The Strange Demise of Jim Crow: How Houston Desegregated Its Public Accommodations, 1959–1963*). In the decades before this civil rights breakthrough—and in truth, for considerable time thereafter—most forms of black music (whether secular or religious) were only occasionally performed locally to nonblack audiences. Sure, on any given Saturday night at one of the finest blues and jazz venues (for instance, the Bronze Peacock or Club Matinee in Fifth Ward, the Eldorado Ballroom or Club Ebony in Third Ward) there might have been occasional visitors from the other side of the tracks. But extensive oral history confirms that those cross-cultural exchanges were the exception rather than the norm, particularly before the mid-1960s.

On the other hand, many black blues musicians—the versatile Henry Hayes (b. 1924) is a prime example—also played in combos or big bands that regularly performed a wide variety of popular musical styles for all-white supper-club audiences and the like. But these typically were gigs where black music culture was not so much celebrated as it was modified and assimilated to accommodate a different audience. As Hayes recalls, during one period in the sixties, he found plenty of work playing for whites but relished his opportunity to perform his own style of music when he worked a black club:

> At that time we played five nights a week in a nice white supper club on Milam, doing what they wanted us to do, standards and stuff. Then we'd play at the Tropicana, a black club, on Sundays, a matinee you know, where I liked to come there and play anything I wanted, jazz and blues, everything, you know. . . . It was pure freedom there.

But Hayes also notes that even when playing the all-black venues, he often drew from the expanded repertoire he'd mastered for his white audiences, adapting his interpretations to a bluesier style to suit the venue and audience:

> Aw man, look boy—I'd tear the house up! . . . I used to make ladies miss church to hear me play "Danny Boy" [at the Tropicana]. I'd do it with so much soul, you know, on saxophone. . . . I played it with a gospel-type of feeling, real bluesy. You feel my music. You know, there's some guys play it and you don't feel much. . . .

Hayes understands in retrospect that performing various styles for audiences of different races helped make him a better all-around musician. But the blues numbers that he preferred—as evidenced by his own compositions as well as his collaborations on the initial recordings by Albert Collins (1932–1993), Elmore Nixon (1933–1973), and Joe "Guitar" Hughes (b. 1937), for instance—primarily remained black music for black audiences.

The experience of Henry Hayes exemplifies a general truth: until the last third of the twentieth century or so, multilevel segregation defined most public race relations in Houston, including the blues culture based in its black communities.

Black Houstonians, nevertheless, have significantly embraced, bonded with, and created various forms of blues from the inception of the genre to the present. The city's most crucial period of blues productivity and large-scale social response occurred in the years following World War II and lasted until the era of desegregation in the mid-1960s. But local contributions to general blues culture, like other implications of that culture's existence, are an often overlooked part of Houston history. Why?

The short answer seems to lie, at least in part, in the impact desegregation had on black cultural life in the Bayou City. As the widely acclaimed guitarist Roy Gaines (b. 1937) once told me, "After years and years of being denied the opportunity to visit certain theaters, restaurants, stores, banks, and what-have-you, do you think black people wanted to stay put down on Lyons Avenue? No, and when they began to spend their money elsewhere, all the black businesses—the hotels, the clubs, the restaurants, the shops—suffered severely."

Like most of the blues musicians I've come to know, the now California-based Gaines experienced an essentially all-black cultural environment growing up in Houston—in his case in the Fifth Ward in the 1940s and 1950s. Especially along then vibrant Lyons Avenue, the youngster who began throwing newspapers for the *Houston Chronicle* at age five caught glimpses of the most famous African American celebrities of the day outside establishments such as the Crystal Hotel, Club Matinee, or Caldwell Tailors. Segregation caused the common folk of the neighborhood to share a necessary physical proximity with visiting stars, directly interacting with them—something Gaines now deeply values in hindsight (despite his awareness of the social evil that resisted integration for all the wrong reasons). In such a milieu, kids such as he had real role models readily available on their own turf, people whose hands they could shake and whose presence and professional example (in business as well as in music) could fuel aspirations.

But the socioeconomic and residential dispersal of blacks to other parts of the city, coupled with the homogenizing effect of the ever pervasive mainstream pop culture (which became increasingly accessible via the proliferation of television and Top 40 radio), altered the lives of Houston's original blues people in many ways. The times were changing, right along with musical tastes. And while certain segments of the young, white rock-and-roll generation were starting to "discover" and venerate selected blues artists and their recordings, many of the younger African Americans were beginning to dissociate from blues culture, viewing it as a throwback to an era of oppression.

Yet, somehow, true Houston blues did not completely disappear, even if it no longer dominated black life here. And large numbers of its original musicians and fans, both older and younger than Roy Gaines, kept the local tradition alive (even as they began to modify it) through long-standing weekly gatherings on their own turf—on Sundays at C. Davis Bar-B-Q or El Nedo Cafe, on Saturdays at clubs like the Silver Slipper, at Blue Monday jams and elsewhere.

Since the late 1980s, and especially in the 1990s, there has been a kind of mini-renaissance of outsider interest in Houston's still-functioning authentic blues venues and in the numerous musicians, past or present, who have performed there. And to some degree (albeit only slightly) that expanded fan base and infusion of a few extra dollars likely contributed to their viability through the end of the twentieth century. But in most cases it is clear that the aging of a generation of black Houstonians who cut their cultural teeth on blues and old-style gospel portends the possible end of a legacy that transcends music. One would hope not, but the Bayou City blues tradition—at

Roy Gaines, 2000.

least as it has been defined by its originators—seems to be gradually, inevitably slipping away. In the black community, most (but not all) of its performers and fans are middle-aged or older, and in some cases quite elderly. And with every funeral, there's another tear in the fabric that still makes Houston an unusually vibrant blues town. Though no one can be certain of the future of the cultural phenomenon of Houston blues, it is enlightening to understand how it survives and manifests itself today, as well as with whom it all began.

the seminal itinerant texas bluesman, acoustic guitarist and singer Blind Lemon Jefferson (1897–1929), likely spent some time in the Bayou City back in the old days, especially since he was known to perform at gatherings in nearby Galveston (and elsewhere in the region) during his prime. But Dallas remained Jefferson's primary base of operations for most of his career. It was there, about ninety miles north of his birthplace in Wortham, that what Harry Smith calls "the first authentic recordings of Texas folk songs" were made (reportedly in the rug department of a local store). Jefferson went on from Dallas to Paramount Records in Chicago and became one of the best-selling blues artists of the 1920s, the first era of popular commercial recording.

One of his occasional traveling companions was the early blues songster (and "King of the Twelve-String Guitar") Huddie Ledbetter (1889–1949), better known as "Leadbelly." Born just across the Sabine River in northeastern Louisiana, Leadbelly spent much time in Texas in the early 1900s. He penned his most famous number, "Midnight Special"—with its pointed warning about staying out of trouble and avoiding the sheriff "if you ever go to Houston"—while doing hard time in the state prison unit just down the road in the town of Sugar Land. A more diversified stylist and politically aware lyricist (see "Bourgeois Blues," for example) than Jefferson, Leadbelly lived long enough to enjoy being "discovered" by mainstream America, thanks to the field recordings and subsequent touring of the college circuit initiated by John A. Lomax for the Library of Congress. Some of his songs ("Goodnight Irene" comes readily to mind) have become standards in the common American folk-music repertoire, recorded and performed over the years by a wide range of artists. But though Leadbelly surpassed Jefferson, his one-time rival and peer, in life span and influence on popular culture, his impact specifically on African American blues in the Lone Star state is far less significant. In fact, arguably the two most important figures in modern Texas blues history—Sam "Lightnin'" Hopkins and Aaron "T-Bone" Walker—were direct musical descendants of Blind Lemon Jefferson, though they parlayed his legacy into two radically different styles.

In the case of an eight-year-old youngster named Sam Hopkins, a well-documented encounter with Jefferson at a countryside picnic performance in the Central Texas town of Buffalo served as his public coming-out as a guitar player. As Hopkins later related to the music historian Samuel Charters, Jefferson's engaging display of deft fingerwork and emotive singing was drawing a large crowd of appreciative spectators, and the entranced boy sensed an epiphany: "That man was picking that guitar, and I just felt it was in me." Prompted by the dares of his onlooking childhood buddies, Hopkins eventually began to pluck the strings of his own crudely homemade instrument, playing right along with Jefferson—who suddenly stopped, demanded to know the identity of his uninvited duet partner, and then (after hearing him play a few more measures) insisted that Hopkins join him on the "stage," which was actually the open cargo bed of a farm utility vehicle. "Man, he put me on top of that truck where he was sitting and we had a association!" Hopkins declared.

For the rest of his life following that fortunate initiation experience, Hopkins remained true to the country-style finger-picking technique that Jefferson had established in defining early Texas blues. Though later in his career Hopkins often performed with an electric instrument or with supporting accompaniment, his normal mode of delivery almost always emulated that of his mentor. That is, he mainly played alone on guitar, skillfully plucking strings to create both the bass line and the lead, making music that was simultaneously primal and complex. And much like his original inspiration, Hopkins was master of a vocal style that was unschooled but starkly direct and personal—darkly haunting in its capacity to convey profound truths about the human condition via poetic imagery as well as inarticulate moans.

An immigrant to the big city, Blind Lemon Jefferson had long played the streets of Dallas and later moved to Chicago (where, impoverished, he reportedly died from exposure at age thirty-two). But he personified, always, the *country* blues. Similarly, despite residing for most of his adult life in inner-city Houston (and surely confronting many distinctly urban realities there), Hopkins remained a country blues stylist throughout his career. He seemed never to forget that his deepest roots were in the poor farming community where he was born in Leon County, just outside of the small Central Texas town of Centerville. And, no matter how much he may have been transformed by decades of life in the big city, when Lightnin' sat down alone and made up a song—on a Third Ward porch front or onstage at Carnegie Hall—he drew from the legacy of Blind Lemon Jefferson. Whenever he plucked and strummed those strings, making them sharply resonate across the hole in a wooden guitar box, a part of him seemed connected to distant sounds, to music played from a flatbed truck at a picnic way up country long ago.

Aaron Thibeaux Walker, better known since childhood by the nickname "T-Bone," was also a protégé of the man called Blind Lemon. But Walker's unprecedented innovations on electric guitar, as well as his dapper and sophisticated onstage persona (which included execution of fancy dance steps and doing the splits while dressed in tux and tails), blazed the way toward the future of American popular music, rather than echoing its folk past. As an inquisitive only child from a remarkably musical family, Walker first encountered Blind Lemon Jefferson at weekend house parties hosted by his mother and stepfather in Dallas. "He'd come over every Sunday and sit with us and play his guitar," Walker explained in a 1972 interview with Jim and Amy O'Neal published in *Living Blues*. By 1920 or so, the young Walker knew Jefferson and the streets well enough to function as his "lead boy," steering him through the crowds on Central Avenue in Dallas, where he would play on the sidewalk or in taverns for tips. Completely taken with the older man's guitar work and singing, Walker aspired to be a musician himself. Learning from what he observed at home, he started out playing in string bands like the Satisfied Five, a group led by the father of Houston blues musician Robert "Skin Man" Murphy (b. 1927), who recalls:

> In that time, they had places in Dallas sort of like drive-ins; they called them Pig Stands. And people would drive up there and they'd be sitting out there playing, three or four of them. . . . T-Bone Walker was a member of the Satisfied Five.
> . . . He didn't stay there very long because he moved on to San Antonio or went off with some other group or something. And then he switched to guitar. He played banjo originally, and his [step]father played bass fiddle.

By the mid-1920s through the 1930s, Walker had worked all manner of entertainment jobs—as singer, musician, dancer, and comedian—and had toured widely with various road shows and big bands. During the late 1930s, he'd begun to experiment with the newfangled idea of incorporating electric amplification into guitar playing, a concept pioneered by fellow Texas native Charlie Christian (1916–1942) in the jazz idiom. By the early 1940s, Walker was playing electric guitar in nightclubs nationwide, including a celebrated nine-month stint with a band led by Houston's Milt Larkin at Joe Louis' Rumboogie Club in Chicago. In the process, Walker was also making history, transforming what had once been primarily a rhythm instrument backing lead horns in Cab Calloway–style big bands into a potent new musical force. Soon signed to the Capitol Records label in Hollywood (and various others thereafter), Walker went on to release a succession of hit singles, codifying the concept of the electric guitar solo in blues music in the process. Based in Hollywood, the newly emerging center of the entertainment industry, Walker, who was in his prime during the postwar era of national prosperity and widespread proliferation of recorded music via radio and home phonographs, almost single-handedly established the electric guitar as the lead instrument in much popular American music, from blues to various stylistic descendants. Throughout the 1940s and 1950s, no other musician had such an enormous impact on a generation of would-be blues instrument players. It was a whole new sound.

Guitarist Pete Mayes (b. 1938), a native of the rural swampland community of Double Bayou (in Chambers County, just east of Houston) and a stalwart of the Bayou City blues scene since the mid-1950s, recalls his epiphany on hearing early recordings of T-Bone Walker:

> When I was four years old, I heard that sound. And the sound stuck in my ear; it was just something like I'd never experienced. . . . I'd heard it on a battery radio, see, out in the country. . . . I fell in love with that sound. I wanted to begin playing guitar then, when I heard that; that's what I wanted to do.

B.B. King, 1991.

While Mayes started particularly young, his story is typical for many of the greatest blues guitarists to emerge from Houston (and elsewhere) in the middle of the twentieth century. Even the world's most recognized master of the instrument, B.B. King, acknowledges the dramatic personal impact of Walker's music in terms of head-over-heels infatuation. As he once mused in an interview televised on *Bravo Profiles,* "Ah, T-Bone [sigh], that was the guy. If I'd have been a girl, I would've tried to marry him."

In the case of Mayes, his total crush on the music of T-Bone Walker dominated his imagination throughout childhood and into adolescence. Several years after first hearing that bright new sound on the radio, he was with his uncle attending the segregated, all-black version of the county fair in the town of Liberty. To the youngster's uncontainable excitement, they happened to hear that T-Bone Walker was playing that night at Club 90 in nearby Ames. Mayes pestered his older relative to take him to catch a glimpse of his idol, someone he had only listened to on recordings but had never seen until then.

> *Well, man, you know I wanted to go to that. So what my uncle did was, you know I couldn't go in the place at the time, so what he did, he went to the back window and got a block or a stool and put it right there close to that window, and I got up on that and watched T-Bone for most of the time he was up there, you know. And I understood and saw what he was doing. Then when I went home, I really was practicing trying to do what he was doing. And I got it down pretty good.*

Like numerous others, Mayes eventually first performed in public in a school talent show, his two-song repertoire consisting of T-Bone Walker hits. "Boy, that talent show went well for us, I'm talking about real well," he recalls. "They clapped us back on two or three times." By the age of sixteen he had mastered enough material to perform whole sets of nothing but Walker tunes, a skill that came in handy when, one night in a small joint at Barrett Settlement (a black community east of Houston, near the town of Crosby), he finally got to meet his idol, who graciously invited the teenager onstage to perform. As Mayes tells it:

> *So I went up there, and T-Bone took his guitar off and handed it to me. . . . That was a Gibson L-5 he had. And I did something you don't normally do—the reason I got away with it was because I was a child. As a grown man, you don't do this type of thing: Everything I played was T-Bone. So I started on one of his songs, and he stood there—he had on a suit with suspenders—and he kind of put his thumbs in his suspenders and stood there and watched me. When I finished that one, he said, "Go on, kid, do another one!" He kept me up there at least thirty minutes or more. I'm talking about doing one song right behind another—of his!*

Pete Mayes, at home, 1996.

Roy Gaines tells a similar story of Walker's generosity onstage at a big show in Houston, a meeting made possible because the then fourteen-year-old Gaines had made a local reputation for himself of impersonating the master's style at the old Whispering Pines nightclub in the north-side Trinity Gardens neighborhood.

When T-Bone came to town, they told him there's this little boy, fourteen years old, playing like you. He said, "Well, that's good." Anyway, I heard that T-Bone knew about me, and I went to see him at the City Auditorium downtown. And it was people in line—man, I mean all the way around the corner! . . . They let me in, and I got the chance to go backstage and tell him that I was in the house, you know, and that I admired him so. And he called me onstage! He said, "You stay right here. Don't you go no place. I'm going to call you onstage." And when he went onstage and had played about three songs, he told the people that he was going to bring me on, and boy, I was standing back there about to pee on myself! I don't know what I was thinking, but I was ready to go. I was all keyed up. Anyway, he called me on . . . He didn't let me sing. He said, "I'm going to sing, and I want you to play behind me." He said that to me over the mike, to all the people. And he said, "Do 'Cold, Cold Feeling.'" And that was one of my favorites! So I played the intro to that, and he came in singing, and I played, man, . . . and the people screamed and hollered.

Just as he did for Mayes and Gaines, T-Bone Walker showed the way to numerous other Texas-raised blues guitarists who came of age in the early 1950s. Walker's influence via popular recordings was immense, but his regular tours through Houston and the surrounding region during the heyday of his fame made meeting him and, as evidenced in the oral histories quoted above, actually sharing the stage with him real possibilities. In contrast to the loner Lightnin' Hopkins, whose style reached back to the era of the younger generation's grandfathers, Walker's electric sound and fashionable appearance appealed directly to their desire for something exciting and new. Joe "Guitar" Hughes succinctly sums up the difference between Hopkins and Walker, at least in the minds of the next generation of Houston bluesmen: "I really didn't talk about music with Lightnin' because I also knew about other guitarists that were into a more *modern* way of playing," citing T-Bone Walker and his Texas rival Clarence "Gatemouth" Brown as players in whom he was much more interested at the time. Almost apologetically, Hughes explains, "I was mainly into the Lightnin' only because my stepfather listened to him all the time. But T-Bone Walker was something cool, man."

Over a quarter century after Walker's death, his legion of loyal Texas blues disciples tend to remain steadfast in their veneration of the man who took what he first learned from Blind Lemon Jefferson—how to punctuate a vocal line with a guitar lick, how to bend the strings in a burst of fluid fretwork romps—and made it all new and electric, a fresh sound. Roy Gaines, who recorded a tribute album to Walker in 1998, puts it bluntly: "To this day, nobody can beat 'Bone on stand-up singing and playing the guitar at the same time. . . . 'Bone is the true king of blues."

And on a visit to Pete Mayes' house during 1998, I noticed that a framed photograph—taken in 1960 at Club Raven in Beaumont, Texas—holds a special place of honor on the otherwise mostly bare walls. Both of them in suits and ties and grinning broadly, the late Willard Mayes holds a bass on the left while his twenty-two-year-old brother, Pete, clutches a guitar on the right. In between them, the shorter, older T-Bone nestles his large Gibson L-5 and smiles demurely. That black-and-white image documents the fact that Mayes eventually graduated from a child prodigy imitating the amused elder onstage to his professional cohort. "We were the band behind him for many gigs," Pete sighs. "And he was the best there ever will be."

Mayes' 1998 CD on the Antone's label, *For Pete's Sake* (a nominee for the W. C. Handy Award for Comeback of the Year), provides a good illustration of the sonic legacy of T-Bone Walker's musical style, as interpreted by one of his personal friends. While the twelve-track collection includes a cover (a performance of a song previously recorded, and written by, someone else) of one Walker composition, the T-Bone influence is generally omnipresent—now an inherent element of Mayes' artistic vocabulary, both as instrumentalist and singer. It's there in his precisely phrased vocal articulations. It's there in the full sound of a well-orchestrated ensemble dominated by clean solos on electric guitar—the sound Joe Hughes earlier referred to as "modern" in contrast to rough-edged acoustic blues stylings from the country. And it's really there in the driving groove that makes the music rock with a certain passionate yet elegant swing. As the Austin-based record producer Derek O'Brien (a major Texas guitar player himself) once explained to me about Mayes:

> He does swing the blues—that is just Pete's pocket, you know. It's real Texas swing—the way the piano plays, the way the bass plays, the way the drums play, they all add up to a type of Texas blues-swing thing. . . . The characteristics are a band with a horn section, as you hear on that record, and the bass and drums playing almost like jazz musicians, or swing players from an earlier era. . . . What it boils down to—the walking bass, sometimes doubled by the left hand of the piano, and the drums playing a shuffle or swing beat, and the horn section doing the call and response with the singer. . . . It's really the Texas blues style.

And that sophisticated style goes far beyond the creations of Pete Mayes to color the work of countless Houston blues guitarists who discovered the electric guitar in the 1950s.

It's the type of music that folks at a 1998 Blue Monday jam session respond to most heartily—the base sound from which subsequent genre-blurring forms emerged, including golden era R&B, soul, and early rock and roll. And it's this polished urban sound, partly jazz, that—in its contrast to the old-style folk blues—tells the second half of the story of many of these people's lives.

Like Sam "Lightnin'" Hopkins, Pete Mayes, Roy Gaines, and others, a sizable number of the Houston blues musicians I've interviewed (as well as their fans in the old wards) have family roots in the country communities of East Texas or southwest Louisiana. Many of them can talk knowingly—from direct personal experience in their youth—about picking cotton, slaughtering hogs, tending cattle, and other distinctly rural and agrarian experiences. As revealed in Hopkins' published interviews with Samuel Charters (as well as in Les Blank's acclaimed 1968 documentary film *The Blues According to Lightnin' Hopkins*), long after the man who called himself "Po' Lightnin'" had settled permanently near downtown Houston, he retained vivid memories of (and family connections to) the Leon County farm region of his birth and visited there from time to time. And as Blank also points out in his *Living Blues* obituary for the man, Hopkins loved the old ways of life, such as fishing and going to rodeos, and often distrusted the new, such as flying on airplanes or maintaining a telephone. As such, Hopkins typifies the mindset of some of the older African American blues people still residing in Houston. But just as most of those folks have eventually left behind a world of fieldwork and barn chores and adapted to new ways of life in the city, they also tend to have moved past the primal blues personified by Hopkins, its most recorded practitioner. Most of them readily acknowledge country-style blues as the foundation for their musical culture, and happily revisit it on occasion. But by the 1990s it is no longer their common mode of expression—nor should it be.

That fact disappoints some misguided outsiders who seem to define blues authenticity only in terms of the rough-edged folk stylings of an older, unschooled era. I have witnessed a visiting "expert" from a prestigious out-of-state institution bemoan the alleged dearth of "pure" blues he discovered in Third Ward clubs. Like many other white intellectual students of the music, this fellow seemed to harbor some romantic (and perhaps unconsciously racist) illusion about the "primitive" Negro and "real blues," offensively dismissing any stylings that suggested jazzlike sophistication or R&B-flavored melodicism as "not blues," and ignoring the fact that the African American performers and audiences in these very clubs mainly describe the music he heard played in terms of the simple "b" word.

To each his own tastes, and if someone's personal preference is only for gritty, relatively simplistic folk blues, so be it. But to seek to discredit a living culture based on a snapshot idea from some mythic past is absurd. Who is in the better position to define the state of the blues at the end of the twentieth century—some scholar and nostalgic record collector from a distant northeastern metropolis, or African Americans in neighborhoods rich with blues history in the South's largest city, people who have remade the music anew with each generation, continually updating it the better to identify with it? If the music these city dwellers play and hear is generally more complex, more media influenced, more progressively urban than that of their rural ancestors, well, so are their lives. And if they understand the core reality of this evolving musical form as blues, what outsider is really qualified to argue against them?

What the big city is to the cotton patch, T-Bone Walker seems to have represented in relation to Lightnin' Hopkins—at least in the musical lives of many black people in Houston in the decades since World War II. The dapper, city-raised Walker—whose family moved to Dallas from rural Cass County when the only child was two years old—never stooped among rows of cotton or tossed fresh-cut bales of hay onto wagon beds out in the countryside. His upbringing, like the overwhelmingly influential sound he would develop as a mature recording artist, was distinctly urban. As such, it was antithetical to that of Hopkins, who once marveled (in detached recollections of his youth during an interview with Samuel Charters) at just how much he had routinely struggled to extract even a two-dollar profit from cotton picking. That struggle informed his music, no doubt, and imbued it with a special antiquated power. But Walker's flashy electric vibe had its own undeniable power too. And together, these two men personify the dialectically opposed forces underlying the evolution of Texas blues.

Even so, if contemporary Houston blues-based music reflects a synthesis of these two styles, it's a lopsided one that tilts heavily in the direction of Walker, the Duke-Peacock recording empire, the old jazz-blues territory bands of Larkin and Cobb, and the concomitant evolution of a West Coast sound in California. Although Hopkins himself journeyed briefly to Los Angeles in 1946 (with talent agent Lola Anne Cullum [1903–1970] and pianist Wilson "Thunder" Smith) to make his earliest recordings on the Aladdin label, he never changed his signature folksy repertoire, or home address, as a result. On the other hand, Walker not only developed his early electric sound while working in California nightclubs but established permanent residence there too, as early as 1934. He thus foreshadowed a still active tradition of black musicians leaving their native Lone Star state behind and becoming stars once located in or near the West Coast entertainment capital.

Among blues artists born or raised in Houston, those who left to find commercial success in Los Angeles include contemporary performers such as Roy Gaines and guitarist Cal Green (b. 1935), as well as many others who are now no longer alive. Some of the latter group include the seminal R&B pianist and vocalist Charles Brown (1922–1999, a native of nearby Texas City); the great lyricist and singer Percy Mayfield (1920–1984); the guitarist and singer Peppermint Harris (born Harrison Nelson, 1925–1999); the "Chicken Shack Boogie" piano king Amos Milburn (1927–1980); the female vocalist Esther Phillips (1935–1984); the funkmeister Johnny "Guitar" Watson (1935–1996); the singer and saxophonist Eddie "Cleanhead" Vinson (1917–1988); and the aforementioned Telecaster guitar slinger extraordinaire Albert Collins, who found his greatest commercial success after relocating to California and starting to record in Chicago, home of Alligator Records.

However, Houston-to-California migration is not the only historical path to more widespread exposure for local blues artists. For instance, Third Ward's great guitarist, singer, and blues ambassador to the world Johnny Copeland (1937–1997) finally found the international acclaim he was due only after leaving Houston for New York City. Jazz-blues tenor sax man and bandleader Arnett Cobb, a lifelong Houstonian, recorded some of his most important work in New York too (for labels such as Apollo and Prestige). And at least two classic singers, truly noteworthy Houston-born early blueswomen, ventured north (not west or east) to develop their careers: Beaulah "Sippie" Wallace (1898–1986), who also played piano, and Victoria Spivey (1906–1976), who played multiple instruments.

Sometimes, for various reasons, a Houston-born blues artist has returned to reside in his or her hometown following a period of professional breakthrough in California. Such is the case, for instance, with the Fifth Ward–born "swamp boogie queen" Katie Webster (1939–1999), who went on to make records first in Louisiana and then became a major recording star for Alligator Records, following her move to California. Yet after a series of medical complications a few years ago, she chose to return to the Houston area to be closer to her family. During the final years of her life, Webster created quite a stir with her surprise appearances onstage at a couple of special musical events (most notably the September 1998 Living Blues Bash II, hosted by the Houston Blues Society at downtown's Aerial Theater). Another returnee from the West Coast, the late Teddy Reynolds (1931–1998) first established himself playing with Bobby Bland for Houston's Duke-Peacock Records. However, as an in-demand musician, he relocated to California for a dozen years (1958–1970) before coming back to his hometown, where (following a period out of music working for local industry) he remained an active sideman until ill health sidelined him. During the last ten years of his life, Reynolds laid down some of the finest blues keyboards ever heard in local clubs, backing lifelong friends such as Grady Gaines (b. 1934) and Texas Johnny Brown (b. 1928). He also recorded with Gaines on several CDs on the Black Top label and is featured on three tracks on Brown's self-produced 1998 W. C. Handy Award–nominated CD *Nothin' but the Truth*.

Then there's the occasional rarity of an established artist from elsewhere immigrating to Houston. Perhaps the best example of this phenomenon is the classic blues shouter Jimmy "T-99" Nelson (b. 1919), who was born in Philadelphia and came of musical age in California (where he recorded his breakthrough 1951 hit "T-99 Blues," as well as 1952's "Meet Me with Your Black Dress On," for Modern Records). But luckily for Houston, Third Ward was the place where Nelson fell in love with a local woman, during an extended stint playing at Club Ebony in the mid-1950s. He had worked there for several weeks with the band led by Arnett Cobb, who had previously toured with blues singers such as Big Bill Broonzy (1893–1958) but was most famous for his relatively highbrow affiliation with jazz bandleader Lionel Hampton (1908–2002) in the 1940s. Cobb was a serious jazz artist who was naturally at home with the blues, regularly employing "blues phraseology and wild swoops and hollers in his music, bringing audiences to a frenzy," as his style was so aptly described by writer Keith Shadwick. That combination appealed to Nelson. And his happiness in collaborating with Cobb, as well as his growing disillusionment with his record label (and the

Katie Webster, at home, 1997.

Jimmy "T-99" Nelson, 1998.

constant touring he'd endured), prompted him to take a day job and settle permanently in the Bayou City with the woman who would become his bride, Nettie. Following a twenty-year hiatus in which he made a good living working for a construction company, Nelson eventually resumed his rightful role onstage singing the blues in Houston clubs. During the 1980s and 1990s, he also began to perform at major festivals at home and abroad, impressing audiences with his swinging vocal style and knack for witty lyrics. In 1999, in his eightieth year, Nelson made his comeback complete by releasing the CD *Rockin' and Shoutin' the Blues* (a double W. C. Handy Award nominee) on the Bullseye Blues label. Meanwhile, now a widower who has never stopped missing Nettie, he still resides in their longtime homestead on Calumet Street. And if you ask him, he'll swear he's a true *Texas* bluesman, a title he's proudly earned the right to claim over the years.

The lists above are not intended as complete catalogues but rather as brief representations of the types of Houston blues artists who ventured elsewhere, or started out elsewhere, to pursue their careers in music. Nevertheless, there were scores of others who came to Houston from the surrounding region or, in the case of natives, chose to stay in the Bayou City—especially in the era from the late 1940s through the early 1970s, when a fair amount of independent recording activity occurred in Houston. In addition to the relatively large Duke-Peacock operations (about which more will be said later in this book), several smaller Houston companies released important blues recordings during this time period.

One of the most significant companies was owned and operated by a transplanted New Englander named Bill Quinn (1903–1976), whose Gold Star label started out calling itself "King of the Hillbillies" (and first scored big with Harry Choates' 1946 recording of the Cajun standard "Jole Blon" [*sic*]) but also waxed some of the best early material by Lightnin' Hopkins, Peppermint Harris, and others. Another was the short-lived (1949–1951) Macy's label, which advertised itself as the "Queen of Hits," alluding to its female proprietress (a rarity), Macy Lela Henry (1912–1991). Macy's did, in fact, release two nationwide hits: "Wintertime Blues" by Houston's Lester Williams (1920–1997) and "Bon Ton Roula" by transplanted Louisiana native Clarence Garlow (1911–1986). There was also Ivory Records, owned and operated by musician and entrepreneur "King" Ivory Lee Semien (1931–2002), which issued singles of various local performers (including Hopkins) but is most noted for producing the primary sonic documents of Houston's late blues genius of the lap steel guitar, Harding "Hop" Wilson (1921–1975). Before folding in the early 1950s, Freedom Records, an enterprise started by Saul M. Kahl in 1948, released seminal sides on former Bayou City regulars such as guitarist Goree Carter (1931–1990), pianist Little Willie Littlefield (b. 1931), pianist Lonnie Lyons (b. 1929), and singer L. C. Williams (1924–1960).

Of special note, no less an authority than Robert Palmer (1945–1997), the late music critic for the *New York Times* and the author of various influential books, argues in his *Rock and Roll: An Unruly History* that Carter's 1949 Freedom Records hit "Rock Awhile," though largely unrecognized as such, was really "the first rock and roll record." In making his case, Palmer debunks the now fairly widespread belief that the 1951 Chess recording (in Memphis) of "Rocket 88" by Jackie Brenston and His Delta Cats (featuring Ike Turner on piano) is the original African American progenitor of the new "rock" sound. As John Nova Lomax has pointed out, Palmer also indirectly reminds us that, in this case as well as other instances, Houston's significant role in modern American music history has been overlooked, especially given the Delta-centric or Chicago-centric assumptions of many music writers.

Chris Strachwitz (b. 1931), of California-based Arhoolie Records, taped some of his most important blues and zydeco sessions in Houston during the 1960s, including the definitive recordings by Fifth Ward's blues poet Weldon "Juke Boy" Bonner (1932–1978), one of the last local song stylists working almost exclusively in the tradition of Lightnin' Hopkins (whom Strachwitz also recorded in Houston on several occasions). The Bayou City is also where the Arhoolie founder was introduced to early zydeco music, where he made his groundbreaking field recordings of the form in 1961, and where, in 1964, he initially recorded the label's all-time biggest selling artist, the late "King of Zydeco" Clifton Chenier (1925–1987). As Strachwitz recalls:

> When I met up with Lightnin' Hopkins one night later on, he said, "Let's just go hear my cousin." And so he took me over to this little beer joint in Houston in an area they call Frenchtown. And here was this black man with a huge accordion on his chest and playing the most unbelievable low-down blues I'd ever heard in my life—and singing it in this bizarre French patois! His name was Clifton Chenier. . . . I don't think the place had a name. It was just a beer joint. And since Houston has no zoning laws, you could build a beer joint anywhere you feel like, as long as the neighbors don't shoot you down. I just remember it was in the neighborhood called Frenchtown, in Fifth Ward.
>
> So as soon as Lightnin' introduced me, Clifton said, "Oh, you're a record man. I want to make a record tomorrow." . . . When I first heard Cliff, I heard him singing in Creole patois. That was his first language. And I didn't think his phrasing in English was nearly as good. So it was a battle, then and every time we recorded. Cliff would say, "I've got to make rock-and-roll records—that's what sells." And I begged him to sing in French. So he said, "Okay, Chris, I'll make you a deal: If you let me cut one side of the album rock and roll"—as he called it, [but] it was really R&B—"I'll make the other side French for you." And from that session, we did have a regional hit, but it was the French one that sold. It was a low-down blues, "Tous les Jours la Même Chose," something like that. I said, how do you spell that? And he said, spell it any way you want to. Then I asked if I could just call it "Louisiana Blues," and he said "Okay." So that's what I put on the label—and it sold.

Strachwitz's anecdote suggests just how significant certain events that took place in the city of Houston—with its large population of Creole immigrants from southwestern Louisiana—have been to the popular development of zydeco music (even though most people seem to regard the genre as an exclusively Louisiana phenomenon). In truth, the vitality of local zydeco culture has contributed in many ways to Houston blues (and vice-versa)—via the interchange of musicians, songs, stylistic techniques, and instruments, as well as the evolution of a sizable audience that appreciates both styles of live music (which often share the same venues, sometimes on the same nights).

In fact, as Michael Tisserand and others have pointed out, the now standard spelling of the term *zydeco* (which is derived from black Creole pronunciation of the first two words in the Louisiana French expression "les haricots sont pas salé," meaning "the beans are not salted"—a metaphor for hard times) was first formally established in Houston by the folklorist Robert Burton "Mack" McCormick (b. 1930). As McCormick noted the use of the term in the city's Frenchtown district, it referred simultaneously to a style of music, a dance step, and the event at which the two could be found. And the first two records to use the word in this sense, as opposed to the original French meaning referring to a bean, were produced not in Louisiana but also in Houston in the late 1940s. Significantly also, these records were made not by artists playing the accordion or in the traditional Creole style. Instead, the first (titled "Zolo Go" by a confused Bill Quinn in the production booth at Gold Star), was issued possibly as early as 1947 by Lightnin' Hopkins, who makes a rare appearance on boogie-woogie organ (on which he roughly imitates the sound of the accordion). The second was the 1949 recording of the rumbalike "Bon Ton Roula" on the Macy's label by the previously mentioned R&B guitarist and singer Clarence Garlow. Then, in 1964 in Houston, Chenier—the musician most responsible for popularizing zydeco—would record the genre's theme song "Zydeco Sont Pas Salé," in which Strachwitz, following McCormick's lead, officially abandoned the French phrase *les haricots* for the potent new word *zydeco*.

In addition to Chenier, whose unique blues-based accordion sound and French idiom Strachwitz introduced to the world, another of Strachwitz's most significant discoveries occurred during a one-day field trip to the Grimes County town of Navasota, approximately seventy-five miles northwest of Houston. Following a lead provided by his generous and knowledgeable guide McCormick, the visiting music enthusiast met Mance Lipscomb (1895–1976), one of the last of the great country-style African American pickers and singers to live out his life on the farmlands of his birth. Like his friend Lightnin' Hopkins, with whom he went on to share the bill at major festivals (and at Houston folk venues such as The Old Quarter and Liberty Hall) during the folk music revival of the 1960s and early 1970s, Lipscomb typically performed alone on guitar, making up ditties and drawing from the traditional nonmediated repertoire he had absorbed while working the fields and playing Saturday night dances in the fertile Brazos River Valley region. Because Strachwitz could not initially afford to pay Hopkins the price he demanded, Lipscomb became the featured artist on the very first LP album issued by Arhoolie, *Texas Sharecropper and Songster* (1960). But though the venerable Lipscomb always lived nearby and made occasional visits to Houston (referring to the city in numerous songs), he was never really at home there, nor in any other urban environment. And his life, like his exclusively acoustic style of playing, epitomized the country past that so many black people were leaving behind as they gravitated toward big cities.

Perhaps no other formerly Houston-based blues artist better illustrates the cultural movement from the countryside to the city streets—and as such the synthesis of the Lightnin' Hopkins/T-Bone Walker dialectic—than a genre-blurring musician named Clarence Brown, better known for half a century as "Gatemouth." Born in southwestern Louisiana, Brown moved with his family to rural southeast Texas when he was only three weeks old. His father was a versatile musician (and particularly accomplished as a fiddler), so Brown grew up exposed to a variety of instruments and styles of Gulf Coast folk music. But to advance his professional career (which has since included scores of albums, multiple Grammy awards, and frequent global touring over many decades), he—like so many others—had to relocate to a big city.

By the mid-1940s Brown was living in San Antonio, playing drums with the Hart Hughes Orchestra. Then in 1947, at age twenty-three, he abruptly left his room in a boardinghouse (where he shared space with the man who would eventually follow him eastward and become known as the blues singer and pianist Big Walter "the Thunderbird") and hitchhiked to Houston. Ever since then, Brown has been a multidimensional force to be reckoned with in American roots music. Though he actually started his professional career playing drums (and has mastered fiddle, mandolin, viola, and various other instruments), Gatemouth reigns as one of the all-time great virtuosos of Texas blues guitar. That reputation caught fire one night when, as a daring, still practically unknown kid, he reportedly emerged from the audience in Fifth Ward's old Bronze Peacock nightclub and literally stole the show from an ailing, offstage T-Bone Walker.

As Brown once related in a *Living Blues* interview:

> He [Walker] got sick one night and laid the guitar down . . . and went to the dressing room. I was sittin' on the side of the bandstand and I got up and picked up his guitar. And I can't say I wrote this, but I invented it—"Gatemouth's Boogie." On his guitar. And I made $600 in tips in fifteen minutes. Back in those days, '47, that was a lot of money. And all of a sudden the guy recovered and come back and took his guitar and told me never to pick it up again.

The club's owner, the enigmatic entrepreneur Don Robey (1903–1975), immediately signed the brash electric guitar slinger to a management contract—and a couple of years later created the seminal blues and R&B label Peacock Records specifically to market Brown's many talents.

Initially—like Lightnin' Hopkins, Amos Milburn, and other Houston musicians before him—Brown had traveled to California to record for the Aladdin label owned by the Mesner brothers.

But like Hopkins, he also soon returned to his home turf in the Lone Star state. Because Robey had grown increasingly dissatisfied with the results of his client's affiliation with Aladdin, he eventually pulled his budding star out of the deal, directed his business partner Evelyn Johnson (b. 1920) to figure out how to start a record company, and the Peacock label was born—in the same building that housed (and eventually would supplant) the Bronze Peacock nightclub.

Following a lengthy run of original hits with Peacock—including intense vocal numbers such as "My Time Is Expensive" and big-band swing instrumentals the likes of "Okie Dokie Stomp"— Brown left Houston in the early 1960s, recording extensively and internationally for numerous labels over the subsequent decades. For years now he has made his residence back in his native state of Louisiana. But the Texas Bayou City, home to many of his musician friends (such as his primary saxophonist in recent years, Eric Demmer), has remained a frequent stop on the seemingly constant touring of the Gatemouth Express. And each time Brown pulls his beloved bus into town, the septuagenarian wonder serves notice that nobody dare pigeonhole his music in any ready-made category. As he implies in the song "Born in Louisiana, Raised on the Texas Side," his style is a gumbo of influences reflecting an intercultural heritage. Brown's technique and repertoire intuitively blend elements of Cajun, zydeco, country and western, bluegrass, jazz, and blues. What to call it? When pressed for an accurate classification of his sound, Brown takes a long drag on his ever present pipe, blows out a roomful of pungent smoke, and gruffly says, "American music, Texas drive."

Whatever label one chooses to affix, the music of Clarence "Gatemouth" Brown represents a potent fusion of the rustic folk elements symbolized by Lightnin' Hopkins and the jazz-flavored, electric elegance of T-Bone Walker. Brown's down-home persona—visually signified by the blue jeans, pearl-buttoned rodeo shirts, and cowboy hats he normally wears—finds voice in the decidedly country tones of his playing, as well as in his choice of material. It's there in his drawling vocal delivery and in his instinct for earthy metaphor, even if he doesn't usually play solo and acoustic like the old-timers. Anyone who's ever witnessed him whip up a fiddle frenzy on traditional numbers such as "Up Jumped the Devil" should comprehend that part of Brown that would seem to be more at home cane-pole fishing in a murky bayou with Hopkins than carting spiffily around the manicured greens with Walker, a noted golf enthusiast. On the other hand, ever since that breakthrough night at the Bronze Peacock over fifty years ago, Brown has been recognized as one of the all-time masters of jazzy electric guitar, the source of a polished urban sound—what Joe Hughes called "modern"—rendered in the sophisticated manner of Walker (sometimes also with swinging big-band accompaniment). In Brown, whose career was based in Houston during its early major phase, one detects the yin and yang of Texas blues—opposite but complementary traits associated in the past with Hopkins and Walker, the two most significant protégés of the guy who started it all, Blind Lemon Jefferson.

Joe "Guitar" Hughes, 1998. [detail]

At the start of the twenty-first century, Brown is arguably the most widely recognized icon of classic Texas blues still alive and regularly touring. Only a year younger than Brown and equally active in the music business, the world's indisputably most well known bluesman, Mississippi-born B.B. King, offers a telling contrast to Brown's Texas style. Like the finely tailored suits worn by the genre's most media-celebrated artist, King's musical productions retain an element of uptown slickness, evident in everything from the clothing to the lighting to the stage dynamics of his backing orchestra. His concerts unfold in a closely synchronized plan (with dramatic entrances after big musical build-ups, carefully planned set lists, seemingly iron-clad time limits, and so on) that would seem to mesh with the program requirements of a lavish ballroom venue at the finest hotel in Las Vegas. In contrast, Brown's shows over the past several decades are usually relatively informal, both in physical presentation and in the wide-open, genre-crossing musical possibilities that arise. When the venerable Gatemouth plugs in the guitar, fires up his pipe, and cuts loose, a certain primal wildness is palpable—even if he's eloquently plucking out straight-ahead uptown jazz numbers such as "Take the 'A' Train."

There's definitely an element of that wild cowboy in Gatemouth that seems to appeal to many blues audiences in the old neighborhoods of Houston. But make no mistake: They love their B.B. King too. Most of the folks there can readily relate to the raw *and* the cooked, so to speak. And some of the locals with good memories actually consider King to be one of their own also, given the crucial role that the Bayou City played for him early in his career. Managed for several years in the 1950s through Fifth Ward's Buffalo Booking Agency (operated by Don Robey's colleague Evelyn Johnson), B.B. King has maintained ties to Houston ever since he initially established himself as a blues star. Some of his first great recordings on the RPM label were made here between 1953 and 1955, using material performed with the legendary band led by Bill Harvey (1904–1979)—a group that, like bands backing Bobby Bland, Junior Parker, and others, formed part of a midcentury Houston-Memphis connection that benefited blues culture in both cities. For the last several decades, however, the Bayou City has been for King just another stop on his frequent tours. Yet he has continued to draw supporting musical talent from his old professional home base—people such as drummer Sonny Freeman (1909–1983), pianist Connie McBooker (1931–1984), John Browning, current band member Leon Warren, and two Fifth Ward natives that I have come to know personally: King's former musical director and bandleader, trumpeter Calvin Owens (b. 1929), and versatile keyboardist Eugene Carrier (1946–1997). King's records are regularly punched up on jukeboxes in the older blues venues around town, and his essential sound, similar in some ways to the defining qualities of the great Duke-Peacock recordings, is often evoked by local musicians jamming at weekly blues gatherings.

Some of the best performers at the Blue Monday sessions, the Sunday-afternoon blues parties at C. Davis Bar-B-Q or Mr. Gino's, or the Saturday-night rituals at the Silver Slipper and elsewhere around the city are professionals (past or present), like the aforementioned Carrier and Owens, who actually worked for years with major stars from B.B. King to Gatemouth Brown to Bobby Bland or other Duke-Peacock featured artists. Now comfortably settled down with families in Houston, they are the lifeblood of the blues culture that survives at the turn to the twenty-first century. One such example is guitarist and singer I. J. Gosey (b. 1937), who was a session musician in the Duke-Peacock stable for many years.

Starting in 1957, Gosey performed on recordings by artists such as Junior Parker, Bobby Bland, Al "TNT" Braggs (b. 1934), "Buddy Ace" (Jimmy Lee Land, 1935–1994), Larry Davis (1936–1994), Joe Hinton (1929–1968), Joe Medwick (1933–1992), and Gatemouth Brown. "Just about everything that come out of Duke and Peacock in the late fifties and early sixties, I was playing bass on," he says, and he has the stories to back up his claim. For instance, he gleefully remembers being in the studio the first time Gatemouth, who formerly had recorded exclusively as a guitarist, brought in his beloved fiddle. The legendary arranger and producer Joe Scott (1924–1979) immediately objected to the introduction of this "country" instrument. "But Gate begged him to just listen to him do a blues . . . and when he started playing that thing, man, it just blew us away." Gosey also recalls how, under the direction of Scott, the studio band would work out the arrangements for new songs for Bobby Bland. Often the new tunes would be recorded later with others, but "sometimes they'd just let Bobby sing over our demo and put it out like that."

Along with his fellow studio musician Texas Johnny Brown, Gosey eventually went on the road for a few years with Junior Parker. During this time, the bass man developed an urge to learn another instrument. Thus, Brown claims to have frequently returned to the hotel late at night to find his roommate Gosey "sitting in bed fooling with my guitar." Later, Gosey began to study the guitar in earnest. He credits Roy Gaines with introducing him to his primary teacher, Steve Hester. He also fondly recalls how each of his "three main influences"—T-Bone Walker, B.B. King, and Billy Butler (1924–1991, of the Bill Doggett band)—graciously gave him impromptu lessons for which he would gladly have paid cash. Among those significant mentors who helped him develop as a guitarist, Gosey also cites Johnny Copeland, whose technique he would scrutinize, along with that of Joe Hughes, at Shady's Playhouse in the Third Ward. "Johnny Copeland is the one who made me throw the clamp away and learn how to play all over the neck."

Nowadays Gosey is recognized locally as the man who held the "longest-running steady gig in Houston" in honor of his performances (every week from 1973 till its closing in 2001) at the rustic C. Davis Bar-B-Q, located on Reed Road in a neighborhood known as Sunnyside (south of Third Ward). Seven days a week this down-home establishment served up some of the best smoked meats in town, but on Sunday afternoons and Tuesday evenings, it also delivered some of the sweetest blues in Texas—compliments of Gosey, an amiable bandleader, master guitarist, and vocalist.

I. J. Gosey, 1996.

By the time the Duke-Peacock era ended in the early 1970s, I. J. Gosey and the Supremes had formed, and the bandleader came into his own not only as a lead guitarist but also as a singer. Despite possessing a capable tenor voice, he had previously played behind other vocalists and had never really sung onstage. But eventually "one of those singers stood me up, and I just started singing, doing what come natural . . . and decided why pay someone else to do what I can do."

Of the C. Davis Bar-B-Q, his home base for more than a quarter of a century, he said in 1995, "I've been blessed here, man. Me and Clarence [Davis, the proprietor, 1927–2000], we're tight." And despite the fact that this gig was never advertised or even listed in the local papers, he steadily drew appreciative fans who, once initiated, kept coming back for more. One notable example:

> When Albert Collins left here and made it big, if he was playing anywhere in the radius of Houston, he'd come by Davis Bar-B-Q and park his big bus and come inside and play with me—just like we used to a long time ago out at Walter's Lounge. He'd do that every time he come to Houston. Wasn't getting a dime, but he'd hook up his stuff and we would get down.

Gosey knows it never was the most prestigious blues venue in Houston, but he clearly appreciates what C. Davis Bar-B-Q has meant to him. "I've been all over, and I've played in a lot of nice places, but there is something about Davis Bar-B-Q that I've never found nowhere else I've played. I'm talking about the atmosphere, the way the people appreciate the music, the way they treat you." Until its closing in May 2001 (following the death of its founder), Gosey continued to grace the stage there twice a week, for, as he says, "It's just pure enjoyment." Since then he's moved his base of musical operations, along with most of his fans, to the nearby establishment known as Mr. Gino's Lounge, where he keeps the same Tuesday-night and Sunday-afternoon schedule . . . and the joy continues to flow.

Gosey's life in music is typical of that of many African Americans who still keep the blues alive in little joints all around Houston. The city, even in the year 2002, is home to numerous veteran sidemen and -women—talented artists who first worked professionally during the golden years of Houston blues, an era roughly corresponding to the rise and fall of Duke-Peacock. Now no longer active (for the most part) in the recording industry, many of these folks nonetheless play frequent gigs across town, and some of them seem to find a special joy in playing the blues for regularly scheduled community-based gatherings. These weekly rituals, such as the Sunday-afternoon performances that started at C. Davis Bar-B-Q or the ages-old Blue Monday parties, have become long-standing traditions crucial to the survival of Houston's original blues culture.

among the several houston clubs where blues is still served up live by local performers at least one night a week, at least one, Miss Ann's Playpen, has revived a special type of musical gathering long known as the Blue Monday. This first-day-of-the-workweek event is a practice that was once common in African American clubs throughout the city, as well as elsewhere around the nation. The fundamental Blue Monday concept seems almost timeless, older than the blues itself. In this respect it differs from certain other highly popular weekly blues parties that—as described to me by some musicians who experienced them firsthand—seem to have evolved and faded away in response to specific socioeconomic (and technological) realities of the mid-twentieth-century era.

In collecting oral history on the Blue Monday phenomenon as it has survived in post–World War II black Houston, I have discovered memories of many similar types of daytime blues-music gatherings that occurred in the late 1950s and 1960s. One local analogue to the more widespread Blue Monday tradition was known, at least to some area women, as the Pressure Cooker. In many ways such an event was similar to the Blue Monday party, but just occurred on another afternoon of the workweek. However, the Pressure Cooker phenomenon is especially significant for one key reason: It shifted the audience focus from the working *man* to the *housewife* and thus reflected some major changes in the lives of Houston's original blues people.

Involving musicians and audience members alike in a cathartic and celebratory assertion of the power of live music (usually fueled, of course, by the consumption of alcohol), the historic Blue Mondays and Pressure Cookers granted symbolic license—to men and to women respectively— to enjoy themselves, and in some cases to escape or defy certain establishment-sanctioned, gender-identified responsibilities. The fundamental impulse to participate seems to lie in a decision to embrace an implicit sensuality and wildness (what an academic might call a Dionysian spirit) associated with the blues experience. Whereas the Blue Monday tradition continues to this day to draw community participation (from both males and females), events like the Pressure Cookers are now largely defunct. It seems obvious to me that the latter's creation and eventual demise reflect the evolution of gender roles in the American workplace and the home. But despite the changes, reviewing the history of such phenomena yields insight on the cultural context of Bayou City blues.

What exactly is a Blue Monday, at least in the context of Houston's postwar African American community? Simply put, it's an open blues jam session that historically started as early as eleven A.M. and as late as seven or eight P.M. on a Monday, drawing lots of musicians (for whom Monday is usually not otherwise a working day, following a full weekend of gigs). Traditionally, its clientele included a number of gainfully employed people for whom Monday is also typically a day off (such as barbers, weekend salespeople, and entertainers). But it was largely supported as well by working men who called in sick, took leave early, or hurried straight to the club upon completing that day's labor—in an attempt to extend the liberties of the weekend or to recover from hangover

Blue Monday, Miss Ann's Playpen, Third Ward, 1998.

effects resulting from weekend pleasure taking. Such gatherings were particularly notorious as settings for inspired blues performances by local players, professional and amateur.

No one seems to have documented precisely when or where the Blue Monday jam-session tradition first emerged among African Americans in general, but the basic concept of Mondays being "blue" is hundreds of years old and multicultural at that. The etymology of the phrase "Blue Monday" dates back at least to the Middle Ages. According to William Safire, in its inception it referred to the Monday prior to the period of self-denying penitence known as Lent practiced by medieval Christians throughout Europe. The phrase invoked the already established metaphorical suggestion of the color "blue" to symbolize the sad mood of revelers who suffered hangovers brought on by a wild weekend of pre-Lenten flings. In subsequent eras, the phrase "Blue Monday" has become more generally understood to signify that all-too-common feeling of depression triggered by having to face the return to work after a weekend off. The musicians I have interviewed, most of whom were born between 1914 and 1950, generally cannot remember a time before something called Blue Monday jam sessions existed in Houston, suggesting that the symbolic phrase was appropriated by blues culture early on.

For these people, the 1950s and 1960s were the real heyday of the Blue Monday in the old black neighborhoods, certainly both here in Houston and in other (but not all) American cities. For instance, the widely popular New Orleans pianist and singer Antoine "Fats" Domino (b. 1928) released a song in 1956 called "Blue Monday," which reached number one on the R&B charts as well as number five on the pop charts (and was even featured in a film called *The Girl Can't Help It*). As expected, the lyrics comment on the general drudgery of the working man who must inevitably return to labor every Monday. It thus voices a universal condition that is by no means unique to blues gatherings but which has found special articulation there. However, to my surprise, Dave Bartholomew (b. 1920), that song's author, original producer, and Domino's major collaborator, has told the writer Steve Kolanjian that Monday-afternoon blues jams were *not* common in the Crescent City during that era, and that he first observed such a phenomenon only while visiting the Midwest: "We were playing in Kansas City on a Sunday and didn't realize [until the following day] they had a lot of matinees on Monday. Why wasn't anybody going to work? I was from New Orleans—everybody works on Monday. Nobody had a party." He goes on to explain how memories of that Kansas City serendipity led to the song: "We went from one place to another, jamming with one band after the next. We were having so much fun. On the way home I scribbled out 'Blue Monday.'" Given Bartholomew's impressive insider status in postwar New Orleans music history, he would seem to be particularly well informed about the presence or absence of certain music traditions there. Obviously, what was common practice in Houston or Kansas City (and certainly elsewhere) might not have been the established norm in New Orleans, located just a few hundred miles east of Houston. (Which brings up another point: Despite their relatively close proximity and rival status as major upper Gulf Coast metropolitan areas, New Orleans and Houston sometimes seem like two different universes, musically speaking.) Whatever the explanation, for numerous Houston musicians of the same race and generation as Bartholomew, the Blue Monday concept was deeply ingrained in their musical upbringing.

For example, the late blues singer and keyboardist Teddy Reynolds, who was born in Third Ward in 1931, recalls the community tradition at a now defunct club known as the original Shady's Playhouse (located on Simmons Street just west of the intersection with Sampson). To Reynolds, this establishment (which he usually called just "Shady's") and the Blue Monday jams he discovered there would provide his introduction to a life in the blues.

> My first encounter with Shady's was just the music. You couldn't miss it. You'd be a block from Shady's and you'd hear that music—the best of the blues. The band would be cooking! . . . And whooooo! On Blue Mondays the place was really jumping, great singing and jamming all day long!
>
> Shady's was mainly for the neighborhood. . . . You can see how crowded it was, how close them houses [are]. Plenty of people stayed right in there. A lot of people! So first the neighborhood. And then the outsiders from Dowling Street [actually only a few blocks away], you know, from all them different places, they'd come to Shady's, see, for the good blues.
>
> Albert Collins, Shady's is where he learned at. That's where he learned at, from Widemouth [i.e., James "Widemouth" Brown, brother of "Gatemouth"] at the old Shady's, uh-huh. . . . Widemouth was the one who was teaching them guitar players, like Joe Hughes, Albert, and Johnny Copeland. They'd watch his hands. But he got real close to Albert . . . and Widemouth would show him all the different things.
>
> Blue Mondays'd start early. . . . Yeah, start at three o'clock in the daytime—three o'clock to sometimes twelve, one, or two o'clock at night. Some would say Blue Monday was a sleeping hangover party. [Laughs] And it was a party! You know, you go to work with a hangover on Monday morning, but you had to have a little drink or something and go listen at some blues, you know, after work. So you wind up at Blue Monday out there. . . . Three o'clock in the afternoon, the place be jumping. Five o'clock when the people'd get off, then they'd just pack in there, see. Some folks never even had made it to work on Monday, just didn't go, you know—sleep late, then get back down there. The blues on Blue Monday, that's it.

Reynolds credits this original location of Shady's Playhouse (in an old wood-frame building that previously housed an establishment known as Jeff's Playhouse) with being the locus of the most significant Blue Monday parties of his era—the place that, according to his impressions, triggered an explosion of similar musical events throughout the neighborhood. He adds:

Later on, other places in Third Ward did Blue Mondays, but they was copying it off of Shady's. That was the main thing, the main place, yeah. In the fifties, yeah, all through the fifties. Yeah, I'm telling you the truth, it sure was something back then. . . . See, all them places sprung up after Shady's doing so good. All of them started Blue Mondaying with the blues . . .

However, guitarist and singer Joe Hughes places the most glorious Blue Monday events not at the original Shady's Playhouse but at the club's second location (on the second floor of a still standing two-story brick-and-cement building near Elgin and Ennis), which it moved to in 1958 (the same year Reynolds left for his twelve-year stay in California). Hughes asserts:

[That] is where the most famous Blue Monday was. We'd start up there at like one o'clock and just go on through, playing the blues nonstop. And many people lost their jobs over here on Mondays! People that delivered stuff for their jobs, well you'd see all the trucks here. [Laughs] Oo-weee, Blue Monday! . . . All kinds of musicians would come by, and if they was qualified, I'd let them sit in. Because that's how I learned to play, from cats that would be sitting in.

Many other Third Ward residents concur that both locations of Shady's Playhouse featured some of the best Blue Mondays of the 1950s and 1960s. But by no means does Shady's Playhouse stand alone in the oral histories I've collected. For instance, Houston-born Bobby Lewis (aka Phillip Mystro; b. 1943), the proprietor of Miss Ann's Playpen (where the Blue Monday tradition continues today), finds the inspiration for his enterprise in memories of a club called Nola's that operated in Third Ward in the early sixties:

Because of Nola's, the men would just call in sick on Mondays. Nobody would go to work on Mondays. . . . [As for musicians,] it was whoever would show up. You know, whoever'd show up first would get it started. . . . And that thing jumped off into one of the best Blue Mondays ever. Everybody was in Nola's on Monday. The music was fantastic. It started about eleven o'clock that morning and would go till about twelve o'clock that night. They'd keep it going the whole time, I mean musician after musician, just a steady stream of 'em. . . . That's where I got that from.

No matter which past venue defines the essential Blue Monday memory for my interview subjects (just a sample of which are represented here), they all point out that the weekly jam session offered blues musicians invaluable opportunities to learn from each other. They also clearly associate Blue Monday with the working man's impulse to defy the responsibility of reporting to his job, frequently mentioning the common malady of the hangover as the excuse for, or the result of, Blue Monday.

Bobby Lewis, Miss Ann's Playpen, Third Ward, 1998.

In 1963, Houston's Duke Records issued a single by New Orleans vocalist James Davis (1938–1992) called "Blue Monday" (Duke single 368, b/w "Sing"), his most significant track for the label—and a completely different number from the previously mentioned Bartholomew composition. This second "Blue Monday" song was also re-recorded, first (and most impressively) in 1980 by that veteran of Shady's Playhouse Albert Collins (who retitled it "Blue Monday Hangover") and then again in 1981 by the popular Malaco Records artist Z. Z. Hill (1935–1984), whose version sold far better than the Duke original. Following the traditional AAB blues verse pattern, the lyrics speak directly to the laboring male's desire to skip work. The song incorporates a variation on a frequently recycled blues line in which the employee addresses his employer as "big boss man," whom he hears calling his name; yet the singer defiantly asserts his refusal to report to work, despite the "shame" of his condition. I note in passing that one of the most famous recorded blues songs of all time, T-Bone Walker's 1947 classic "Call It Stormy Monday," articulates even more elegantly the working man's frustration at having to resume another week of labor. But in contrast to the Walker composition, in the Duke label's "Blue Monday," it's not just the "boss man" and the obligation to report to work that the speaker hears calling. Significantly, another stanza also notes the diametrically opposed lure of the neighborhood Blue Monday jam session, whose music he can hear sounding across the neighborhood as he lies in bed at home bemoaning his inability to join that party because of previous indulgences and the oppressive hangover he now suffers.

The drudgery of having to confront the realities of Monday (whether it's metaphorically depicted as "stormy" or "blue") has never been limited exclusively to males, of course. However, in an earlier era in which many women typically labored at home while their husbands reported elsewhere to earn paychecks, the Blue Monday phenomenon seems to have responded to, and given form to, a collective male angst. By all accounts, neighborhood women were present at Blue Mondays in the past—especially the beauticians, for whom, like the previously mentioned barbers, Monday was usually a day off. However, in black Houston during the fifties and sixties, an analogue to the Blue Monday tradition evolved that appealed primarily to the female experience.

Singer Gloria Edwards (b. 1936) was the first interview subject to tell me about the Pressure Cooker phenomenon, a weekly ritual for black housewives that came into being during a time when their husbands could easily find relatively well-paying jobs in Houston's booming industrial economy. Unlike the open jam-session structure of the Blue Mondays, Pressure Cookers typically featured one band hired for the occasion; however, guest singers and players who dropped in would often join the band onstage, creating a freewheeling, anything-can-happen atmosphere for musical entertainment. Recalling a club where she performed during this era, Edwards says:

> That was the place to be. It was what they called a Pressure Cooker. That's where the wives come in. It
> was a daytime job. We'd start at like about noon and played until about five, and all the housewives

would go home with the pressure cooker cooking, you know, with that stew on. . . . It was Johnny Brown's gig. And me and big Martha Turner. . . . We'd be onstage together, and she'd be on one end and I'd be on the other, and we'd be singing blues and battling them back and forth. . . . The women would just go wild.

Such gatherings presumably offered these women a chance to escape from their own domestic drudgery and embrace a type of carnivalesque behavior triggered by the blues performance.

For some readers, it might help to review the now outdated technology of the pressure cooker—and how its introduction proceeded to liberate housewives, to a limited degree, from the kitchen and the task of closely supervising the cooking of a meal. Starting in the 1950s, the availability of this widely popular household device among black Houston homemakers increased the possibility of their being able to escape the kitchen during the afternoon (i.e., once the evening meal was in the pot and starting to cook). Some women took advantage of this convenience so they could attend the traditional Blue Monday parties, and some also used it to create a context for their own gatherings on other workday afternoons. As guitarist I. J. Gosey explains it:

Here's how it started: 'long in then—people don't use them now anymore—but they had a big old pot that they could put their food in, and you'd put it on the stove. And on the top of the pot it had a relief valve, so if it gets too hot it would automatically kick off itself. In other words, the valve on top of it would open up and let it cool down. That way they didn't burn the food and they didn't overcook the food. They called it a pressure cooker. So the women could put their food on and leave home and come to the Blue Monday parties and other things, and when they'd get back home, that food would be done.

However, Gosey, like almost every male I have interviewed, indicates that the identity of these female-dominated afternoon blues gatherings was never officially established as the name of the household appliance that released housewives to attend. He says, "Now that cooking machine is the only 'pressure cooker' that I know about. In the clubs, to the men it would be just an afternoon gig, a blues party, or whatever. To the women it maybe was [called] a 'pressure cooker,' I don't know."

But to Gloria Edwards, Martha Turner (b. 1935), and several other females who performed at or attended such events, the label of Pressure Cooker seems to have been fairly common currency at least for a while. Verta Mae Evans (who is known informally in Houston blues clubs as "the Tambourine Lady" because of her long-running propensity to join bands onstage and provide impromptu accompaniment on the handheld percussion instrument) once told me the term "Pressure Cooker" may or may not have been used by club management or male performers to denote a midweek afternoon blues party, but "the women, they sure knew what it meant." As we conversed, she went on to joke slyly about the appropriateness of the name for such gatherings, as it suggested the women's symbolic need to "heat things up" and "let off steam" as a group.

The confusion over what these daytime blues parties were properly called stems partially from a gender gap, but also from the sheer prevalence of live music events on workday afternoons in black clubs during this era. As guitarist and singer Texas Johnny Brown points out:

> *Hughes Tools, Bethlehem Steel, Brown and Root—all the big industry was booming back then, so they had shifts going around the clock. And the club owners could be open during the day and always find people who'd want to come in and hear some music and have a drink, you know—before noon, afternoon, evenings, whatever. That's when this whole thing got going. The men would all be out at the factories working, and then they would show up at the shift change. You'd have a whole club of ladies, and then the shift change would come and the men would suddenly show up. Some of the husbands would come find their wives at the club and join in with the party. But a lot of them ladies had to get home to get supper out of the pressure cooker for their husbands to eat.*

Oscar O'Bear (b. 1942), another male guitarist from that era, concurs:

> *Around 1958, 1959, and for a while after that, all the blues clubs was packed back then in the middle of the day. . . . And the people would come every day we played, starting around noon. . . . During their lunch breaks or after their shifts changed, men would come by in their uniforms and work clothes, but the women would always be there . . . in the afternoon, then go home and do dinner. Then sometimes they'd be back later on with their husband.*

As for the term "Pressure Cooker," O'Bear says male musicians, club owners, and clientele never called such gigs by that name, but admits that "they [women] used to use that as their own thing, maybe."

By the 1970s, the heyday of the Blue Mondays and the Pressure Cookers had passed in Houston, and though Blue Mondays continued in local clubs, the entry of more women into the extradomestic workforce brought the Pressure Cooker phenomenon to an end.

Yet the Blue Monday remains to this day a galvanizing ritual for men and women in the community of Third Ward, thanks to club owner and singer Bobby Lewis. His small club (named Miss Ann's Playpen after his then four-year-old daughter) faces historic Dowling Street near the intersection with Alabama. On Monday late afternoons (unlike weekend nights on which live music is also featured, but in a slightly more formal context), the performers, patrons, and club employees are typically casually attired, sporting a mix of working-class uniforms along with blue jeans, short

Oscar O'Bear, C. Davis Bar-B-Q, Sunnyside, 1997.

Miss Ann's Playpen (exterior), Third Ward, 2000.

pants, T-shirts, and such. Some customers in their twenties or thirties occasionally drop by, but most of the audience consists of middle-aged or significantly older African Americans—particularly those mature enough to recall the glory days of Houston blues decades earlier.

Most importantly, the regulars—both the numerous musicians (including amateurs and professionals) who show up to jam and the customers who cheer them on—seem consciously to be perpetuating a blues tradition that they realize is endangered by the passing of time. Having proudly dubbed themselves "The Blue Monday Gang"—and even having created blue-and-white T-shirts they marketed in the late 1990s to establish and advertise this collective identity—these people gather each week to request their favorite songs, applaud earnestly emotional displays by musicians and audience members alike, engage in call-and-response, and generally celebrate the blues foundation of their musical culture.

Like the players at C. Davis Bar-B-Q or Mr. Gino's on a Sunday afternoon—or those at any one of several other venues that feature weekly gatherings on other days of the week—the Blue Monday participants regularly demonstrate that, in Houston at least, some black people still *do* play music that they and their predominantly black audiences define as *blues,* even in the twenty-first century. In my opinion, these are the original and ultimate blues people of Houston. No, they're not necessarily the out-for-a-night-on-the-town spectators at big shows at the city's highest-profile entertainment venues downtown or on the southwest side. Instead, the blues performances they attend on a weekly basis have generally never been advertised in the local newspapers and have rarely even charged a cover fee (and only nominal ones at that). And these shows conveniently take place right in the old neighborhood, sometimes featuring friends they've known all their lives. For this type of Houston blues fan, the music has little to do with contemporary show-business realities and everything to do with a deeply rooted way of life.

Ever since that 1982 newspaper announcement of the death of Lightnin' Hopkins hinted to me that I was living in a special place, I've been curious to learn more about the blues culture that survives mostly unnoticed in the old neighborhoods of the Bayou City. Recordings, books, and magazines couldn't teach me much more about the subject, as its existence in the latter decades of the twentieth century has been largely undocumented. To understand it has necessitated my direct involvement—visiting unpublicized little clubs on obscure streets in areas that looked nothing like the suburbs, experiencing the intense live music performed there, and conversing with lots of kind individuals (in clubs, cafes, and homes), usually with tape recorder in hand. I've been doing it for many years now, and I'm still learning. But there's one thing of which I'm already quite certain: If you want to understand the blues, don't rely just on the record labels and packaged road shows. Instead, seek out the real people and places that have a history with the music and keep it alive on its own terms. Lucky for me, I found many such folks just down the street in Houston. But first, I had to open my eyes and ears and go searching.

Carolyn Blanchard, Miss Ann's Playpen, Third Ward, 1999.

Miss Ann's Playpen (interior), Third Ward, 2000.

Eugene Moody, El Nedo Cafe, Third Ward, 1997.

CHAPTER 3

To me, Third Ward seemed like heaven. . . .

One place I never will forget:

Third Ward looked just like heaven to me.

TEDDY REYNOLDS

third ward
From High-Class Joints to Honky-Tonks

any historical account of Houston blues culture must consider, if not begin with, the central importance of a place called Third Ward. The sociologist Robert D. Bullard has aptly described it as "the city's most diverse black neighborhood and a microcosm of the larger black Houston community." Over the last five to six decades of the twentieth century this area (located just southeast of downtown) has been home, at one time or another, to countless internationally famous blues artists—from Lightnin' Hopkins to Albert Collins to Johnny Clyde Copeland and jazz greats such as Arnett Cobb. However, such was not always the case.

Not many years after the city of Houston had been founded in 1836 as part of the independent Republic of Texas, the civic leadership, seeking to make local government more efficient, revised the town's charter to create four quadrants that it called wards. Later, as local population expanded beyond the original areas of settlement, two additional wards were added, making a total of six. These administrative districts elected their own representatives to the city council and

71

developed their own neighborhood identities, with the original Third Ward then being considered home to what Bob Tutt described in a 1996 *Houston Chronicle* article as "a large segment of Houston's 'silk stocking district.'" However, in the early 1900s, as the city grew beyond the boundaries of the six ward areas, a subsequent charter revision made the old wards obsolete as political units. Nevertheless, the neighborhood monikers survived this change in the structure of city government, and today many inner-city residents still refer to certain older sectors of town by their ward names.

The area originally defined as Third Ward extended immediately south of downtown's Congress Street and east of Main to the northern shore of Brays Bayou. That space, which now includes major portions of the central business district as well as an urban-renewal zone known as Midtown, is considerably larger and more diverse in its usage than the African American residential area to the southeast primarily thought of as Third Ward today.

However, determining exactly where to draw the boundaries to define Third Ward—as it exists in the minds of its own people—is not easily done, since a variety of opinions exist. For instance, Joe Hughes once adamantly told me, "Third Ward, culturally speaking, ended at Truxillo, no matter what the technical map might say." His designation of this particular street as an unofficial dividing line seems to reflect the fact that the wood-frame homes north of Truxillo tend to be smaller and more cheaply constructed (and historically were occupied by working-class blacks), whereas south of that line the predominantly brick homes are typically larger and nicer (and have only gradually become occupied mainly by blacks). Hughes goes on to define the eastern boundary of Third Ward as ending in the once low-rent area he calls "Sugar Hill," near the campus of Texas Southern University. Having debated the precise dimensions of Third Ward with various others, I've decided that in common parlance (among musicians, at least), the neighborhood is mainly understood to extend south to Brays Bayou from the downtown intersection of the Gulf Freeway (I-45) and the Southwest Freeway (Highway 59), with Main Street forming its western boundary.

Within that historical neighborhood, various groups and individuals have united in recent years to form the Third Ward Redevelopment Council, which has worked to coordinate plans and efforts for the greater good of the community. Earnestly urging residents to "Be True to the Trey" (signifying pride in the number three, as in Third), the council's billboards were once a ubiquitous presence. Many of the streets in this area, the cultural Third Ward, as Hughes would insist, are characterized by rows of small, aging wood-frame houses built in the simple style known popularly as "shotgun shack," some of which have been continuously occupied and others of which have been long abandoned, boarded up or not.

However, the closer one gets to Brays Bayou on the south end of the community, the more likely one is to find avenues lined with old two-story brick homes, which also vary greatly in condition—from the respectfully maintained to the beautifully renovated to the severely neglected.

Some of these structures are quite grandiose in their original architectural design and landscaping. Built in the early twentieth century (in many cases by the most prominent Jewish families in Houston at the time), they reflect an era before African Americans were the dominant ethnic group in this part of Third Ward, economically segregated as they were then to the shotgun shacks in the blocks north of Truxillo Street. By the 1930s, greater Third Ward's demographic profile included a fairly even number of blacks and whites. But in the two decades following World War II, the main neighborhood rapidly became predominantly black, for most of the white residents (as well as the synagogue for Houston's original Jewish congregation, Temple Beth Israel) moved to the more fashionable southwest-side suburbs as the city expanded.

In the past as well as now, Dowling Street has served as the main traffic conduit running northeast to southwest through the district, intersecting other key thoroughfares such as Elgin, Holman, Wheeler, and Southmore. Once considered "the main street of black Houston" (according to blues singer and longtime Third Ward resident Big Robert Smith, among others), Dowling Street was actually named after Richard William "Dick" Dowling (1838–1867), an immigrant from County Galway, Ireland, who became a Confederate officer and the Texas hero of the Battle of Sabine Pass in the Civil War. Historical ironies aside, in its heyday, Dowling Street was widely recognized as the center of Houston blues culture. In the mid–twentieth century it was a special place where a sidewalk pedestrian might expect to hear either of the two contrasting strains of Texas blues—the progressive stylings in the mode of the electric T-Bone or the homespun fingerpicking of songsters such as "Po' Lightnin'." As Hopkins once told a northern, predominantly white audience in his spoken introduction to the song "I Was Down on Dowling Street" (a live performance included in *The Complete Prestige/Bluesville Recordings*), "That's a nice place to go and get an education."

step out of miss ann's playpen, home to the late-1990s Blue Monday jams, and you're right there on Dowling, the primary artery running through the heart of Third Ward. Once lined with prosperous black-owned businesses—including department stores, shops, professional offices, restaurants, and numerous entertainment venues large and small—following the desegregation of public facilities in Houston that started in the 1960s, the street's economic fortunes began to decline as African Americans exercised their freedom to spend their money and live wherever they pleased. In the 1990s, the thoroughfare remained home to several major churches and a scattering of small businesses (including law offices, laundries, barbershops, cafes, and taverns) that share blocks with vacant weed-grown lots and dilapidated abandoned buildings. However, it's also the location of several special landmarks important to the history of blacks (and their blues) in Houston.

Eldorado Building, Third Ward, 1997.

Just walk a few blocks to the north of Miss Ann's Playpen, the epitome of a small neighborhood lounge, and you're soon at the corner of Elgin and Dowling. On the southwest quadrant of this intersection stands an imposing two-story structure still identified as the Eldorado Building. The ground floor has always been divided into space for a variety of small businesses, but the entire second level (empty for most of the 1980s and 1990s) is distinguished as the former home of one of the finest showcases in Texas for black music, the grand old Eldorado Ballroom. From the late 1930s till the early 1970s this club was the venue of choice for upscale blues and jazz performances, as well as afternoon talent shows and sock hops. It was the centerpiece of several profitable enterprises owned by the African American businesswoman (and eventual philanthropist) Anna Dupree (1891–1977), who had already achieved success as a beauty shop operator before marrying her husband, Clarence Dupree, in 1916. Together they had created the Eldorado Ballroom in order to establish a "class" venue for black social clubs and general entertainment. Almost from the beginning, "the 'rado" (as people sometimes referred to the ballroom) and the large building that housed it became symbols of community pride—Third Ward's most prestigious focal point, especially for musicians.

As the bandleader and trumpet player Calvin Owens once said, upon recalling his first appearance there with the band led by I. H. "Ike" Smalley (1915–1991), "Playing at the Eldorado Ballroom—I mean that's like saying: Okay, I've *made* it." There he was one of the nattily dressed, chart-reading musicians who were creatively shaping blues into jazz and back again, a fusion that is a crucial distinction of the Texas sound in modern black music. Looking back, he considers the place to have been like a "finishing school" in his early musical development.

For John Green (1931–1998), who worked behind the scenes of Houston's blues business for many decades, including a stint in the mid-1950s booking acts at the club, there was no doubt about it: "The Eldorado was top of the line. Oh yeah, back in those days, people would really get dressed to go hear a band there." Asked to describe the building in its prime as he remembered it from the 1950s, Green responds with a detailed survey of the scene:

They had a restaurant downstairs, with the liquor store on that corner. The club didn't serve liquor in those days; it was a "brown bag" joint. They sold beer and setups. Right next door to the restaurant on the bottom level was Playboy Sport Shop, a clothes store. Then there was a Walker-Brantley Appliance store—that was in there. And then, later on, Lloyd Wells and Herbert Provost had a photography shop down there too.

To get to the club, you'd go up the steps, then you'd make a left turn and go up another flight of steps, and then you were in the ballroom. They had a bar at the back, on the Dowling Street end. The stage was on the right-hand side.

Now the old building—before they remodeled it [following a fire, ca. 1952]—the stage was on the left-hand side. . . . It was real high, a raised stage. They had little off-the-wall dressing rooms, really a hat-check room. There wasn't really a formal dressing room for the artists per se, so they would just use part of the hat-check room.

They had good tables, little square ones. It was really nice. They put all new furniture in when it burned down and they reopened it . . . some really good stuff.

On a good Saturday, I guess you could get maybe five, six hundred in there. But they would be stacked in there like cardboard, yeah.

There was always a cover charge. They had Ladies' Night on Wednesday night, and women were free, and the guys had to pay a dollar. They closed on Monday and Tuesday—unless they had a social club in there. Wednesday night, then Friday, Saturday, Sunday—that was the main nights. And a long time ago when it first opened, they would also have matinees on Sunday afternoon.

Everybody that was anybody played at the Eldorado in the fifties: Etta James, Bill Doggett, Ray [Charles], Jimmy Reed, T-Bone [Walker], Charles Brown, "Guitar Slim" [Eddie Jones], you name it, they all came through.

It's no wonder that for countless musicians the Eldorado Ballroom represented the pinnacle of local success. But it also stimulated the imagination of mere youngsters. Teddy Reynolds, who was born and raised just a few blocks away on Hutchins Street, eventually played professionally there too, but he actually earned some of his first money as an entertainer by "busking" (i.e., dancing on the street for tips) outside the building as a child, around 1940. The enterprising lad had mastered a primitive but innovative form of barefoot tap dancing by clinching bottle caps beneath his toes and making a rhythmic racket on the sidewalk as he improvised various steps and moves. Recalling the place and the times, he adds:

So I used to whistle and tap-dance for tips there. There used to be a drugstore at the bottom corner of the building, with a Victrola in it, down there on the ground level. A shoe-shine parlor, a liquor store too, yeah. That corner downstairs has been everything, you name it. . . . Anyway, I used to dance out there at night, when people were going into the club. They'd put some money in the jukebox, see, and we'd tap-dance. And people'd give us tips, see, yeah. . . . I was about nine or ten. The Eldorado, that's where it was at, that main corner in Third Ward, yeah.

Though the late-1960s, early-1970s decline of the Eldorado Ballroom, like that of Dowling Street, is largely attributable to the negative economic impact (for black-owned businesses in the old wards) triggered by desegregation, other factors contributed to its demise. For one thing, musical tastes were changing, and many younger African Americans were abandoning the old-style

John Green, 1997.

Teddy Reynolds, at home, 1995.

jazz and blues of their parents' generation for more progressive sounds. Also, according to some accounts, in the late 1960s, the local affiliate of the Black Panther Party established its office in a building approximately one block north of the Eldorado Ballroom on Dowling Street. For a variety of reasons, that headquarters of black activism and its surrounding environs soon became the focal point for increasing tensions and showdowns with the Houston Police Department, prompting some former Eldorado Ballroom clientele to begin avoiding the whole area, especially at night.

And ironically, the increasing ability of local black people to achieve the common American dream of driving a personally owned automobile (a mentality on which the sprawling city of Houston has long depended) also hastened the end for the Eldorado Ballroom. As Joe Hughes astutely points out:

> In the old days, people would walk everywhere they was going, all over Third Ward, or they took a cab. Wouldn't be nothing but thirty-five cents, or a nickel a mile, or whatever. And most people didn't have cars then. And here's what destroyed the Eldorado: Because as the people grew, and got cars, they had no place to park their cars there. There was no parking at the Eldorado, and no place to make a [parking] lot or anything. So the club died. That's what happened to it.

Hughes says that during this same time, on nearby side streets at the smaller, less prestigious clubs (located mostly in old wood-frame houses, thanks to Houston's notorious resistance to zoning legislation), "you'd have cars all around here and all around there, up and down the way." But he acknowledges that these cheaper, usually cramped-for-space venues never drew the types of crowds long customary at the Eldorado Ballroom, adding, "and most of those poorer people in the little joints, who wouldn't be going to the Eldorado anyway, still didn't have cars then."

His analysis is validated by various others, including John Green (whose career included serving as Bobby Bland's road manager from 1957 to 1969). Regarding the downfall of the once mighty establishment, Green explains:

> When I came back to Houston in 1969, the Eldorado was in decline, on the way out, then. It would open, but just for special occasions. . . . One thing, they didn't have parking around there, no parking at all. See, back when the Eldorado was jumping, people used to ride the bus and get off right on the corner. But then after the Korean War and everybody started getting cars, there was nowhere to park. They used to park on Elgin, on both sides, and around the corner. And those schoolkids would go and jack the cars up, take the tires off, and strip 'em! So that went on and helped kill the Eldorado.

Today the Eldorado Building still looms over the corner of Dowling and Elgin. Until recently, the structure had long been posted for sale, its second floor hopelessly available for lease as office space, silent and empty for years. However, in December 1999, the Eldorado Building (along with the entire seventeen-lot block on which it sits) was acquired by Third Ward–based Project Row Houses, a nonprofit arts and community service organization that plans to restore the facility as both a special performance venue and a meeting site, while maintaining small-business tenants on the first level. Old-timers may recall a once glorious past up in "the 'rado," jumping and jiving to the fully orchestrated blues of the eight-piece band directed by Pluma Davis (1919–1988) and other groups at Houston's self-proclaimed "Home of Happy Feet." But to the younger generation, which has yet to witness the transformation envisioned by Project Row Houses, the structure is simply home to a few modest business establishments on the ground floor. At the corner, there's the Lunch Box Diner; until its recent closing, it served cheap breakfasts and soul-food lunches that the owner bragged about on advertising slogans hand-painted over the picture window facing Dowling. There's still a barbershop and a beauty parlor as well as an insurance agency around on the Elgin side, plus one other tenant—the recently relocated Caldwell Tailors, an establishment with its own unique place in Houston blues history.

Since 1951, Booker T. Caldwell (b. 1923) has operated a tailor shop that has provided sartorial splendor for a wide range of black leaders, athletes, and entertainers—including numerous blues singers and musicians. Caldwell Tailors was originally based across town on Lyons Avenue near Fifth Ward's analogue to the Eldorado Ballroom, the Club Matinee. Another important business neighbor there was the Crystal Hotel, which Caldwell and others remember as "the nicest hotel in town for blacks." As Caldwell explains, between the clientele at the huge club with its twenty-four-hour restaurant and the guests at the major hotel, "that just brought the customers to us." One was the Duke-Peacock Records and Buffalo Booking Agency kingpin Don Robey, who also owned a nearby barbershop and office space. Robey's patronage and subsequent referrals of his performers only enhanced Caldwell's access to black entertainers wanting to look sharp onstage.

Among the hundreds of musicians Caldwell and his staff have clothed over the past half century are Buddy Ace, Charles Brown, Clarence "Gatemouth" Brown, Texas Johnny Brown, Ray Charles, Clifton Chenier, Johnny Copeland, Grady Gaines, Clarence Green, Lightnin' Hopkins, Joe Hughes, B.B. King, Pete Mayes, Jimmy "T-99" Nelson, Calvin Owens, Junior Parker, Big Walter Price, Jimmy Reed, and many more. During the heyday of Caldwell's Lyons Avenue operations, tour buses full of musicians staying at the Crystal Hotel or performing at the Club Matinee would "park right there, right in front of the shop. We used to *like* to see those buses pull up! Yeah."

However, in the post-segregation era, as onetime centers of black culture such as Lyons Avenue and Dowling Street lost their status as locations for profitable commerce, the ensuing socio-economic changes sealed the fate of once vibrant venues like the Club Matinee and the Eldorado Ballroom. And though some of the major businesses of that era, such as Caldwell Tailors, have managed to survive, most of those have been forced to downscale their operations.

Booker T. Caldwell, Eldorado Building, Third Ward, 1997.

When Caldwell moved his business into the old Eldorado Building a few years ago, he too was downsizing. But even though he's now in his late seventies, he continues to sell custom-designed suits and all manner of fashionable accessories to the general public as well as to entertainers. Every now and then Caldwell still sees longtime patron B.B. King. "He bought ten tailor-made shirts last time he was here," the proprietor notes. But after reciting names of former famous customers who have passed away, he acknowledges that times have changed and sighs, "Don't have all those guys coming through now."

Nevertheless, Booker T. Caldwell is a living reservoir of memories of the glory days of Houston blues culture. As Joe Hughes attests, "He was the top tailor in town." Now, through a fluke of real estate dealings, Caldwell Tailors occupies space in Third Ward's most historic building from the era when a lot of blues was big and brassy, and its performers impeccably well dressed.

From the sidewalk in front of Caldwell's shop, looking just across Elgin (i.e., toward the northwest quadrant of the Dowling-Elgin intersection), you can't help but notice a large urban greenspace far older than the Eldorado Building. That's Emancipation Park, so called ever since the land was purchased in 1872 by the congregations of the nearby Antioch Missionary Baptist Church and Trinity Methodist Episcopal Church, who worked together under the leadership of the Reverend John Henry "Jack" Yates (1828–1897) to procure the property and donate it to the city. Yates was a former slave, and the son of slaves, who promoted his idyllic vision of the park as a special place for black people (who at that time were apparently not welcomed in other city recreational facilities). As its name suggests, Emancipation Park was for many generations also a major site for the annual Juneteenth gatherings in which Texans celebrate the belated end of slavery in the Lone Star state. In that capacity, through the end of the nineteenth and most of the twentieth century, it hosted large concerts with big bands and impromptu musical performances by individuals and small groups.

A true patriarch of the Houston jazz and blues community, Milt Larkin was among those who played "way back when" in Emancipation Park. Born in 1910 in nearby Navasota (home of Mance Lipscomb), Larkin had moved with his family to Houston while still in his childhood. A trumpeter and trombonist as well as a vocalist who loved to sing the blues, Larkin is mainly remembered as a bandleader whose orchestras and groups promoted the "big-foot swing" and "honking" that defined the Texas sound in the 1940s. Locally, he is equally respected for the musical talent he cultivated in others and introduced to the world, including great saxophonists such as Arnett Cobb, Illinois Jacquet (b. 1922), and Eddie "Cleanhead" Vinson.

But despite his jazz credentials, Larkin always identified strongly with his roots. As he told Alan Govenar in *Meeting the Blues,* "Any time there's a Texas band, blues and jazz fit together." And he collaborated readily with blues artists such as Jimmy Nelson and Johnny Copeland (who appeared on Larkin's LP *Down Home Saturday Night,* released on his own Copasetic label). In fact, one of the bandleader's fondest memories was topping the bill as the featured act at the 1931 Juneteenth

Calvin Owens, Emancipation Park (opposite the Eldorado Building), Third Ward, 2000.

Big Robert Smith, Third Ward, 2000.

Celebration in Emancipation Park. As Rick Mitchell notes in his 1996 tribute article, Larkin had recalled that experience in a previous interview: "They loved us, especially our blues. You never saw such dancing and carrying on. The whole town turned out to celebrate. It was wild." By the 1970s, however, the large Juneteenth concerts had been moved to the state-of-the-art Miller Outdoor Theater in the city's finest public recreational space, Hermann Park. Consequently, the tradition of large-scale musical celebrations (on Juneteenth and other special occasions) at Emancipation Park gradually waned, corresponding to the general economic decline of Dowling Street in the post-segregation era.

But the park remains the historic center of Third Ward and Dowling its major street, even if the finest music venues that were once located there (Club Ebony and Club Savoy on the south end, in addition to the Eldorado Ballroom) have long since gone out of business. Yet even in its most prosperous years, Dowling was also home for small dives and beer joints that catered to a relatively impoverished clientele quite different from those who frequented the upscale clubs. In addition to the ubiquitous jukebox ambience, any of these little hangouts might feature live musical performances from time to time. But they weren't performed by slick orchestras backing touring stars. No, the music there was stripped-down-to-the-essence blues played by often ragged-looking individuals, either solo or in small groups with their peers. And the most famous of the down-home acoustic minstrels who wandered up and down Dowling, in and out of the open-door taverns, was a fellow described by Mack McCormick as "a cocky, loping figure with a guitar slung across his back, pausing now and then to gather a crowd and coax their coins into his hat"— Lightnin' Hopkins, of course.

In many ways, Dowling Street was Lightnin' Hopkins' home. He made frequent references to it in songs and interviews, and, locally, some old-timers still refer to the intersection of Holman and Dowling as "Lightnin's corner." Among the various addresses he established over the years in Third Ward, one of the longest running was in a row house on Hadley Street just a few blocks west of the main drag. And in published interviews, Hopkins more than once recounted how, when he first settled in Houston, he naturally gravitated toward the bustling Dowling Street scene.

Among the factors that appealed to Hopkins about the area were the friendships he formed with black drivers in the city's then totally segregated bus system, men who regularly drove up or down Dowling in the course of their various routes and who would let Hopkins ride for free because he entertained them. In a variation on his sidewalk-minstrel persona, Hopkins developed the daily habit of boarding one of these buses, guitar in hand, and making the circuit while playing for fellow passengers, who usually rewarded him with good tips. One driver evidently enjoyed this diversion so much that (according to the Hopkins interview included in *The Complete Prestige/ Bluesville Recordings*) he would make unauthorized stops so the bluesman could run into a liquor store, purchase a pint with some of his just-earned income, hop back on the waiting bus, and

Third Ward \ **85**

continue the rolling concert. Hopkins also claimed that sometimes commuters would choose to miss their stops and just keep riding because they were having such a party, complete with schoolgirls dancing in the aisles.

In retrospect, Dowling Street is emblematic of the down-home/upscale dichotomy that characterizes Houston's original blues culture. From the 1940s through the early 1970s, it was a place where both vagabonds and sophisticates made music. There a country-style songster might ring out notes that echoed through alleys (or buses) just down the block from where a big band negotiated complex arrangements in a popular floor show at the Eldorado Ballroom. Both types of musicians, despite some obvious differences in instrumentation and presentation, identified with the blues, as did their respective audiences. But each group seemed to define the form in ways that reflect a class consciousness. For some, it was the musical link to a rural culture they had abandoned for life in the city; for others, it provided the conceptual foundation for the media-influenced exploration of progressive musical ideas. The sociology of Third Ward blues encompasses both the crude and the refined.

the few previously published accounts of Houston's blues history have usually noted in passing the important role of the largest, finest, and most famous of the city's African American nightclubs—for instance, Club Ebony, the Eldorado Ballroom, the Bronze Peacock, or Club Matinee, none of which is still in operation today. These and other relatively upscale showcases flourished during the most commercially productive era of Houston blues by featuring major black recording artists, popular combos, and big bands in finely tailored suits. Collectively, they nurtured the black community's taste for what the writer Albert Murray describes as "the fully orchestrated blues statement." It was in such prominent nightclubs that patrons who were still subjected to racial segregation elsewhere in the city could experience first-class amenities and entertainment—the finer side of black social life. And it was in such establishments that well-trained, chart-reading musicians could experiment with new and sophisticated artistic possibilities as they pushed their orchestration beyond basic blues toward R&B and the rich complexities of jazz. However, despite the obvious cultural and historical importance of the upscale nightclubs, a large portion of popular Houston blues as we know it today traces its roots to coterminous but considerably lower-class Third Ward establishments, the type of place where Lightnin' Hopkins might just wander in. And of special significance was the unique environment at the previously mentioned Shady's Playhouse.

In the oral histories of many Houston blues musicians, Shady's Playhouse arises again and again as the social antithesis of the nearby Eldorado Ballroom. And for a core group of local players—some of whom went on to become major stars—it was clearly the most important location in their early musical development. Why? During the 1950s and early 1960s, Shady's Playhouse served a key role in the education and maturation of numerous young blues artists who were often otherwise instructionally and economically deprived (and thus somewhat alienated from the musical and social milieu of the more prominent clubs).

If our historical consideration of the environment in which Houston blues has evolved focused solely on implications of *racial* segregation, Shady's Playhouse—if it were acknowledged at all—might simply be added to a list with other more famous black clubs, as if there were no difference between them. But my interview subjects make it clear that there definitely *was* a crucial difference, revealing a type of intraracial *class* segregation at work in the community. And this reality had an ironically fortunate educational impact on certain blues musicians.

Possessing little formal training or funds, these guys didn't fit in at places like the Eldorado Ballroom, at least not at first. But they were welcomed at Shady's Playhouse, which provided them with the experiences and atmosphere that served as the closest they'd ever get to a program of professional education. Ultimately, some of the "graduates" of this schooling were transformed by their experiences in ways that enabled them to cross over—that is, to participate in the first-class blues culture of the 1950s and beyond in which they initially were outsiders.

In short, despite its reputation among Third Ward residents as more of a juke joint than a ballroom, and despite reports that various illegal activities may have occurred there with some frequency, Shady's Playhouse also functioned as the fundamental instructional center for a long list of Houston bluesmen, including Albert Collins, Johnny Copeland, Johnny "Guitar" Watson, Elmore Nixon, Joe Hughes, Teddy Reynolds, Joe Medwick, L. A. Hill, and numerous others less well known.

Before proceeding I should make it clear that when I say "Shady's Playhouse," I am referring to the original location of the nightclub on Simmons Street, just east of the intersection with Sampson, in the same wood-frame building (now destroyed) that previously housed a club founded in the late 1940s and called "Jeff's Playhouse." Vernon Jackson (b. 1926), known to most people only by his nickname "Shady," took over operation of the club there from 1953 until 1958, when he moved it a few blocks away to a new and larger location on the second floor of a still-standing brick building near the corner of Elgin and Ennis (at Beulah and Sauer), where it continued operation until closing in 1969. These dates were provided by Jackson—Shady himself—who is now in advanced age and poor health and has thus far been unable or unwilling to be interviewed beyond the few questions he has already answered for me.

The musician Teddy Reynolds remembers Jackson with a fond sense of awe:

Man, he had Houston by the back of the neck at one time! Really, he did. Even Don Robey and them wouldn't mess with Shady. And he was heavy uptown, with the law, you know. They'd let him do what he wants, know what I mean. . . .

He was a big dude, man, very big dude. His hat would touch the top of that door. And he had a big heart! Man, he was crazy about the musicians. Yeah, he looked after us. I was real young, and he was older than me, you know. . . . Shady's one of the finest persons you could find.

Joe Hughes acknowledges that "Shady was a gambler and a hustler," but he too is grateful for the way the club owner promoted the blues. So is the longtime Third Ward resident Henry Hayes: "Shady was a friend to musicians; he would help them," he says, noting that this support was crucial to young players who had never seen the interior of places like the Eldorado Ballroom.

To recall the reality of class distinctions among black nightclubs in Houston (and elsewhere) in the early 1950s, consider for a moment the tripartite classification of entertainment venues as articulated by Marie Adams (1925–1998) in one of Peacock Records' earliest national-chart hit records, "I'm Gonna Play the Honky-Tonks" (Peacock single 1583; recorded in Houston, 1952, with Bill Harvey's Band). The well-known refrain features the singer-songwriter's defiant assertion that she will cross class boundaries and do as she pleases by having fun in all types of venues. Proclaiming that she is no longer willing to submit to other people's notions of what she should or should not do, she announces her intention to patronize "high-class joints" as well as "low-class joints" and even "honky-tonks." I will leave it to you to ponder the precise difference between the latter two. For my purposes, grasping the basic binary distinction between "high" and "low" is sufficient to understand the presumably intraracial class awareness of this 1950s black female.

At the time Adams' song was most popular, Third Ward's Eldorado Ballroom was recognized (along with Fifth Ward's Bronze Peacock) as the epitome of a "high-class joint" for black Houston. But only six to seven blocks away—east of Dowling Street and literally on the other side of railroad tracks that once ran down Velasco Street—stood its cultural opposite: Shady's Playhouse, a nightclub that must certainly have qualified, no disrespect intended, as a "low-class joint," of which Third Ward apparently had plenty. Yet Shady's Playhouse seems to have been different from the rest.

One of the many successful musicians to emerge from Shady's Playhouse was Teddy Reynolds, who went on to record as a solo artist and to play with the likes of Bobby Bland, Junior Parker, Phillip Walker (b. 1937), and others. The Third Ward–born keyboardist and singer explains the different atmospheres of the Eldorado Ballroom and Shady's Playhouse as follows:

Shady's Playhouse was down-to-earth, not that formal. Now the Eldorado Ballroom, that was dressing up, you know. But at Shady's, come as you are! As you are, uh huh—just as long as you got a shirt on your back and some shoes on.

. . . You're going to hang out, you know, and really enjoy yourself, get funky, get sweaty, get, you know, nasty sweaty, dancing.

The guitarist and singer Joe Hughes provides additional elaboration on the contrasting social ambience and musical styles of the two clubs:

Shady's was short shirt, come-as-you-are, whatever. The Eldorado was a tie and jacket, dress up. It was big bands per se at the Eldorado. Here [at Shady's] you could have anything from a three- or four-piece band on up to whatever. What made the sound different was the class and caliber of musicians that you had. Here you could come in here and hear anything. But you wouldn't hear no Lightnin' at the Eldorado. But you could come here and hear Lightnin'—and on up . . . . From real down-home blues, all the way up, you could hear it all at Shady's.

In this quotation, Hughes provides us with perhaps the most fundamental distinction between a "high-class joint" like the Eldorado Ballroom and the numerous "low-class joints" that surrounded it in Third Ward, of which Shady's Playhouse was one of the biggest (capable of holding a crowd of 200–250 people by Hughes' estimate) and, in the hearts of many, the best. Making this contrast might well be referred to as something like the Lightnin' Hopkins Litmus Test: Those who accepted and enjoyed the type of earthy blues associated with Third Ward's most famous blues minstrel would likely be comfortable at a place like Shady's Playhouse; those who did not—preferring instead the sophisticated big-band sound of Pluma Davis, I. H. Smalley, Milt Larkin, and others—would probably feel out of place there.

Understanding these different, class-based attitudes about music provides a sort of template for identifying the two basic currents running deep in Houston blues in particular, and in Texas blues in general—the rough versus the smooth, so to speak. The Shady's crowd was apparently looked down on by a would-be higher-class segment of the black community, which regarded Hopkins' down-home style of music as raw, degrading, and old-fashioned. Similarly, the musicians at Shady's Playhouse perceived this judgment and resented being considered lower class. Hughes adds in a mocking tone:

Club Ebony, the Eldorado—both of them were white-table-cloth kind of places. A guy'd come and take your hat and coat and that shit. [Then, feigning anger and naiveté:] "What! Gimme my coat. Where you going with my coat?!"

And he makes it clear that he did not appreciate what he considered to be the pretensions he experienced at the "white-table-cloth" places:

I didn't like the Eldorado. You were welcome, but I'm just a down-to-earth guy. I can fit in at the White House, or I could fit in down at the garbage dump, in the sewer—and get along with anybody along

*the way. I'm not going to look down at no guy from down at the garbage dump because I'm "up here"
at the Eldorado. And that was the attitude that these people had! And I didn't like that. I didn't feel
comfortable there. I would go there because the talent show was there, you know. And I was trying to get
my foot in the door, somewhere, any door—it didn't make no difference, so long as I could get it open. But
it was the attitude they had at the Eldorado. Now these same guys, I'd see some of them down here at
Shady's, and they were as different as day and night. But they go up to the Eldorado, and they have to cop
that attitude, and that's phony to me. I don't like that. Be who you are, wherever you are, you know.*

The multi-instrumentalist Henry Hayes, who had excellent credentials as a professional musician, nonetheless chose to live, play, and teach others at the apparently less respectful Shady's
Playhouse for a while. He too experienced a type of class conflict as a result:

*I was sometimes criticized by the better musicians [for hanging out at Shady's] because they knew I
was a good musician. I could play with the best, you know. Even when I went to California, you know,
I was still up there—playing with Cannonball [Adderly], Charlie Parker, and all them people. Because I'd had that experience, you know, playing with those types of professional guys like that, well,
they said, "You don't have no business down there with them people." They looked down upon those
guys, you know. They'd say, "Man, you're supposed to be up here with us. You don't need to be down
there at Shady's. You got more going on for yourself," you know.*

Former B.B. King bandleader Calvin Owens, an Eldorado Ballroom veteran since the 1940s,
emphasizes the distinction between the two main styles of popular music in Third Ward at the
time—the raw, unschooled sound he associates with Shady's and the more complex, big-band
sound of the Eldorado. Note Owens' guarded revelation of a sense of class difference as he talks
about the two establishments:

*All of the blues musicians hung out at Shady's, and around in that area. . . . Now I was on the other
side of the track—how would you say it—with the musicians that played the shows, could read the
music, that kind of a thing. I'm not trying to put nothing down; I just never went over much on that
other side of the tracks. . . . It was a little too rough to me—it just was not my place to hang. Because
even in high school I was playing in eighteen-piece bands, six nights a week! . . . So I never really
hung out in that bluesiest part of town . . . with really the religiously blues people.*

Owens' perceptions about different tastes, different levels of class among black musicians playing
in the same neighborhood at the same time (and his implications of musical, or at least educational, superiority) pivot on that gap between the more simplistic, deep blues that he dismisses

Henry Hayes, at home, Third Ward, 1997.

and the more polished, studied, big-band jazz-flavored blues that he respects. This dichotomy also seems to be based on the size of the performing unit, which carries economic implications, since each musician had to be paid. Hence, his reference to "eighteen-piece bands" suggests not only musical and educational but also financial superiority to players who worked at Shady's Playhouse.

Yet one of Owens' good friends, the late Johnny Copeland (who collaborated with Owens on the latter's 1993 CD *True Blue*, as well as on his own album on the Verve label *Flying High*), ultimately locates his true musical home not only in Houston and in Third Ward but specifically at Shady's Playhouse—the very club that Owens seems to put down. Consider, for example, the implications of Copeland's song "Houston." In it, he speaks from the perspective of an expatriated Third Warder (living "up here" in New York, where he had moved to enhance his career) about the desire to come home, to revisit old hangouts such as the corner of Live Oak and McGowen Streets and, in particular, the place he simply calls Shady's. The only musician identified by name in the lyrics is Lightnin', the epitome of the "primitive" Third Ward blues artist. In this song, Copeland recalls his former mentor Hopkins with a fond nostalgia topped only by his subsequent references to the dynamic music scene at Shady's, which he mentions twice. Though his longtime friend Owens, like many others historically affiliated with the Eldorado Ballroom, seems incapable of appreciating Shady's Playhouse, Copeland here immortalizes the old club as the place he most associates with satisfaction and a sense of being "home."

What is the reason that Copeland—like Reynolds, Hughes, Hayes, and others—remembers Shady's Playhouse as something so special? What made Shady's different from the other numerous clubs that existed in Third Ward and offered venues for these same musicians to play? I believe the answer lies in the unique environment of education, support, and a sense of belonging that the younger men found at Shady's Playhouse.

The nineteenth-century American writer Herman Melville once asserted that a sailor's life at sea had been his Harvard and Yale. In a similar fashion, life at Shady's Playhouse was the essential undergraduate school for Copeland, Reynolds, Hughes, Albert Collins, and many other youths who had little or no opportunity to receive their musical education in any formal academic context. What separates the legacy of Shady's Playhouse from that of all the other black nightclubs in Third Ward in the 1950s is what it had to offer these young men—a situation analogous in some respects to the collegiate learning experience.

For instance, Shady's Playhouse uniquely provided its musicians with the equivalent of dormitory space in the form of a courtyard of one-room cabins Shady offered for rent directly behind the club, where many of the musicians lived from time to time. Residents included James "Widemouth" Brown (d. 1971), Joe Medwick, Reynolds, and Hayes, who was not only a musician but also a record producer. Thus, in addition to sleeping quarters, the club offered an on-site job placement office of sorts. Hayes recalls:

When I was attending Texas Southern [University], I moved into the back courts back there behind the club so I could be where the action was when record companies came to town. They didn't go where some of the jazz musicians were; they came in the lower parts of Third Ward looking for talent. 'Cause that's where the low-down blues was. . . . And I was looking for talent, to find somebody that could sing or something and put something together and try and make some records, you know. . . . This is where I ran into guys like Elmore Nixon. Anyway, when the companies would come—like Modern Records, King Records, Mercury, Aladdin—all these different companies, they usually would come in that area looking for blues talent.

But regardless of the potential music deals that might be made at Shady's, the rental cabins proved to be a major convenience to a wide range of people. Reynolds adds:

Some of the cats'd be too loaded to go home, and they'd go back there and spend the night at Shady's. And you had working people that stayed back there too. You know, a cheap place to stay. . . . He had about twelve cabins, all of them one room, shotguns, yeah. . . . And I had me a little old place back there. And all the guys, all the musicians—one guy'd get a place back there and all the guys'd move in, you know. . . . And that's the way it was. We had so much fun. . . . And they'd all chip in, put in a dollar and a half, two dollars, you know. To help him with the rent. That's the way it was.

The living quarters behind Shady's Playhouse were especially significant because they offered access to a well-qualified on-site instructor and guidance counselor, mainly in the person of Henry Hayes. Not only was he a musician, composer, and producer but also a certified public school teacher who informally taught music theory and composition, as well as the ins and outs of the music business, to the younger men he took under his wing, so to speak, at the club. Hayes says:

I was the man there. Most of the guys that hung around Shady's Playhouse, they hadn't had any formal musical training, like Teddy Reynolds or Elmore Nixon. They had beautiful talents, but you know, they just played by ear. They couldn't read music and everything. . . . I taught guys like Teddy Reynolds so that then he could later learn from someone like Joe Scott [an acclaimed producer at Duke-Peacock Records]. You see, all those guys, I put 'em in position where they could move in through the door when they got the chance. . . . In other words, I brought a lot of guys out of the ghetto so that they actually had a chance in the music business. Just like Albert [Collins]; Albert might not ever have been the big star that he was without what he learned at Shady's.

Reynolds reminisces about Hayes:

Shotgun shacks, 1997.

Man, all the cats'd come there 'cause he had that good knowledge, all that musical and school knowl-
edge. . . . Hayes'd do nothing but write and arrange; that's what I remember about him. Nothing but
that—and take care of us, you know. He'd write our music, teach us, and just look after us. . . . He's
a schoolteacher too, see. . . . The cat'd be like with music all around on the floor. [Laughs] Sheets of
music everywhere, stuck on the wall, music everywhere, you know. Henry Hayes'd remind you of one of
them old hippie musicians, the vagabond, you know—just by himself, music around all over the floor,
you know. . . . And everybody dug him!

In addition to Hayes, other older musicians frequented Shady's Playhouse and informally served as mentors and teachers, generously giving advice and demonstrations of technique to the younger players. For instance, Reynolds also reports how singer-songwriter Joe Medwick patiently taught him the art of composing via repeated brainstorming sessions on the site: "Joe Medwick would come back there in the back too. We wrote our songs there—in his cabin and in the club too. He'd be writing. Joe'd be penciling, . . . writing, all the time!" In addition to acknowledging James "Widemouth" Brown as the on-site guitar tutor to Albert Collins, Joe Hughes, Johnny Copeland, and others, Reynolds notes the help he received from keyboard-playing elders such as Bill Johnson, Lonnie Lyons, Earl Gilliam (b. 1930), and "a lot of them old-timer guys at Shady's."

Moreover, Shady's Playhouse provided the young musicians not only with a place to hang out but also with consistently available rehearsal space as well as well-maintained musical instruments, such as a piano, that they otherwise could not afford. Reynolds remembers, for instance, that "they kept a piano in there all the time, all the time. Piano, man, and keep it tuned, keep it tuned! An upright, kept it tuned, kept it in good shape. Yeah, didn't let nobody bam on it." To someone trying to develop his keyboard skills, access to such a piano was obviously quite valuable.

Shady's Playhouse was also one of the few places in Third Ward where a struggling musician knew he could usually get free meals when times were hard, whether provided by the proprietor, who regularly cooked barbecue on-site, or by Hayes, to whom musicians lacking money often turned. As Reynolds tells it:

It wasn't mainly a restaurant then but a music place, yeah. Now you could get some beans and rice or
barbecue. Yeah, Shady was barbecuing it up! He had that barbecue pit on the side. That's what he had
going. . . . Sometimes Shady started cooking on a Thursday night and cook all night. They'd drink
beer out there on the side of Shady's, you know, him and some of the customers, drink beer and cook all
night. So Friday, it's well done. It'd be so tender, cooked in them big pits. You talking about good food!
Boy, we sure had some good food there!

Reynolds' many fond memories of his mentor Henry Hayes also often involve food:

[In Hayes' cabin] that's where we'd put on a pot of beans and neckbones, you know, and let it cook all day. And that's enough to feed the whole band! . . . We'd all meet there at Hayes' house every morning, back of Shady's, yeah. . . . There was a hot plate, two hot plates, where you could cook and boil food, see. Yeah, and Hayes would cook. We'd put on a big pot of peas and some neckbones and—you talking about having a meal! Oh man, yeah. Then we'd put on a pot of rice, sure. The cats'd come by, you know, they'd come back there and eat. See Hayes would do that when we didn't have enough money to go around and buy no food. . . . Yeah, that's the way we survived, see.

Finally, Shady's Playhouse offered this group of young, mostly poor Third Ward musicians coming of age in the 1950s three other things they sorely needed if they were to graduate from this basic learning experience and succeed as professional artists: regular work, management, and transportation for road trips. The chance to make music for money at Shady's Playhouse was readily available, several nights a week, and players split the tips earned during the legendary Blue Monday celebrations there. Professional management was eventually provided by Big Frank Newsome (1920–1970) (who also, I'm told, happened to be the stepfather of the club's proprietor), who booked and promoted shows throughout South and East Texas for the musicians, launching people like Johnny Copeland on their first road trips as performers. During this time, Shady's Playhouse served as the home base for Copeland's band. The drummer, Johnny Prejean (b. 1938), recalls, "We would go on out-of-town gigs, the old country gigs . . . to Corpus Christi and go down in the [Rio Grande] Valley. . . . Big Frank was kind of managing the band, and he had a Buick, and we'd all pile in there and go to the gig, man."

Along with his partner, Big Frank (who had previously made a living working on cars and hauling grease), Shady introduced a whole generation of underprivileged blues players to the wheelings and dealings of the entertainment industry. Although the success Newsome and Jackson achieved in the world of professional music was outside the realm of the more prestigious venues, it nevertheless opened doors to such places for several younger musicians.

Certainly an unusual learning environment existed at Shady's Playhouse in the 1950s, making it historically significant in the lives of numerous blues musicians from Houston—young men who by and large did not fit in, at least initially, at the more famous clubs, the "high-class joints" such as the Eldorado Ballroom. The legacy of the original Shady's Playhouse is therefore important for two main reasons: (1) the club fostered a relatively spacious musical environment in which the "down-home" blues was welcome, providing an alternative to the more sophisticated tastes of the Eldorado Ballroom and its ilk; and (2) the club gave various young men, many of whom never completed high school, a place to learn and really grow as musicians. Consider the testimony of Teddy Reynolds, an elementary-school dropout who never experienced much academic success, who says of his experience at Shady's Playhouse:

Oh man, it was just like going to school. Like a child would love his school. And getting the kind of lessons that he likes. . . . And he's the only one getting the lesson right! That's the way it was at Shady's, see. That's the way it was. You'd be glad because you'd be the only one getting the lesson right, you know. That's the way Shady's was for me. . . . I wish they could have preserved that first Shady's . . . put a fence around it and kept that place. That place is full of history. You talking about history! Oh yeah.

Of course, the structure of the first Shady's Playhouse wasn't preserved, but you can still find the now shabby building where the second manifestation of Shady's Playhouse was based, near the intersection of Elgin and Ennis (just a few blocks east of the old Eldorado building). Today, the upstairs location to which the club relocated is silent and boarded up. The first level is mostly empty too, except for a little beauty parlor staffed by young women who stare blankly and collectively shake their heads when posed the question, "Does anybody here know anything about a blues club called Shady's Playhouse that used to be upstairs?" But a lot of people in the neighborhood still remember the second Shady's—fondly or not.

For some of the musicians who loved the original Shady's Playhouse, this second location never had a chance. Reynolds tries to explain:

I never did hang out there. I was at the real Shady's in the old days, man. When they moved it to the other place, it kind of did something to us, to a whole lot of cats. A lot of cats that went down to the old first one, they wouldn't go upstairs up there [i.e., the second location]. It just did something to it.

Yeah, the original was a place to live, man, a place to learn. But not the upstairs one. Couldn't do it, couldn't do it. It was upstairs, and it was bigger, but it just wasn't like the old place. The old place was our old place, and that was it.

Yet for slightly younger players such as Joe Hughes, the second incarnation of Shady's Playhouse will forever remain a very special place, an extension of the comfortable, come-as-you-are, down-home blues-club environment that contrasted with the more upscale, jazz- and pop-flavored scene at the major establishments. And for Hughes, Shady's #2 eventually became home. "When Shady's first moved from the other location and opened this club, this was still Johnny Copeland's house," he explains. "This is where he played. See, when he left and went on the road, I got the job, and I took over Shady's, as far as the music. But Johnny was up here three or four years."

Though Hughes has fond memories of the second Shady's Playhouse, he understands why older guys such as Reynolds always preferred the original location.

Joe "Guitar" Hughes, Shady's Playhouse (second location), Third Ward, 1998.

The scene at the old Shady's was different—especially with the motel right out back. You know, guys'd come in, dance awhile, "catch" [i.e., pick up women]. Then sneak around back to the cabins, come back, dance some more, and "catch" again. . . . I never did go to the motel back there because I was too young. I was just starting then. But I knew most of the guys, and I'd see them going in back and forth. I'd see Hayes and them going back there, Teddy Reynolds. They lived back there for a while, but I was too young to go back there at that time. By time I got old enough to really kick around, Shady had moved over here.

But Hughes, like Reynolds and others, will also remember the original Shady's Playhouse as something unique because of the direct musical education he received there. "That's where I got started, sort of cut my teeth there," he sighs.

On a 1997 tour of the structure that formerly served as the second Shady's Playhouse, Hughes points out that the old building first housed the Swan Motel, and "after Swan dropped out, Shady got the building, tore all the partitions and stuff out, and made it into a club." During that era, there was a pharmacy located in the downstairs portion of the building, and the "front" of the building used to face the opposite direction (i.e., toward Beulah Street rather than Elgin). From the sidewalk, patrons climbed an exterior stairway to the club entrance. "Once you got to the top of the stairs, that's where they had the little opening where you buy your tickets and what-have-you, like a little cloakroom-type thing." Although there was a kitchen on the premises, according to Hughes—who should know, given his tenure there (and the appetite he surely worked up playing onstage)—Shady's #2 did not sell food.

It was tables and chairs, with a raised stage. . . . It was live music. He had this thing going seven days a week . . . cold beer, setups, and all that. . . . It wasn't fancy. They had these regular square tables, the kind of chairs you folded. And they always used those red-and-white polka-dotted table cloths. . . . It would hold between two [hundred] and two fifty jam-packed, and I've seen it jam-packed a whole lot of times.

So did many others, a good number of whom went on to become blues musicians. One such person is a guitarist and singer named Don Kesee (b. 1943), who grew up in the country, about seventy miles west of Houston. In the 1960s, Kesee started driving into the city to hear live music on weekends, and he found a favorite venue in Third Ward. "Yeah, I went to Shady's Playhouse upstairs there, and oh it was a jamming place! It was one of the jammingest places in Houston at the time," he recalls. "The atmosphere, the blues fans, the blues lovers—that's what I remember—and dancing!" he says with a grin, relating several anecdotes about the attractive females that frequented the club. But most important to Kesee was the indirect musical education he picked up by close observation of players onstage there. "You had some good musicians coming through Shady's Playhouse, yes sir. They had Travis Phillips, Joe Hughes, and Johnny Copeland, and Albert Collins, and many others. I learned a lot just by watching all of them."

In addition to local talent, touring musicians were also booked at the second Shady's Playhouse from time to time. Hughes remembers leading bands there that backed the likes of Nappy Brown (b. 1929), Ted Taylor (1934–1987), Roscoe Gordon (b. 1928), Lowell Fulson (1921–1999), Joe Hinton, Barbara Lynn (b. 1942), and many others during his years as guitarist in residence. And the work was surely steady. "I was here seven nights a week, and two times in the daytime. On Sunday he had a matinee, and on Monday he had a matinee," Hughes asserts. "We played them all."

Until its closing in 1969, the second location of Shady's Playhouse functioned as the music center for a Third Ward block that encompassed soul-food restaurants, a rooming house, a place known as Black Joe's club, the neighborhood pharmacy, and other establishments. "This was *the* corner. You know, for this particular area," Hughes reflects, adding:

> See, everybody had their club. My club was Shady's. Albert Collins' club was out on Lockwood, Walter's Lounge. . . . Guitar Slim's [Rayfield Jackson, b. 1936] club was the Cozy Corner. This was areas you went in, and they owned those areas, per se. I was like the governor on this corner. Yeah, a lot of memories on this corner here.

Interspersed among the larger commercial structures in the area were numerous residential shotgun shacks, some of which also contained home-based businesses—little cafes, tiny beer joints, beauty shops, and the like. Though most of those commercial enterprises are now defunct, many of the old buildings still stand, boarded up and vacant, and folks still make their homes in some of the little houses.

At the eastern end of the block, near the corner of Beulah and Velasco, a rickety two-story structure leans and sags under the shade of a huge oak tree. The bottom level houses a barbershop, as it has for many decades; the upper floor consists of cramped living quarters. This dilapidated but still occupied wood-frame building was the childhood home for one of Third Ward's greatest blues success stories, an unconventional electric-guitar stylist named Albert Collins.

After moving to California in 1968 (at the urging of the seminal West Coast blues-rock band Canned Heat), Collins experienced a career renaissance, becoming one of the most internationally popular blues guitar slingers of the 1970s and 1980s, especially after his affiliation with Chicago-based Alligator Records began in 1978. When he died in Las Vegas in November of 1993, the world lost a true original—a fiery and physically animated instrumentalist who fingerpicked his Fender Telecaster in D-minor tuning with a capo clamped far up the neck. During his Alligator years, Collins had also developed into a more confident vocalist who relied on a sharp, self-deprecating wit and natural story-telling abilities to infuse songs with vibrant narrative power. His death was mourned literally by thousands of people all over the world, but many of those who knew Collins best—the real man, not the star—first met him when he resided above that modest Third Ward barbershop just down the block from the second location of Shady's Playhouse.

Born in 1932 on a farm near Leona, Texas, Collins moved to Houston at approximately seven years of age, settling with his family in the same neighborhood that would be home to his older cousin, Lightnin' Hopkins. In the Bayou City, he bought and mastered his first guitar, attended public school (and took piano lessons), made friends with neighbors such as Johnny "Guitar" Watson and Johnny Copeland, and (around 1948) formed his initial group, the Rhythm Rockers. By the early 1950s, he was a regular at the original Shady's Playhouse, where James "Widemouth" Brown tutored him on two subjects close to Collins' heart: guitar playing and truck driving. Teddy Reynolds recalls:

> That's where he learned at, from Widemouth, at the old Shady's. Uh-huh . . . Widemouth was the one who was teaching them guitar players like Joe Hughes, Albert, and Johnny Copeland. They'd watch his hands. But he got real close to Albert because Albert drive a truck, and Widemouth loved to drive a car! He was a freak for cars and trucks! So Albert got close to Widemouth, and that's when they'd get their guitars and Widemouth would show him all the different things. That's why Albert could sound so much like Widemouth back then.

As his skills developed, Collins began to compose original instrumental tunes. So when Henry Hayes formed Kangaroo Records, his first of several independent labels, he serendipitously also became the initial producer to capture Collins' signature "icy" sound on wax in the seminal hit "The Freeze."

> The way I hooked up with Albert, a friend of mine, who was also a music teacher, decided—you know during this time it was hard getting on a record label—so we decided . . . that we was going to put our funds together and start a little record label. . . . And the idea was to put out records on different talent, build 'em up, get some company interested, and then get a lease with them. . . . Kangaroo Records, that was my idea, Kangaroo Records—because it jumped! . . .
>
> See, I was the producer in the studio . . . and Albert came along with Joe Hughes, and Teddy was there, and several other musicians. So the piano player that used to play with Albert told me, "Man, Albert has a number that he's playing out at the clubs—boy, people are going wild about it! Man, you've got to hear that number."
>
> So Albert came out that day, so when we got through recording the others, I told him, I say, "Albert, I heard about this number 'Freeze.' . . . A lot of people been going wild for it in the clubs. . . . They've

been telling me about it, and you haven't recorded it with anybody. Do you want to record it with me?"
He said, "I guess so." I said, "Okay." We'd never rehearsed on it or anything.

So I say, "Well, okay, you start it off, and when you get ready for me to come in on the tenor, let me
know. Just bow your head, and I'll come in . . ." And the first time, he came in, played with the
drummer and the rhythm behind him and everything, and then after he played it, told me to come in
on the saxophone. Then he came back and played another chorus and played it out. And the man that
was over [i.e., in charge of] the studio, he shouted, "Whoa, that's a hit!" [Laughs] The first time down!
And that's how I recorded Albert Collins.

Joe Hughes provides further explanation of the fortunate sequence of events that led to this Hayes-Collins collaboration. The session on that fateful day was supposed to include recordings for a local girls' group called the Dolls, as well as for Hughes (who waxed his first single, "Ants in My Pants," on Kangaroo). However, Hughes had left his guitar at Shady's Playhouse, which was still locked up and closed during the morning hours of the scheduled recording session. After banging on the bolted nightclub door to no avail, Hughes thought of the closest place where he could borrow a guitar and still make the studio appointment on time—his friend's little cubby-hole apartment above the Beulah Street barbershop. "So I had Albert go out there with me, and that's how 'The Freeze' got cut, by accident," he says. "I went by there and got his guitar and took him to the studio."

From that 1958 session date until his departure for California a decade later, Collins would go on to record numerous sides in Texas for a variety of labels. Though he developed a productive songwriting partnership with his wife, Gwen, and became more comfortable singing, it was and will always be that unusual guitar playing—what Collins called "ice picking"—for which he will be most remembered. "That tone, that sound that Albert had!" as Hayes puts it. "Especially when he first start[ed] off, he had one of those crazy old amplifiers, made that old weird funky sound. That's what would catch you about Albert."

A lifelong Third Ward resident who knew Collins well is the eccentric guitarist known as "Little Joe" Washington (b. 1939). Though he started out playing piano as a child and then worked professionally as a drummer and vocalist, Washington—whose birth name is Marion—got the "Little Joe" moniker when he switched to guitar and then later began to emulate the playing style of Joe Hughes (who eventually married Washington's cousin Willie Mae). But Washington's earliest six-string influence was Collins, who lived just around the corner in the space above that barbershop on Beulah.

"I first picked up a guitar when I was playing drums with Albert Collins. I taught myself after that," Washington explains. "I figured it out on my own." Once he began to experiment with the guitar, however, the diminutive and now perpetually scruffy-looking fellow developed a unique

Albert Collins, 1986.

style that is best described as raw and unpredictable—some people would say wild. "I play with my teeth, my tongue, my head. I used to hang on the rafters when I was in Old Mexico," he says.

By the late 1950s, Washington had begun what would be a decade-long tenure working the border-town bars between El Paso, Texas, and Ciudad Juárez, Mexico—where he sometimes shared the stage with his old acquaintance Long John Hunter (b. 1931), a Louisiana native who had first played blues in the southeast Texas city of Beaumont, then in Houston, before ending up out west (where his thirteen-year stint at the Lobby Bar in Juárez remains the stuff of legend). During this era, the younger Washington also recorded a few sides for small labels such as Freedom and Donna. Unfortunately, however, and by his own account, the crazy lifestyle prevalent in the wide-open border-town entertainment district led him into bouts with alcoholism and substance abuse that took their toll on his health and artistic achievement.

On and off over the years that followed, Washington returned to live at the site of his initial affiliation with Albert Collins, maintaining his own makeshift residence in the dilapidated wooden structure where he grew up, which sat on the still unpaved road (formerly a railroad line) called Velasco. However, that house burned down in 1997, forcing Washington back onto the streets (and inspiring his freewheeling narrative song, "Who Started the Fire?," an especially plaintive blues). Dispossessed of a regular residence following the demolition of the fire-ravaged family home-stead—where he essentially used to camp out in a structure that already lacked utilities or a cohesive roof—Washington has somehow managed to hold on to life. He continues to play blues, especially at open jams such as the Blue Monday sessions at Miss Ann's Playpen not far away.

And in the year 2000 he even reformed a band to play a steady "Happy Hour" gig on Wednesdays at the eclectic Continental Club on Main Street in nearby Midtown. His work at this venue has exposed him to an entirely new audience, as documented in a prize-winning 2001 cover story Jennifer Mattieu wrote about Washington for the *Houston Press*. And his popularity there—both with customers and the management—eventually led to him being invited to reside, full-time, in the otherwise empty living quarters on the second floor of the old building housing the club. As a result, Washington now has a home, and he has become something like the club's resident mascot, hanging around pretty much all the time, sometimes sitting in with visiting bands, and regularly playing his weekly gig to an admiring, predominantly white crowd. This relative stability has also led him to book gigs at other venues around town, both within and well beyond his home neighborhood.

Sometimes performing without a guitar strap, Washington frequently engages in full-body contact with the instrument onstage, erupting into all-out assaults that suggest a primal expressionism. (On more than one occasion I've witnessed him do the same with a piano keyboard.) Musically, the results vary: He can produce crudely basic boogie riffs ad infinitum, be pointlessly

Little Joe Washington, C. Davis Bar-B-Q, Sunnyside, 1997.

profane in his language (both body and verbal), and then suddenly and unexpectedly unleash a series of brilliant improvisations laced with sonic quotes that range from Negro spirituals to B.B. King to jazz composers such as Charlie Parker. Along with his high-pitched, weathered voice and his often spontaneous lyrics, his instrumentation can communicate anything from the most tender melodicism to gut-bucket blues to abrasive noise. Houston blues-club audiences are never sure what they'll get from Little Joe, but they know it will flow straight from his stream of consciousness. He's a rather unique figure on the local scene, and at the start of the twenty-first century, Little Joe Washington has evolved into a Houston folk hero of sorts.

From the now vacant lot where Washington grew up and still resided until recently, heading straight north on the dirt path that Third Warders consider to be an extension of Velasco, hundreds of shotgun shacks and leaning two-story wooden houses define the area. One of these, up on Trulley Street, was the childhood home of Louisiana-born Johnny Clyde Copeland, a passionate and personable guitarist and vocalist who eventually left Third Ward to become a blues star. Amazingly, according to Joe Hughes, Copeland became a guitar player almost by accident when, in their midteens, they formed their first musical enterprise, a neighborhood band called the Dukes of Rhythm:

> Actually, we started out as a vocal group, singers. And then as we went along, that wasn't working out that well, so then we decided to add the instruments. And I had first put Johnny on drums, you know, and I had Herbert Henderson playing second guitar. We were using two guitars and a drum. But Herbert kept better timing on the drums than Johnny did, so I switched them around, and it came together then. But he came real close to being a drummer.

Once Copeland got settled on guitar, a good-natured and inspirational rivalry developed between him and Hughes. As the latter recalls:

> We were competitive. In those days, we used to do a guitar thing, what we called "cutting head," you know: "I got the best of you," like "I cut your head up" and vice versa. And that was very big during that time; all the guitar players did that, you know. But Johnny would tell me stuff, like what he's going to do to me on the guitar out on the stage, . . . and that's how we got better and better. . . . I was his teacher, but I didn't teach him everything. [Laughs]

And in an interview published in Kathleen Hudson's book *Telling Stories, Writing Songs,* Copeland confirms this account, saying of Hughes, "He was my teacher, and you always want to beat the teacher."

Copeland amicably departed from the Dukes of Rhythm when he was approached by saxophonist L. A. Hill to take the place of Albert Collins in another band, which soon became the house band at the original Shady's Playhouse. Though they never really worked regularly together in a group after that, Hughes and Copeland remained spiritual brothers, if not bandmates, right up through Copeland's departure from Texas, his big breakthrough in the music business, and his eventual heart transplant and death. "He was my best friend in the world," Hughes says.

Copeland had relocated to New York in 1975, and it turned out to be a major career move. He remained based there throughout a subsequent recording career that included albums on Rounder Records and Verve (as well as the Grammy-winning three-way collaboration with Collins and Robert Cray, *Showdown,* on the Alligator label). But Copeland always acknowledged his Houston roots in live performances all over the globe, and was typically introduced onstage as being "from Third Ward, Texas." After all, it was in Houston that he grew up, learned to play, and made his first records (as far back as 1958, on labels such as Mercury, All Boy, Paradise, and many more).

One of his cohorts in those earliest studio sessions was drummer Johnny Prejean:

I played on the early recordings with Johnny Copeland, "[Down on] Bending Knees," a bunch of others. I was his regular drummer for years.

. . . Shady's Playhouse, that's where I first met him. . . . I guess we might have been sixteen or seventeen years old. So I'd started off playing at Shady's with Big Frank [Newsome, the manager]. And I wasn't there maybe a week or two and Johnny Copeland and Joe Hughes and them had broke up, and so we needed a guitar player, and that's when Johnny came, and when Johnny came we made him the bandleader, you know. We had some gigs, so we started using his name, you know, Johnny Copeland's band. I might have did maybe fifteen years with him.

He was playing guitar and singing, or helping doing some of the singing. Teddy [Reynolds] would help sing, and L. A. Hill would sing one or two songs every now and then, the saxophone player, so it was kind of versatile like. . . . We had a pretty good little band back then.

We would go on out-of-town gigs, the old country gigs. I know we would go to Slippery Hill— that's a place somewhere back off by Lufkin, way back off in the woods. They had a little old club in Jasper we used to go to every weekend. . . . What we called "on the road," like when we would go to . . . the [Rio Grande] Valley and play. You know, and try to play our way back home—we would call that "on the road." We'd be gone about a week or two. . . . I don't know how we did it now. [Laughs]

Teddy Reynolds, who goes back even farther with Copeland, confirms Prejean's memories of the early days in Houston, especially the environment of mutual learning and teaching that the young musicians shared:

Johnny Prejean, Billy Blues, 2000.

We were all having fun and learning music. The chord structures, they was taught to me first, and then I'd teach the chord structures to Johnny and them. The piano man had to learn it first. The King Bee [radio DJ] had a talent show, and all the youngsters used to come and sing, and we'd play.

I did "Rock and Roll Lilly" with Johnny; that was his first recording. . . . We used to tell jokes on each other: "Hey man, if you don't stop that noise back there, I'm gonna hit you with a copy of 'Rock and Roll Lilly'." The sales was so bad, couldn't get nothing started back then, so we had stacks of copies sitting around wasn't doing nothing.

Me and Copeland, we've had a lot of fun together. Up and down the highway, playing Richmond, Rosenberg, Wharton, El Campo, all the little country towns, man. . . . He played at Shady's some with me too—till Big Frank would get a gig and take us out of town again. . . . Before then, he'd come down to Shady's with his guitar, but he didn't know how to play, so he'd sit there and want to learn how to play and watch us. Picking on that guitar and trying to learn, you know. Finally he caught on to it, and he ain't turned it loose yet . . . playing those blues.

First in Houston and later far beyond that city, Copeland universally impressed people not only with his stingingly precise guitar picking but also with some of the most rousingly soulful singing in recent blues history. There was an emotional honesty and intensity in his vocalizing that complemented his considerable technical skills on the guitar fretboard. Oscar Perry (b. 1943), a significant presence on the Houston scene for the last forty years—as a composer and producer as well as a multi-instrumentalist and singer—describes that intangible quality that made Copeland so special:

I played bass with Johnny for a pretty good period of time, about four or five years. . . . He felt his music when he performed, I mean really felt it. You know a lot of guys use other things to . . . help them perform. . . . But Johnny was more a natural. He would just use his own feelings to do what he had to do as an artist.

Though Johnny Copeland and Albert Collins became world-famous blues artists only after leaving Houston for cities more closely linked to the commercial entertainment industry, they would likely be quick to point out that major media centers and real-deal blues culture are often two starkly different realities. Beyond instrumental prowess or passionate singing, what made these two products of the old Shady's Playhouse scene such powerful performers was the spiritual connection they seemed to offer to the fundamental blues experience. In a marketplace full of poseurs—especially in the 1980s and 1990s when they both really hit the big time—these guys clearly stood among those players whose blues credentials, both musical and personal, were impeccable. And they both could tell you that Third Ward, even in the nineties, remained home to numerous lesser-known folks from the same stock.

Johnny Copeland, 1988.

the dichotomy between the jazzier, big-band style once popular in high-class joints such as the Eldorado Ballroom and the grittier, hard-driving combo sound of honky-tonks such as Shady's Playhouse is reflected in the socioeconomic status and musical orientations of current blues-playing residents of Third Ward. At one end of the spectrum you've got the likes of the elegant Jewel Brown (b. 1937), who was a featured vocalist from 1961 until 1968 in the world-famous band led by the great Louis Armstrong (1901–1971). Nearby you've also got the regionally prominent big-band maestro Conrad Johnson (b. 1915). At the other end of the spectrum, you'll find rustic front-porch players such as Francis Street resident and popular shade-tree mechanic Leonard Tyson. They all live only a few blocks from each other—Brown and Johnson in similarly well-built brick homes with neatly trimmed lawns, and Tyson in a one-room shed behind an un-painted wooden house in a weedy yard stacked high with automobile parts. Their living quarters, like their musical performance styles, suggest the contrast of uptown and down-home elements still common in Third Ward.

Brown, a successful insurance agent and businesswoman who sings only on special occasions these days, is aptly described as an accomplished jazz singer who loves to revisit the blues. "This is where I was born, right here in Houston, Third Ward," she says. "In the area I lived, blues was all I heard, other than gospel," adding that when it came to public performance beyond the church house, "We *all* started with the blues." Indeed, some of her early local associations—before being discovered while singing in a Dallas club (owned, incidentally, by Jack Ruby, who would later become known worldwide as the assassin of Lee Harvey Oswald) and before going on the road with the Louis Armstrong Band—included a 1955 recording session for the Duke label and singing with the Elmore Nixon group. And as she has demonstrated at infrequent public appearances in more recent years (e.g., occasional nightclub dates, a college concert, a brief European tour, and an August 2001 appearance in New Orleans at the "Satchmo Summerfest" honoring the centennial birthday of Armstrong), Brown proudly retains a connection to her roots.

> As the years went by and we established ourselves, they called some of us jazz singers, and you know, that's hip. You do whatever it takes to make a living, whatever club you can work in and whatever they want in that club. . . . But jazz is a derivative of the blues, and without the blues, it wouldn't have been jazz! . . .
>
> I would say the blues is a feeling, basically, and it was a feeling of expression from the times that especially black folk went through. That's how they relieved, you know. It was a form of moaning that they put words to, and it was a release of pain that was suffered in those years. . . . If it don't be for the blues, there'd be no jazz.

One of Brown's distinguished neighbors, just a few streets over, is Johnson, the man known to

Jewel Brown, Houston Community College, Third Ward, 1997.

countless musicians simply as "Prof," a tribute to his status as perhaps the most widely recognized and beloved music educator in black Houston. Highly respected as a versatile, passionate saxophonist and leader of the band Conrad Johnson and the Big Blue Sound, the diminutive octogenarian has for over fifty years been a major force, along with Milt Larkin and Arnett Cobb, in shaping the local sound into a rich synthesis of blues and jazz.

"Well, why do you want to separate them?" he demands. "They are part of each other, definitely!" Like Brown, Johnson ultimately argues that jazz is only a natural extension of the blues form, the flower that must be connected to its root.

> Blues is one of the basic forms of music that can be changed to any degree, any complicated way that you would like to take it, because it's only a matter of putting more chords in it to express more precisely what you feel. So you can dig it if it has maybe just three different chords, or you can take it and put in a multitude of chords, and it's still the blues. . . . Blues is the fundamental music. It's where all jazz came from. So if I, in my playing, don't have any blues reference, I don't feel like I'm doing a good job. . . . And I feel that all that we are doing has come from the blues.

A Houston resident since the age of nine, Johnson was a high-school chum of jazz-blues dualist Eddie "Cleanhead" Vinson (and claims to have directly inspired him to take up the saxophone). Johnson later attended the old Houston College for Negroes in Third Ward and then graduated from Wylie College in the East Texas town of Marshall. He began teaching in public schools in 1941. His thirty-seven years of classroom service were highlighted by an amazing tenure as director of the Fifth Ward's Kashmere High School Stage Band—which won victories in forty-two out of forty-six festivals entered between 1969 and 1977, recorded eight albums featuring more than twenty original compositions by Johnson, and traveled throughout Europe, Japan, and the United States.

Of his former students Johnson says, "I've got some I'm extremely proud of. Just like Don Wilkerson [1932–1986, a saxophonist who made seminal recordings and toured for years with Amos Milburn and Ray Charles, as well as played with T-Bone Walker, Joe Turner, and others] . . . Oh man, oh, he just turns you on." Johnson thinks for a couple of seconds and then adds with a smile, "and Sherman Robertson [b. 1948, guitarist and singer] came out of my band in high school—and he played about seven years with me professionally." For his part, Robertson, who is an internationally recognized blues recording artist, gives much of the credit to Conrad Johnson as the key to his success: "Kashmere High was *the* thing for me. . . . Prof tutored me, helped me, instructed me, showed me, and pointed me in the right direction."

Although officially retired from teaching since 1978, Johnson—who has never stopped performing onstage—continues to give private lessons and train his own band from his home today. Conrad Johnson and the Big Blue Sound practices every Tuesday night at the little "studio" addition on the back of his house in Third Ward. In addition to a full complement of horns and rhythm section, the group regularly features female vocalists such as Carolyn Blanchard (b. 1941), Gloria Edwards, fellow Third Ward resident Mickie Moseley (b. 1943), or Johnson's sister and longtime collaborator Liz Grey. Concerning the challenge of squeezing up to eighteen musicians with instruments into the small space, Johnson quips, "I get all of them in here. And some of them are *big—wooo—big* dudes, man!" [*Laughs*] Regarding the volume of sound they generate, he smiles and adds, "And I've never had any complaints from the neighbors [*shaking his head as if in disbelief*]. Boy, sometime we be *bearing down* in here!" Asked to define his group's fundamental sound, he says it's part of a long-running Texas tradition:

> We are very well accused of having certain idioms and certain sounds that are not present in a lot of other blues. And one of them is the big tenor sound—the Texas tenor sound. And you'll find the guys that come right out of Texas are the ones that really perpetrate this sound. Oh man, like Arnett Cobb, Eddie Vinson, Don Wilkerson, and so many more. . . . Well, I hate to say this, but maybe it's just because everything coming out of Texas is big! You know, it's a concept that we live with. But for some reason, the tenor sound here is not a puny sound. It's just not puny! It's a rich, vibrant sound. So I guess that's it.

Way back in 1947 Johnson recorded "Howling on Dowling" for Gold Star Records. It's a raucous jazz instrumental tribute to Third Ward's main street, home of the Eldorado Ballroom where Johnson regularly performed with his big band. A year later, Connie's Combo, a smaller group also led by Johnson, recorded on the Freedom/Eddie's label with folk-blues singer L. C. Williams, who was also known as "Lightnin' Jr." at the time. In the half century since then, Johnson has made music ranging from the relatively simple, old-style blues of Williams to the most complex orchestrations of the form, and he still delights in experiencing the full range of creative possibilities. "You can get anything in it, almost, that you could want. And you can get it bright. You can get it dark. You can get it bluer. You can get it smoother. You can get it rich. You can get it poor. It's just no end to the blues!"

On the opposite side of Dowling, just east of the middle-class enclave where Brown and Johnson live, Leonard "J. T." Tyson surely knows that a blues player "can get it poor." That's how the Arkansas native has lived, economically speaking, since moving to Third Ward about thirty years ago. A onetime Memphis-based professional guitarist who worked with prominent bandleaders such as Phineas Newborn Sr. and Bill Harvey back in the 1950s, Tyson hasn't gigged for money in years. But he stills loves to play (and informally teach) the blues around the impoverished section of the neighborhood where he makes a living as a home-based auto mechanic. Despite his humble status as a high-school dropout, this World War II veteran has a vast knowledge of blues music and its history, which he articulates in conversation with uncommon rhetorical force.

Conrad Johnson, at home, Third Ward, 1997.

They got W. C. Handy's statue up there in Memphis, but for what's been going on for the last forty years or more, Bill Harvey and Phineas Newborn should be where he is. They are truly statue-worthy too! See, W. C. Handy did the blues way back many years ago. But I'm talking about Bill Harvey and Phineas Newborn are the roots of what you've got going on today, modern blues. . . . So many fine musicians sprung from these two guys, all around Memphis and all the way down to Houston. Bill Harvey brought B.B. [King] here for Don Robey [to manage]. . . . Bill played tenor and Phineas played drums on many of those first sides cut here in Houston—on B.B., Bobby [Bland], and Junior Parker.

Tyson had started out in 1946 playing trumpet with Will Brown and the Brown Bombers in northeastern Arkansas, but he soon switched to guitar and was eventually recruited by the senior Newborn to play in his legendary Memphis band during its mid-1950s heyday. However, a few years later, legal difficulties derailed his career, as he explains:

When I was with Phineas' band, my second old lady sued me for nonsupport, and they come to Memphis, picked me up, and taken me back to Arkansas, put me in jail for six months. And I never did make it back in with Phineas' bunch no more after that. That incident just cut me off from them. I was supposed to have been their next big guitar player. They was going to make me cut that first record and get my own name. . . . [Phineas] gave me good advice, and see, if I'd been able to stay there, he'd a made me. Today I'd be a different guy.

Though Tyson's story of missed opportunity is sad, he did rebound from his break with the Newborn band to land other gigs, first with Bill Harvey in Memphis. "We were both staying up there in Sunbeam's place—that's above that old drugstore on Beale Street," he recalls. "And Sunbeam [Andrew Mitchell, 1906–1989] put a band together, and I was with it, plus with Bill Harvey too. We used to leave Memphis and come here to Houston to play." Before departing Tennessee for good, Tyson also worked for several years backing Roscoe Gordon.

Eventually, Tyson got fed up with the rough life on the road playing the so-called chitlin' circuit and settled for twelve years in Shreveport, Louisiana, where he worked day jobs and put together a weekend group he dubbed Jimmy Tyson and the Hurricanes. Then, in 1970, he moved to Houston to work with his former brother-in-law in an automobile body shop. On the side, he performed with trumpeter Frank Mitchell for a few years, then formed his own group. "I taught a bass player to play, got a drummer, and just started my own little thing, called it J.T.'s Express. We played around Third Ward in little joints and stuff," he says. However, over the years, Tyson tired of dealing with club owners and audiences and just quit gigging. But he didn't stop making music. These days he entertains himself and passers-by with occasional impromptu performances on guitar—an electric model that rarely gets plugged into an amplifier but can softly yield impressively bluesy sounds nonetheless. Among neighborhood kids who live within blocks of Tyson's front porch, the old fellow is affectionately known as "the guitar man."

A similarly down-on-his-economic-luck but talented guitarist is Kinney Abair (b. 1946), who moved to Houston decades ago from his small hometown of Refugio, 170 miles to the southwest. As a guitarist and singer, he mainly performs his own compositions—or favorites by Lightnin' Hopkins, his late friend (whom he depicted in the 1999 local original theatrical production *Third Ward Griot,* co-written with Ed Muth). But despite the pronounced influence of the elder bluesman, Abair has always defied any attempt to classify his music using convenient labels. He just writes and delivers songs that draw from wide-ranging roots to comment on life and the place he's now lived in longer than anywhere else, Third Ward.

As it had done to Lightnin' and others before him, the big city eventually pulled or pushed Abair into the heart of the old neighborhood just beyond downtown's mirrored towers. He was soon immersed in this environment—particularly its musical culture and street life—so he made himself at home there, even when a house fire put him out in the alley for a while. For almost thirty years now he's been knocking around and beyond Third Ward, taking just about any music gig available, mesmerizing people with his narratives, and making up scores of songs—usually based on episodes from his stories.

The songs are a reflection of the artist and his environment, both of which have the capacity to surprise. Although the majority of his compositions are the strange fruit of Abair's Texas blues roots, and though his biography qualifies him as having led what many would define as a "blues life," he is not exclusively a blues musician—anymore than Third Ward is exclusively a blues community. In Abair's repertoire, diverse musical elements, from Motown to straight-ahead jazz, appear and blend. Never one to fret over labels, he selects sounds and structures to suit himself. Thus, what the Houston musicologist Mack McCormick wrote over thirty years ago of Mance Lipscomb, whom he could not label strictly a "blues singer," just might apply today to Kinney Abair: "You will hear the firm, brisk rhythm meant for dancers, the clear ring of expressive song, and the energetic melding of traditional and personal creation. And if you describe the artist with accuracy, it will be with his own apt word: songster."

Of course, Lipscomb's folksy self-definition comes from an earlier generation of mainly rural African American culture. However, updated and urbanized, it still validly applies to an unusual artist such as Abair. He may be electric, rooted in post–World War II blues, wise to jazz, funkified with R&B, and open to a world of other influences, but in his own strange way he's a Third Ward *songster*. Unfortunately, he's mainly seemed content to make up songs without capitalizing on them in a professional sense. Combined with his apparent aversion to maintaining a steady day job, that characteristic has left Abair temporarily homeless more than once in the 1990s and into the twenty-first century. Yet he perpetually resurfaces, just sitting in at a local jam session or booked for a real gig with fellow musicians who—though they may have trouble finding him at any given time—know and appreciate what he can do with that big blond Epiphone guitar.

It's people such as Leonard Tyson and Kinney Abair who personify that strain of 1990s-era Third Ward blues that only rarely, if ever, travels beyond the boundaries of the neighborhood. Though numerous well-known performers still reside there—such as Calvin Owens or Jimmy "T-99" Nelson—these days they mostly play elsewhere in (or well beyond) the city of Houston. Tyson, on the other hand, hardly ever leaves Third Ward at all. To a slightly lesser degree, the same is true for other local blues people.

For instance, an artist occasionally featured at the Blue Monday jams over at Miss Ann's Playpen is William "Candyman" Hollis, a fine singer who was probably in his late sixties or early seventies when I came to know him. In the last few years, he's gigged a few times with guitarist and bandleader Milton Hopkins (b. 1934) at venues in the suburbs of the city. But mostly he stays close to his longtime home base. A tall, well-dressed man with very dark skin, he prompts shouts of "Candyman!" as soon as he enters the door at the jam session on Dowling. Dressed in a canary yellow suit and still sporting his wraparound shades, he later takes the stage to interpret old favorites such as "Call It Stormy Monday," which he renders in a finger-snapping jazzy style. The crowd loves him, waving uplifted palms and repeating his nickname as he holds the final note. Hollis relishes the positive attention too, smiling broadly and grasping offered hands as he moves back to his table. Performing the blues isn't really an income-producing endeavor for this Candyman; it's just one of the main ways he finds, and gives, joy in living.

In addition to Miss Ann's Playpen, several other old Third Ward venues still offer low-key, comfortable environments for musically talented area residents to make blues. The atmosphere at such places is far closer to (but likely much tamer than) the old Shady's Playhouse model—and certainly nothing like the former Eldorado Ballroom milieu. These are come-as-you-are cafes and taverns where local professionals share microphones, amps, and instruments with amateurs who have proven themselves worthy of joining them onstage.

One of my favorite such places is El Nedo Cafe, a soul-food restaurant located in a sagging wood-frame building on Ennis (not far from the second location of Shady's Playhouse). Until recently, Maxine Williams (b. 1917)—the genial octogenarian proprietor who's run the place since 1950 and is known to all as "Miss Maxine"—regularly served up tasty lunches and dinners (including the initially unexpected special of the house: cheese enchiladas) to a lively mix of old-timers, middle-aged working men and women, and teenagers. By 2002, she had started to limit her hours of operation only to late afternoons and evenings. For years, between the formerly regular lunchtime rush and the supper hour, as well as later on in the evenings, El Nedo has been a friendly, no-pretense place to sit and sip ice tea or beer, watch the television news, chat with neighbors,

Leonard "J. T." Tyson, Third Ward, 1997.

Kinney Abair, 1995.

Eugene Moody and Maxine Williams, El Nedo Cafe, Third Ward, 2000.

play dominos, and listen to a jukebox stacked with blues and R&B records that span the last five decades.

But for fans of the music there's more. Each Sunday night, the back room is opened up to form a larger L-shaped space, with a little stage area tucked into the right angle where the two rooms meet. The house is perpetually packed for this weekly ritual. Third Warders representing a relatively diverse range of ages crowd around tables, jam into booths, and stand along the walls—all there for the same reason: It's blues time.

For over a decade now, the Sunday-night show has been anchored by a uniquely raspy singer and guitar player named Eugene Moody (b. 1949). Fronting his Blues Back Band (usually a trio including bass and drums but sometimes featuring keyboards too), Moody mixes his own take on classic Willie Dixon tunes such as "Wang Dang Doodle" with fresh treatments of more recent Johnnie Taylor hits such as "These Last Two Dollars." Happily taking requests from the audience (though jiving and signifying when someone asks for a song he considers unworthy of his repertoire), Moody clearly enjoys the relaxed, all-in-the-family atmosphere that prevails there.

> *I became aware of El Nedo in 1957 [when] I went to school across the street at Blackshear Elementary. Most folks, unless they live right in the neighborhood, wouldn't know about it. But some of the patrons have been coming for fifty years. For me, it's like coming home every Sunday. . . . I like what I'm doing. I don't write songs. I don't read music. It's a cleansing, helps to relieve pressure; it gives me joy to do this. . . . I sing from my heart—what I feel, what I know, what I'm comfortable with. What I'm about is blues and R&B. I know there are guitar players who can outplay me all day long—but that's not what it's about to me. I don't want to play like them [because] I like the way I play. If you're not feeling it, it's no good. I tend to have more fun in a joint than on a big stage. It don't get no better than this.*

On and off through the late 1990s, Moody's band featured a woman named D. D. Bret on bass. Self-taught and still learning, this short, jovial gal is mainly known as "Boots" around El Nedo. Like Moody, she knows she's not the most accomplished player on her instrument, but she's a crowd favorite nonetheless, occasionally coaxed by women in the room to step up to the microphone and sing a number. As you might expect, Moody always readily encourages her to do so. In fact, between songs, he frequently calls out to any musical friends and acquaintances he spots in the audience and good-naturedly orders them to "Come on up here and play us a song." For some of those who do—such as a black cowboy I once saw warble "Sometimes I Feel Like a Motherless Child"—El Nedo is probably the grandest stage they'll ever play. For others, such as the late Eugene Carrier, a college music school–educated keyboardist who played for years on tour with B.B. King, Moody's Sunday-night gig has long offered a much appreciated retreat from the world

Grady Gaines, Evening Shadows, 1996.

Big Robert Smith, 2002.

of show business and professional demands. There are no stars or overinflated egos there, just neighbors who love to be part of a communal blues experience.

Moody's Sunday-night performance at El Nedo usually concludes around midnight, that pivotal moment when the weekend technically shifts into another Blue Monday. But patrons or musicians who aren't yet ready to call it quits have one more option. Over on Scott Street on the far eastern edge of Third Ward, saxophonist Grady Gaines hosts a late-Sunday-night jam each week at a delightfully funky club known as Etta's Lounge. Located in the back of a ramshackle wood-frame building with a modest cafe and barbershop up front, this venue is home to some of the deepest blues in town. Guitarist Milton Hopkins (who backed B.B. King for years on tour) initiated the weekly gatherings in the early 1980s, eventually handing the host job over to Gaines, who's been playing there since the start.

In terms of both musical tastes and atmosphere, Etta's is similar to El Nedo, though it's better known to outsiders and draws a more diverse crowd that usually includes some curious students from nearby University of Houston. The level of professional musicianship is generally more advanced at Etta's—starting with Gaines, whose credits as a bandleader date to before the period when he fronted Little Richard's (b. 1935) original group, the Upsetters, in the 1950s. An accomplished sideman who also played with major R&B stars such as Little Willie John (1937–1968) and Sam Cooke (1930–1964), as well as with local Peacock Records artists such as Gatemouth Brown and Big Walter "the Thunderbird" Price (b. 1914), Gaines emerged as a recording artist in his own right with several fine albums on the Black Top label in the late 1980s and 1990s. Given his impressive résumé, Gaines attracts some of the top local talent to his Sunday-night jam sessions, where gritty blues and chitlin'-circuit soul rule the night. It's a relaxed atmosphere that mainly features older, predominantly African American musicians who grew up with this music and relish the opportunity to sit in and jam. For Gaines and many others, Etta's is a refuge they can retreat to once a week to nurture their musical roots. As he says:

> We are really a blues band. I consider ourselves a blues band, but we also play a lot of other functions, like weddings and parties and such. We play all the hotels and all the country clubs and all of this kind of thing—for private parties and things like that. A lot of people think that because we play those things that we are not solid blues, you know. But we are blues.

Anywhere from five to fifteen guests may join in the jam before the night ends, but it's Gaines' full-time band, the Texas Upsetters, that opens the show and provides the core backing ensemble. No matter the song selection they play, most of their versions are indeed characterized by a strong gospel-blues feel, compliments of Gaines' reedy honking and the emotive delivery of featured singers such as Big Robert Smith (b. 1939), Patrick Harris, Paul David Roberts (who also plays trombone in the band), and others. When Roberts steps forward to reprise "Looking for One Real Good Friend"—a popular original that appears on Gaines' 1992 CD, *Horn of Plenty*—he testifies that he's had "a whole lot of lovers" but has now quit the sex game and craves a true soul mate. Though secular in its focus (referencing, among other things, a fear of AIDS), this musical tale of personal conversion draws its impressive power straight from the church house.

Likewise, when Third Ward resident Smith—a genial 325-pounder with processed pompadour and mutton-chop sideburns—takes the microphone, he's transformed into an enraptured preacher, remaking B.B. King's "Sweet Sixteen" into a bluesy sermon on unwavering devotion to a woman. And when he shifts into a medley of Otis Redding (1941–1967) tunes, he's filled with a spirit that makes the big man bounce and sway in defiance of the powers of gravity.

In addition to songs by members of Gaines' regular band, any given Sunday night is likely to feature a few numbers by Third Ward residents such as the lanky guitarist and singer Oscar O'Bear or the classic blues shouter Jimmy "T-99" Nelson. Though O'Bear is just as apt to show up at several other blues jams elsewhere around town, the eighty-plus-year-old Nelson rarely makes the weekly rounds these days. But when he does, one of his favorite places to blow the rust out of his pipes is Etta's Lounge, backed by his good friend Gaines on saxophone.

Nelson's got another good reason to like the place. It was there, back in the mid-1990s, that he met trombonist Carl Querfurth, then a member of the popular New England–based recording and touring group known as Roomful of Blues. Their friendship and subsequent affiliation eventually led to a three-way co-production, along with Houston blues radio DJ and promoter Nuri A. Nuri, of Nelson's 1999 comeback recording *Rockin' and Shoutin' the Blues*.

As Querfurth recalls it, his initial meeting with Nelson occurred by chance after Gaines, whose band had opened for Roomful of Blues at a local appearance, invited the visiting musicians to drop by Etta's later in the evening to join the jam.

> *Grady told us all to bring our horns down, and we were sitting there listening, and someone said, "We're going to have Mr. Jimmy Nelson come up and sing." And I hadn't heard that name in ages.*
>
> *. . . I didn't realize he was still going, in Houston or anywhere. So I got real excited, got the horn out, and told the other guys, "C'mon, let's go sit in now. This is the time!"*

An avid collector of early blues records, Querfurth remembered Nelson mainly for his signature hit "T-99 Blues" (named after a highway formerly known as Texas 99), which rode high on the Billboard charts for twenty-one weeks back in 1951. That song, which was followed the next year with another hot-selling Nelson single, "Meet Me with Your Black Dress On," once had the large-framed vocalist primed for major stardom. But a dispute with his label, Modern Records, occurred when the owners (L.A.'s legendary Bihari brothers) chose to devote all of their resources

Jimmy "T-99" Nelson, inside Eldorado Building, Third Ward, 2000.

Houston skyline view from Third Ward, 2000.

to promoting their latest discovery, a young hotshot guitarist from Memphis. "They went down and got B.B. King and recorded him, and that cat hit five in a row, man. And that was the money, right there, so they put me down, dropped me like a hot potato," says Nelson.

Though a series of recordings for numerous other companies occurred thereafter, Nelson could not duplicate the phenomenal success of "T-99 Blues." That disappointment, combined with his growing distaste for the "Jesse James contracts" that dominated the R&B industry, prompted him to get out. "That's how I ended up settling in Houston and going into the construction business," the Philadelphia-born singer explains. "I was booked here at the [Club] Ebony, over on Dowling, and I didn't want to leave because people were so nice. So I decided to stay here and joined the laborers' union, Local 18." As a mason tender, Nelson later made good money forming concrete walls for a massive, long-term project—the construction of the Astrodome stadium.

Though he still sang sporadically, Nelson essentially dropped out of professional music—forsaking a calling that dates back to 1941, when in a California nightclub he saw the Kansas City Rockers led by Harlan Leonard (1905–1983) and met Big Joe Turner (1911–1985), who would become his role model and personal mentor. By the late 1980s, Nelson had comfortably retired from the Hartney Construction Company and had time on his hands. Thus, when his wife passed away, he decided to refocus on his singing career. He had never ceased songwriting, so he possessed fresh material, and he had also cultivated an instinct for reinterpreting standards the "T-99" way. That combination, plus his past reputation for tastefully swinging the blues, led to major festival appearances and guest slots on a few CDs.

Yet Nelson envisioned something more—a complete album made on his own terms. At first there were setbacks. He bankrolled a 1996 session in Houston with a band led by Milton Hopkins, but that project remains on the shelf. He has also endured a seemingly interminable legal battle over the unauthorized 1992 CD release of old "T-99" material on the Collectables label. Those disappointments have been significantly abated, however, by Nelson's full-force glee over his subsequent projects with Querfurth (including material for another CD, *Take Your Pick,* released in 2002, featuring Duke Robillard on guitar). It's a partnership that owes its genesis to the late-Sunday-night jam sessions at Etta's Lounge.

And Nelson, along with countless other musicians, feels he owes something to the cosmetically deteriorating but still finely functioning Scott Street club. After all, it's a place he can depend on, week after week—one of Third Ward's deepest wells for old-school blues.

as I reflect on this wonderful and commonly misunderstood place called Third Ward, I realize again that one of the deep joys of my life has been my friendship with the late Teddy Reynolds. He was an especially passionate musician and a kind, loving man. As Joe Hughes told me following Reynolds' death in 1998, "Teddy was just one big ball of soul, you know. If he weighed 150 pounds, he was 175 pounds of soul." Reynolds' detailed stories offered me an especially valuable link to local music history (as you've already witnessed in my frequent quotations from him in this book). But on a personal level, he was also special as a rich source of knowledge and insight about so much more than blues music. I honestly cannot think of any other person who gladly taught me more about the city I now call home, and especially about life in the neighborhood where I have worked since 1981, Third Ward.

Reynolds was born and raised at the corner of Elgin and Hutchison, about eight blocks from the college campus where I teach, just opposite the South Freeway that chopped its way through the neighborhood decades ago. That new highway might have once been perceived by some people as a sign of progress reflecting and facilitating Houston's growth. Yet, until I got to know Reynolds, I could not have begun to conceive how much Third Ward, like the entire city, has radically and irreversibly changed in one man's lifetime.

Today glass and steel skyscrapers loom nearby, reminding one at a glance that the big city is ever present. However, the old neighborhood just southeast of downtown was once a remarkably different place, a place that still lived in a native son's vivid stories.

Reynolds told convincing tales about rabbit hunting in the dense woods on the land where Texas Southern University now stands, narratives that revealed his lifelong love of good dogs (whether they hunted or not). He described Brays Bayou, before it became a concrete-lined drainage ditch for the city, as a waterway that pulsed with wildlife—especially the catfish and perch that he used to catch and eat. The bayou banks were also thick with blackberries that could be picked and sold for profit (if the urge to consume them on the spot could be resisted).

Perhaps his most amazing memories of this time and place recalled his Huck Finn–type existence when, as a rebellious twelve-year-old, he ran away from the overly strict home life of the grandmother who raised him and actually lived in the woods for a while, sleeping in an abandoned shack huddled under army surplus coats.

To hear the tales, one would think that this talented musician had grown up in some remote rural area, but in fact his basic connection with the outdoors was cultivated in the heart of what is now a densely populated inner-city environment. Teddy Reynolds helped me remember that before there was a city, there was land, and before there was culture, there was nature—and that human attention to this fact can be a source of enlightenment and strength that surpass explanation.

Teddy Reynolds, at home, 1995.

Wilfred Chevis, Silver Slipper, Fifth Ward, 1997.

CHAPTER 4

fifth ward

Blues with a Creole Accent

smiling contentedly, the guitarist sways in rhythmic step with the two saxophone players behind him. His left-hand fingers glide along the neck of a red Gibson ES-335, right hand meanwhile shaping the solo, striking precisely against the worn pickguard. The drummer, tucked behind his percussion kit in a little foam-rubber-padded alcove at stage's rear, pounds a funky pulse, accented on electric bass by a bandmate whose wide-brimmed hat brushes against the sloping ceiling.

A slightly raised floor, featuring isolated Plexiglas squares illuminated from below by rotating bursts of colored light, draws an overabundance of dancers (perhaps more per square yard than any other I've witnessed around town). Dressed in a variety of styles, from the semiformal chic of glistening dresses or suits to the Lone Star state standard of cowboy shirts and blue jeans, they happily bounce and spill against each other—and anyone else seated or standing along the perimeter of the shuffling mass.

The dimly lit but spacious room, heavy with cigarette smoke, is shaped like a fat rectangle, the stage and adjacent dance floor nestled in the corner to one side of the main entrance, and the bar (backed up by a small kitchen) diametrically opposite at the far end. Along a wall partially covered with sections of mirror, a paperboard sign declares in ten-inch handmade letters: "WELCOME TO THE SILVER SLIPPER." The text is adorned with two paper cutouts, one of a high-stepping couple in silhouette and the other of a shiny specimen of the namesake footwear. On each side of the sign hovers an oversized artificial crab, a Gulf Coast–theme wall decoration mass-produced in red plastic. From wall to wall the floor is crowded with sturdy chairs and cloth-covered tables, some temporarily abandoned by those squeezed into the dancing area, but most occupied by patrons who talk, drink, flirt, and good-naturedly argue—all while still attuned to the music.

Since tonight's soundtrack is a steady mix of blues and R&B classics, it's got to be Saturday here in Frenchtown, a special district of Houston in the larger area known as Fifth Ward. On Fridays and Sundays, true to its ethnic heritage, this venue features authentic zydeco performers whose instrumentation highlights accordions and washboards—and whose lyrics are as likely to be rendered in a Creole patois as in heavily accented English. But on the day of the week that T-Bone Walker immortalized as the time to "go out and play," the Silver Slipper—the last of the great old Frenchtown clubs—continues a decades-long tradition of serving up the blues.

Some of the old-timers here occasionally slip back and forth between English and French in their verbal expression—a linguistic ebb and flow that parallels the historical relationship between blues and zydeco in their lives. It's also a reminder that mobility, assimilation, and double consciousness have long been fundamental realities for the people known as black Creoles. And that's especially true for those who have left backwoods farms and little towns of southwestern Louisiana and migrated to the urban magnet of Houston (a process that began with emancipation from slavery, boomed with the early-twentieth-century creation of the petrochemical industry, intensified following the devastating Louisiana floods of 1927, accelerated even more rapidly after World War II, and continues to this day).

Inside the Silver Slipper, physical mobility might be a bit restricted by the close proximity of so many bodies, but almost everyone is somehow moving to this music—not just those on the dance floor but also people seated in chairs and standing along the main aisle running the length of the room. A waitress, balancing a tray aloft on an upturned palm, hypnotically rotates her head and swishes wide hips, almost dancing herself, as she navigates the throng of bystanders. An elderly couple in the corner leans close together, gently rocking to the beat, her hand nestled in the crook of his jacketed arm. Nearby, three males in their thirties trade wisecracks and observations as they collectively peer through the partial darkness toward a gathering of seemingly unattached women. Though obviously focused on the females, one of the men clutches a sweating brown beer bottle and subconsciously taps its round base against the tabletop, keeping time to a swinging blues instrumental.

Curley and Alfred Cormier, Silver Slipper, Fifth Ward, 1998.

Elmo Robinson, Silver Slipper, Fifth Ward, 1998.

Eventually, the band hits the final chord, holds it (while the patrons respond with handclaps, shouts, and whistles), then modulates into a revue-style introductory theme. Speaking over the looping musical motif, the guitarist announces it's now time to bring out one of the featured singers, whose name triggers a roar of approval. And from the kitchen area at the back of the room, a short, overly wide man in tuxedo shirt and cummerbund emerges to stroll toward the stage, his right hand waving a white handkerchief each step of the way.

Disconnecting the microphone from its stand, he raises it like a wine bottle from which he'll sip, and bellows "Oh yeah," holding the second syllable for several seconds. The band stops, and he immediately steps away from the stage and disappears back into the midst of the dance-floor crowd, microphone still in hand. As bottles clink and voices murmur, the singer—now lost from general view—suddenly shouts through the public-address system, "People, has love ever made you feel low-down? Has your heart been broken by love?" Pausing briefly to allow the enthusiastic audience response to subside, he then screams, "A lady broke me down for love! A lady broke me down for love! I say, my lady broke me down!" As the room's fervor swells, he sighs, "Let me tell ya 'bout it all, the way she broke me down." The band kicks in on cue, and a song begins, its scripted stanzas frequently interrupted by segments of improvised dramatic monologue echoing the rhetorical flair of the most sanctified pulpit.

And the people—many of whom (more than you might expect) will dutifully be hearing actual church sermons in the morning—momentarily lose themselves in gospel-flavored blues. This music, secular in focus and often blunt in its lyrical documentation of human imperfections, provides a special kind of soul balm for some folks who, by and large, take the concept of *soul* very seriously.

Several hundred Saturday-night revelers will congregate here for hours, well past that midnight pivot into Sunday's early morning. Cheering a succession of featured vocalists, as well as the instrumental talents of the band, they may seem to live only for the dance, the drink, the moment. But for many, this weekly release proves absolutely necessary for them to live fully, to connect honestly with the full range of human experience. And, consciously or not, by gathering to hear blues at the Silver Slipper, they perpetuate a long-standing connection between a sound and a larger community called Fifth Ward.

each of the six wards that subdivide the older core of Houston has its own distinct history, its own persona. And most, if not all, of these places are known to have contained some section—small or large, disreputable or not—where blues has been played and lived, at least at some point in the past. For instance, during the 1920s and 1930s, the Fourth Ward was home base for a number of itinerant barrelhouse pianists (such as Robert Shaw, Buster Pickens, Pinetop Burks, et al.) known as the Santa Fe group—named after the dominant railroad line, whose trains they rode and whose rollicking sound they imitated on the keyboards. But for the generations of the city's black men and women who grew up with the music and have perpetuated it through the year 2002, the primary corollary to Third Ward's impressive cultural legacy, past and present, is the Fifth Ward, sometimes called "the Nickel."

Originally settled by freed slaves and immigrants from various ethnic minority groups, the Fifth Ward was formally incorporated in 1866. Its relationship to central Houston is defined by two natural boundaries: It lies north of Buffalo Bayou but east of White Oak Bayou on the east/northeast side of downtown. Waco Street officially (though not necessarily culturally) forms the ward's eastern border and Jewel Street the northern edge.

As the scholar Diana J. Kleiner notes in the *Handbook of Texas Online,* the Fifth Ward was already considered a predominantly black neighborhood by 1900. The numerous Germans, Italians, Jews, and other Europeans who had lived there in the late nineteenth century were increasingly displaced by newly arriving African Americans moving in from the surrounding farmlands of eastern Texas and southwestern Louisiana. Among those from the latter area, black Creoles—descendants of the old French-African slave class—formed a significant presence. Settling in what originally was only a four-block area (but eventually expanded many times over), they established an enclave that in 1922 formally became known as Frenchtown.

As the major urban cultural center in Texas for transplanted Creole folklife, early Frenchtown was home to hundreds of musicians who played the old-style syncopated music first known as "la-la" and mainly performed at house parties in the area. But this acoustic form—characterized primarily by plaintive vocalizing in French to simple accompaniment on accordion and percussive washboard—would eventually metamorphose into something radically new. As the newly citified Creole players absorbed the musical elements and instruments of urban blues—which they were exposed to primarily in Houston's largest black nightclubs (such as Fifth Ward's Club Matinee or the Bronze Peacock, or Third Ward's Eldorado Ballroom) and via the increasingly popular medium of radio—their sound evolved toward the post-1950 phenomenon now known as zydeco.

That distinctive, highly danceable style of black Creole music—for many years restricted to obscure nightspots on the circuit between Houston and New Orleans—emerged into mainstream popular culture in the 1980s, where it has generally been misconstrued as a musical genre totally unique to Louisiana. But though the seminal black Creole dance music la-la surely originated there, modern electric zydeco is arguably the product of a syncretism that was first triggered in Texas, especially in the Bayou City. Of course, that new sound, once realized, was naturally carried back to Louisiana, where its dominant features soon became the norm. As Michael Tisserand—author of the definitive history of the genre, *The Kingdom of Zydeco*—has noted, "Although Houston is often overlooked in zydeco history, the city's relationship to the music can roughly be compared to Chicago's impact on the blues." That assertion may sound like an overstatement to some, but Houston has undeniably been the migration destination of many generations of expatriated Creoles—as well as the focal point for the modernization of their music. And two of the most important venues in the history of zydeco music (at least west of the Sabine River) are old Frenchtown clubs that have also hosted more than a few blues artists and fans over the decades.

Doris McClendon (1936–1997) reigned for years as the matriarch of the most well known of such establishments, the Continental Lounge and Zydeco Ballroom. While still in her early teens, the Louisiana-born McClendon (who had moved to Fifth Ward at age eleven) established her first connection, via a family member, to the large barnlike structure at 3101 Collingsworth that she would later come to operate as the Continental. Her grandfather Charley Johnson originally owned and managed his Johnson's Lounge there, a nightclub that first featured big bands playing blues and swing, until around 1951 when he began booking Creole accordionist Lonnie Mitchell (1925–1995). As the Indiana University folklore professor John Minton notes, "By the mid-1960s Johnson's, often featuring Mitchell six nights a week, was Houston's premiere Creole nightspot." Upon Johnson's death in the mid-1960s, Mitchell assumed operation of the club for five years, until his lease expired and reverted to Johnson's heir, McClendon. She renamed the club the Continental Lounge and Zydeco Ballroom and for the next twenty-five years continued to book mainly zydeco music, but also Texas blues artists such as the nationally known Sonny Rhodes (b. 1940) as well as locals such as Big Roger Collins (1935–2001) or Little Buck Green.

During McClendon's tenure as owner of the club, she hosted practically every major artist in zydeco. In an interview I conducted as research for her *Living Blues* obituary, Stephen Harris gratefully recalls how McClendon "took me as her nephew." Harris, who worked as the parking attendant at the Continental for twenty-one years, adds an impromptu role call of zydeco greats he remembered formerly playing there:

> All of them started in Houston right here: "Buckwheat" [Stanley Dural], "Boozoo" [Wilson Chavis], "Rockin' Dopsie" [Alton Rubin], "Rockin' Sidney" [Simien], John Delafose, Clifton Chenier—he played his last gig right here [1987] . . . "Beau Jocque" [Andrus Espre], Paul Richard, Wilfred Chevis, L. C. Donatto, Wilbert Thibodeaux. Lonnie Mitchell, he played his last gig here too [1995].

Chevis, the leader of the Texas Zydeco Band, concurs: "All the main bands out of Louisiana, when they came to Houston, this is where they played at—the Continental and some of the Catholic Church halls." As a younger Texas-based recording artist, "Li'l" Brian Terry (b. 1973), of the Zydeco Travelers, once told the *Houston Chronicle* writer Carol Rust, "Playing there was like being in the hall of fame."

Although the Continental's historical significance and spacious floor plan certainly contributed to its popularity with performers and fans during her proprietorship, McClendon herself was the key to the club's continuous operation. As Harris points out, "A lot of the musicians accepted her, you know, as an auntie. . . . The majority of them that started out young here, they would call her Mama." And McClendon labored diligently to promote the legendary zydeco venue, often appearing on the early-Sunday-morning KPFT radio blues program once hosted by Big Roger Collins to announce upcoming events, only a few hours after having closed from the previous Saturday night show.

Guitarist Ashton Savoy (b. 1928) remembers: "Doris was a good woman, and she worked hard at that place, man." He cites her unwavering commitment in spite of recent difficulties, including a seemingly interminable freeway construction project that hampered access to her club, the dwindling population of older Creoles in Frenchtown, and her own health problems. Chevis adds, "She pushed zydeco a whole lot. And she kept it going till the day she left."

McClendon continued to invite people into her red-and-white painted zydeco landmark until ten days before her death. Inside, among the year-round Christmas lights, tin-foil decorations, mirrors, and balloons, she greeted what would be her last customers with free food and a warm smile. Unfortunately, despite the considerable efforts of daughter Carolyn Rose McClendon to continue her mother's legacy by keeping the club opened, it was indefinitely boarded up and vacant by the end of 1998. As University of Houston folklore professor Carl Lindahl once told me, "The Continental was Doris' life-token, as if neither could live without the other."

But the symbiotic relationship between blues and zydeco survives in Frenchtown even beyond the year 2000, just a few blocks north of the old Continental building in the sagging wood-frame structure that houses the Silver Slipper. Curley Cormier, a soft-spoken gentleman fond of three-piece suits, is the proprietor there and is much beloved by his loyal customers. Yet unknown perhaps to some people who've ventured in only on Fridays or Sundays (i.e., zydeco nights), he's also the Saturday-night bandleader and a widely respected guitarist who, despite a temporary hiatus due to the effects of a stroke a few years back, still mixes stinging blues runs with jazzy chord changes, making music with his five-piece band, the Gladiators.

Cormier was born in Cecilia, Louisiana, but—like so many other Fifth Ward Creoles—has actually lived in Houston since childhood (that is, since his father moved to the city to find work around 1950). In 1962, after several years in the construction industry, the senior Cormier capitalized on his well-proven talent for throwing a house party by opening a club—a little cafe with live down-home music—in a shotgun shack on Crane Street in Frenchtown. Known then mainly as Alfred's Place, it featured a mix of live blues and zydeco six nights a week, providing a steady gig for former Houston resident Clifton Chenier for over five years. "Two pieces—just he and the scrub board," the younger Cormier recalls, was the usual setup, as it had been for decades in the

Doris McLendon, Continental Zydeco, Fifth Ward, 1996.

The Silver Slipper, Fifth Ward, 2001.

old la-la tradition. But by this time Chenier was already collaborating elsewhere with larger, more instrumentally sophisticated bands and arrangements as he was gradually becoming known worldwide as "The King of Zydeco"—a title that evolved following his 1964 recording (in Houston, for Arhoolie Records) of the signature anthem "Zydeco Sont Pas Salé."

The Silver Slipper was, and to this day still is, a place where zydeco and blues just seemed to fuse organically. Each remains a separate entity, as red beans are to rice; but properly blended together, each defines the other's perfect complement. And the Cormier family long ago figured out the right proportions of musical ingredients to keep their patrons satisfied.

That recipe goes back to those countless occasions in the 1960s when Chenier was the rice, so to speak, to Lightnin' Hopkins' beans—or vice versa. According to the Cormiers, the Third Ward bluesman often visited the club (located a few miles northeast of his home turf) whenever Chenier was there. Cousins by marriage, the two musicians reportedly were good friends who enjoyed each other's company, offstage and on. When Hopkins showed up, the two would often treat the audience to an impromptu showdown between guitar and accordion, trading licks and improvising arrangements, recycling and inventing songs on the spot—surely blurring the aesthetic line between blues and zydeco in the process.

Word of such savory jam sessions enhanced the popularity of the club well beyond Frenchtown, so that the clientele eventually came to include blacks from Third Ward and other parts of the city. As business increased, the elder Cormier opted to buy the property next door and expand, building onto and remodeling the original establishment to its present relative spaciousness. But the club nonetheless remained crowded. "Even after [my father] enlarged it, it was still the same thing," Cormier says. "Just jam-packed."

Following his father's tenure as proprietor, Cormier's older sister managed the place for a while, rechristening it the Silver Slipper but maintaining tradition and booking both zydeco and blues performers. Then around 1973 Cormier, who was already well established as a versatile guitarist backing the likes of soul-blues singer Luvenia Lewis (b. 1940) at local clubs, assumed operation of the popular nightspot. Though he is "not really a zydeco player" himself, Cormier has continued to book Houston zydeco bands led by traditional-style Creole accordionists such as L. C. Donatto (1932–2002), Wilbert Thibodeaux, and Wilfred Chevis (b. 1945).

Meanwhile, he now reserves one night a week, Saturday, just for his own band, just for the blues and old-school R&B. That's when he brings out his precious Gibson guitar, and the Gladiators reign triumphant. And whether he's jamming a B.B. King–inflected solo, faithfully rendering classic soul riffs, or providing gospel-toned backup for featured singers such as Joe Hill or Elmo Robinson, Cormier always seems to play with a cool poise, comfortably at home on a stage that's been in his family for over four decades.

Zydeco players, Silver Slipper, Fifth Ward, 1998.

Grady Gaines, Silver Slipper, Fifth Ward, 1997.

The blues legacy of the Silver Slipper reaches back to the primal musings of Lightnin' Hopkins and extends through the more "modern" sounds of guys like Floyd London (1911–1979), Clarence Green (1934–1997), Joe Hughes, I. J. Gosey, and other blues players who've gigged there regularly over the years—right up to the Saturday-night sessions the guitar-playing owner now hosts himself. As Cormier remarks about the club's role in the development of numerous local musicians, "Everybody's played here—I mean everybody that can play a little bit has played here."

The turnout at a very special October 1997 show at the Silver Slipper proved the point to me. This event, which was a fund-raiser benefiting Cormier during his recovery from the stroke, took place on a Wednesday (a night the place is usually closed), but it drew several hundred patrons and scores of musicians, crowding the house during midweek the way it used to be back in the heyday of Alfred's Place. Featured entertainment included blues players such as Gosey, Hughes, Grady Gaines, Texas Johnny Brown, Oscar O'Bear, Faye Robinson (b. 1952), Ashton Savoy, Sherman Robertson, and many others—most of whom ended up sharing the stage with equal numbers of zydeco players at some point during the evening. It was a very fine night: one historic venue, one massive and appreciative audience, and two styles of music, distinctly different though related. And in Frenchtown it all seems, then and now, perfectly natural.

The Silver Slipper no longer serves, as it once did, as a full-time neighborhood hangout and grill, and years ago it abandoned its six-nights-a-week schedule of live entertainment. But the legacy founded by Curley's father, Alfred, who still resides across the street from the club, lives on. "Just three days a week, and live music basically is all we want to deal with," the younger Cormier asserts, confident in his priorities. And the appreciative fans who regularly pack the house—whether they come to hear zydeco or blues—enthusiastically agree.

of course, presuming to classify many of the local musicians as either strictly zydeco or strictly blues players can be a fallacy, especially given Fifth Ward's (and greater Houston's) heritage of going it both ways. As I've discovered over the years, some of the best blues instrumentalists in town, especially guitarists, occasionally "disappear" from their normal haunts to enjoy random gigs or steady work with zydeco outfits—free from the hassles of fronting (and often managing) their own bands.

I recall, for instance, one Friday night in the mid-1990s when I had escorted some curious out-of-state visitors to the Silver Slipper, eager to share with them the wonders of *chanka-chank* rhythms and squeezebox harmonics. As we parked in an adjoining lot and walked around to the main entrance, my friends marveled aloud at the exotically funky sounds that already filled the evening air, pulsating from the walls. Primed for immersion in real-deal Frenchtown zydeco, they were later stunned to witness one of the more unusual blues guitarists they'd ever seen, the inimitable Joe James (b. 1937).

Though he was once the leader of an R&B group called Joe James and the Flames, had long ago accompanied major blues stars (including Joe Turner, Jimmy Reed, and Freddie King), and still occasionally (through the 1990s) headlined his own shows at local blues venues, this personable Houston native was dutifully fulfilling a supporting role as a member of the Texas Zydeco Band at the Silver Slipper that night. As such, most numbers called for him to concentrate on rhythmic guitar chording, deferring the leads and solos to the front man, accordionist Wilfred Chevis. Little bluesy riffs and accents surfaced now and then, but James' guitar playing was, by design, mainly a part of the larger background of syncopation, nothing that stood out as remarkable or unexpected.

But during the second set, the sound shifted, starting with a sizzling zydeco treatment of "Turn On Your Love Light." That classic blues song, written by Third Ward's Joe Medwick and originally recorded in Houston in 1961 by Bobby Bland (Duke single 344), had been introduced to many rock-and-roll baby boomers such as myself by the seminal California hippie band the Grateful Dead, who covered it on the 1969 *Live/Dead* album (Warner Brothers) and often included it in their concert repertoire. My visiting friends likewise recognized the number immediately and grinned to hear it now performed with accordion and washboard. It was something at once familiar and foreign, kind of cool—and now being reinvented once again, back in the very city where it had first been created decades ago. But after a couple of stanzas, the cool quotient of this performance would shift into overdrive as Chevis nodded to James, unleashing him for the first extended guitar solo of the evening. It would not be the last.

James, suddenly transformed, proceeded to mesmerize the audience with his fleet fretwork, artfully squeezing the strings to wrench out vintage blues licks and improvisations while finger-picking with a deft right hand. Later, as he made the guitar moan and wail in sync with a chunky groove, he walked to the front of the bandstand. Chevis generously yielded the floor with a simple shout: "Go, Joe!" And for the first and only time in my several visits there, I witnessed a floor full of dancers cease their steps in midsong and turn as one to watch an inspired instrumentalist. James expertly worked the guitar from every angle—strapped across his chest, slung down around his knees, arched behind his head, even held to his mouth (so that he could pick it with his teeth). "Who *is* this guy?" one of my companions gleefully screamed at me across the table. Before I could yell back an answer, he bellowed, "And what's he doing in a *zydeco* band?"

As the music and audience fused in a roaring crescendo, I shrugged, smiled, and shouted in response, "That's Joe James. Welcome to Fifth Ward."

Meanwhile James had stepped down from the stage and had begun snaking his way through the ecstatic onlookers on the dance floor, soloing at full speed the whole time. Pausing once to

Joe James, at home, demonstrating his headstanding guitar-playing technique, 1997.

survey the room, he spied his target and moved slowly toward it, still jamming, occasionally bowing to enthusiastic patrons along the way. Then, sidling up to a small, unoccupied table, its red cloth cover empty except for a butt-filled ashtray and one long-drained beer bottle, he quickly pushed the items aside with one hand. With his amused bandmates blaring away in the background, James clutched his guitar, tucked his hat-covered cranium, and rolled over onto the tabletop into a headstand, legs extended so his feet could brace against the low ceiling. The now upside-down guitarist promptly resumed the solo to squeals of delight from throughout the room. But he wasn't done yet. Topping it all off, he began to shuffle his feet in little steps so that he soon rotated in a 360 degree circle, the crown of his head pivoting on the table cloth. And through it all, James was creating a spicy blues solo—served with lots of relish over an almost trance-inducing zydeco beat.

A minute or two later, what James modestly refers to as "my little show" had come to a rousing end. After a few high fives from nearby spectators, he quickly returned to the stage, resumed his earlier spot beside the drummer, and morphed back into the efficient zydeco role player he can be, saving the next solo (without the acrobatics) for later in the evening. While the Creole bandleader occasionally grants James such license to follow his blues muse and unshackle the head-standing showman within, the guitarist understands that such diversions are, by necessity, only temporary. After all, this gig is with a zydeco band, in which, as always, the accordion ultimately reigns supreme.

That's a reality that many a blues-loving Creole guitarist has had to come to terms with in Houston. Especially since the 1980s—when traditional Creole and Cajun cooking emerged as a national culinary craze, and the related musics became popular with much broader audiences—many of the most reliable and well-paying gigs in town are with zydeco bands playing not only in clubs but also at high-profile restaurants and festivals throughout the region. Simply put, some blues guitar players have discovered that they can get more work and make better money just going with the flow and doing the zydeco. For purely economic reasons, some even decide to pursue it full-time. But there are many others (such as James) who straddle the fence, who just can't walk away from straight blues—no matter the fluctuations in the musician job market.

That's long been the case with Ashton Savoy. Born to Creole parents in 1928 in Sunset, Louisiana, he was introduced to the old pre-zydeco la-la tradition from his infancy. But Savoy has identified mainly with Texas blues since his teens, when, like so many of his non-Creole counterparts, he was turned on by the electric sounds of T-Bone Walker. So even though he's performed with some of the most esteemed patriarchs of black Creole dance music, including Clifton Chenier and Boozoo Chavis, Savoy asserts: "Man, I didn't want to do zydeco. I wouldn't play nothing but blues if I could! Just blues!"

Perhaps the key to understanding this man and his almost single-minded attitude is his passion for the guitar, which was mainly relegated to simple rhythm work, playing behind an accordion or a fiddle, in the rural la-la culture of his youth. "I didn't like that too much," he says. "My daddy was a musician who played guitar [and some violin] in backyards and barns and stuff, you know. But T-Bone Walker was the style of playing I would like—him and, later, Lightnin' Hopkins." Handling a prized Gibson Epiphone, Savoy sighs, "A good guitar is just like a piece of clothes you like to wear."

Onstage he wears it well, playing blues in the style he first developed after leaving home at age sixteen and moving to Lake Charles, where he bought an amplifier and got his initial gigs. Following a stint with the Blue Notes, he started his own band and expanded his territory: "Ain't nary a place around south Louisiana I ain't played." He credits his popularity with the ability to emulate his primary inspiration. "Everybody was grabbing me then because T-Bone Walker was it! He was about the hottest thing on guitar, and because my style was patterned after his, everybody wanted me."

Through the late 1940s and 1950s, Savoy led a blues band and helped many others get started, including pianist and vocalist Katie Webster, a native of Fifth Ward whom he met one night in Port Arthur, Texas. "Yeah, I hired her right then—and raised the price for the band. We made some good money too." Webster and Savoy "shacked up" for about five years, he wistfully recalls.

During that era, Savoy was often in the studio with Louisiana-based producers Eddie Shuler (b. 1913) in Lake Charles or J. D. Miller (1922–1996) in Crowley, recording as frontman and session player for various small labels, such as Goldband, Zynn, Hollywood, Storyville, and others. He further established himself on the regional scene playing before huge crowds at places like the Harlem Club in Opelousas, where "me and Clarence [Bon Ton] Garlow used to battle the blues."

After an amicable breakup with Katie Webster (who went on to become a major blues star, especially after leaving the Gulf Coast), Savoy moved permanently to Houston in 1960. "Back then, everybody was working, and man they had clubs all around Fifth Ward, all over town, everywhere," he explains. Like many of his peers, he auditioned at Peacock Records for Don Robey, who turned him down for allegedly sounding "too much like Jimmy Reed." Years later he took a day job driving a truck for Safeway, but he never stopped playing the blues on evenings and weekends.

During the 1980s and 1990s, having retired from the trucking job, Savoy occasionally took work playing in various Houston zydeco bands, including one led by his cousin, accordionist Wilbert Thibodeaux. But he also continued to perform in blues ensembles, fronting his own group from time to time and often sitting in with others—right up till late 1999, when a freak accident that occurred while fishing left him badly burned and with limited use of his left hand.

Before that misfortune, Savoy maintained a refreshing presence on the local blues jam circuit, usually arriving early and always sporting his trademark cowboy hat and one of his cherished guitars. No matter the venue or the crowd, at some point he would stand and deliver his unique repertoire, singing hard blues in both French (e.g., "Tous les Jours la Même Chose") and accented English, picking the guitar in a style that blended fluid T-Bone Walker runs with the swampy riffs of former Louisiana cronies such as "Guitar Gable" (Gabriel Perrodin, b. 1937).

Ashton Savoy, Big Easy, 1995.

Though his Creole mannerisms and zydeco roots will always define part of his identity, Savoy has now lived in Houston—and been a part of its music culture—for most of his life. For sure, he can still speak and play in the manner of his native state, but as he told me in a 1995 interview, "I just can't help loving them blues, yeah."

The same goes for some Fifth Ward–raised blues players even a generation younger, such as internationally known recording artist Sherman Robertson. "I started at twelve years old, and I'm fifty-one now," he told me in 1999. "So I'm just as old as some of the elder guys playing, not in age but in time playing, you know." Indeed, his résumé is impressive, highlighted by tours while he was still a teenager as lead guitarist backing Duke stars Junior Parker and Bobby Bland, as well as a later lengthy affiliation as the six-string wizard for Clifton Chenier's Red Hot Louisiana Band, a studio appearance on Paul Simon's 1986 Grammy-winning Album of the Year *Graceland,* and (through the 1990s) three major-label CDs as a solo artist—featuring his own singing and songwriting, in addition to the instrumental mastery for which he's best known.

"I can't speak totally for the next generation," he says, "but the old brothers had to do it for a reason, to lay the format. And that was their role, to lay the foundation. Now if we don't take that gift and continue with it, the struggle was for nothing."

When Robertson was growing up in the 1950s and early 1960s in Frenchtown, talented people were making the music all around him. Literally just around the corner was Alfred's Place (the Cormier family enterprise later known as the Silver Slipper). Years before his first appearance onstage there (at age thirteen), Robertson couldn't help but overhear and absorb the funky rub-board rhythms and accordion riffs of the zydeco players, or the guitar leads and shouted vocals of the blues bands. In an era of open windows and far fewer electronic distractions in the homes, such sounds saturated the neighborhood most nights of the week.

"The guy that first taught me, Floyd London, used to play there on the weekends," says Robertson. "He was just blues, straight-ahead blues, just a regular old blues guy. . . . But he was still a virtuoso at what he was doing. And he wasn't aware that the several notes that he played, man, was so perfectly spot on. I've tried 'em, what he used to play, put the notes in the same places, but I still can't do it."

Robertson could certainly dig the earthy zydeco and acoustic blues that often emanated from the club, but he was obviously most turned on when the more progressive performers—such as London or Clarence Green—would plug in their electric guitars and make the adjacent houses vibrate with modern blues and R&B. A Creole baby boomer, Robertson associated the traditional folk sounds with a way of life his family had left behind upon migrating to Houston from Breaux Bridge, Louisiana, in 1950. In the big city, things were different, and, like most kids, he wanted to believe his music was something new.

After school each day, he knew where to find this new music: 2809 Erastus Street, once the site of the most prestigious nightclub in Fifth Ward, the Bronze Peacock. By the time Robertson was old enough to navigate his bicycle to the place, the building had evolved into the home of Duke-Peacock Records. In his early teens, Robertson would loiter hopefully on the sidewalk out front, eager to glimpse label giants such as Bland or Parker, or at least to speak to respected session guitarists such as Clarence Hollimon (1937–2000) or Wayne Bennett (1933–1992). "I was on almost every session," he claims in jest, then explains, "but I was on the *outside* wall. I was right by the door, but I couldn't get in! I rode my bicycle there and laid my ear to the wall." His imagination invigorated by the palpable presence of the record industry as well as by his natural-born love of music, Robertson dreamed of someday being part of it all.

By his midteens, those fantasies would be fueled by his own rapid mastery of guitar. Supported fully by his father, John "Choo-Choo" Robertson, a hard-working auto mechanic who spared no expense to get the best musical instruments and instruction for his son, the younger Robertson soon began to distinguish himself as the fleet-fingered kid behind the fancy new guitar.

Like many black Creoles of that era, the senior Robertson had embraced urban life in Texas as a means of escape from a tradition of rural poverty and degradation back home.

My father was a sharecropper who went off to fight World War II, a man who was driven to be somebody. I was born in 1948, after he had returned from the war in '46. When he came to Houston from Breaux Bridge, he left the mules and the plow hitched. He abandoned his field. Because he had been to World War II, and then to come back and say "I've got to get back in the sharecropping groove," well, he just didn't fit that groove anymore.

In a variation on an ages-old theme—the father who pushes his own unfulfilled aspirations onto his son—the elder Robertson was driven to see his boy establish himself as a great guitarist, a dream he had never been able to pursue himself.

So as soon as I said, "Daddy, I want a guitar," he started living his dreams through me. Now I was in trouble! He was like, "Practice, practice, practice, practice!" "Dad, can I go play some basketball?" He'd say, "Nope, practice your guitar." . . . So I didn't get to be a kid, because he wanted me to be the best.

By the time the son had mastered the basics, his father was determined to show him off around town. "My dad took me to every little joint in Houston and would say, 'I want you to let my boy play.' I'm like twelve or thirteen now. And the only thing I can play is 'Honky-Tonk.'" Curley Cormier over at the Silver Slipper concurs, "Yeah, his dad used to bring him here when he couldn't even really get in a club, bring him here to play." Robertson explains, "What he was doing, he was really doing me like the guy that taught him how to do auto mechanics. He didn't know how to teach or tutor, so he just put me in the situation and made me figure it out."

The strategy paid off, and Robertson went on to form his own bands and make a good name for himself on the regional circuit, playing weekends and evenings. Meanwhile, following his father's lead, he had learned auto mechanics and taken a day job to support his own household, which now included a young wife and child. As the years passed and Robertson more fully matured as both a performer and a bandleader, his aspirations as a professional blues musician were eventually discouraged by the dawning of the late–1970s disco era. But he stuck with the music—out of defiance of popular culture as much as his growing sense that blues was his natural calling, a perception that dated back to his first inspiration (via recordings), Freddie King. Robertson's perseverance eventually led to an opening slot on what was then one of the premium annual local gigs, the SumArts Original Juneteenth Blues Festival (now defunct) at Miller Outdoor Theater.

"My break came when I played on the Juneteenth Festival in the summer of '82," he recalls. "My band, the Crosstown Blues Band, we had seven pieces, with horns and piano, and . . . I came and played my tail off." Buoyed by the enthusiastic reception he earned from the crowd, Robertson departed the stage to stumble into good fortune. "The lucky thing was Big Mama Thornton's band didn't show up," he recalls.

> So she said, "Get that little fat-assed boy out there—the one that just got through playing that guitar. Tell him he's got to play behind Big Mama Thornton." They came to ask me . . . and I already had the guitar in my hand. I said, "Man, sure!" I was already supposed to back up Peppermint Harris—which I did too. But I got to back up Big Mama Thornton. Wow! All in one night.

Though he relished the opportunity to perform the blues on a large stage for thousands of fans—with his own band as well as backing up a pair of living legends—Robertson never anticipated what that one night would ultimately do to change the direction of his career. His inspired playing had caught the eyes and ears of the evening's headlining act, zydeco master Clifton Chenier. The older musician sent word inviting the hotshot guitarist to visit him backstage, discovering in the process that Robertson's father was one of his own childhood friends from back in south Louisiana. Then, about a month later, Chenier called to ask Robertson to join the Red Hot Louisiana Band on tour, an opportunity he seized and never regretted, even though that meant shifting away from his primary focus on Texas blues to play zydeco instead.

Looking back now, Robertson comprehends that the half decade he worked with Chenier provided priceless training and enlightenment. "It was so much fun to see places I hadn't seen—and not to have to front the band. It was fun to be a sideman and just to enjoy myself." It also gave him a mentor, someone who taught lessons he would utilize years later as leader of his own blues band. As he explains:

> The thing I took from Clifton, I learned how to work a crowd. He would never miss. I don't care where we went. It was not the thing where he played the same show every night—because he didn't, like most guys do. He didn't have a set show. He'd say, "I know what will work tonight," and that's what we'd do. He could feel the people. . . .Whatever it was, it was right on the target. . . . He taught me. He'd say, "I don't know what I'm going to do up there tonight. But when I get up there, I'll know."

In addition to daring to trust his instincts, Robertson learned from Chenier to keep the proper perspective about his entertainer's role in relation to his audience, whether playing for the masses at a major European festival or for the locals at a little Blue Monday jam.

> He used to tell me—he'd drill this in my head: "Don't ever play for you. Don't you play for the club owner. Don't you play for no woman. Don't you play for no drink. Play for the people! Never forget the people." He taught me that. He'd say, "That man in the audience is always right. Even though he's sloppy drunk, he's right. He deserves it. He's worked hard all day, and you taking his money." For a while I'd say, "Yeah, okay, sure." But then I thought about it. It is for the people.

Following his departure from Chenier's band, Robertson emerged as an in-demand guitarist, right during the mid-eighties' zenith of zydeco's breakthrough into popular culture. High-profile stints followed with Terrence Semien and the Mallet Playboys, as well as Good Rockin' Dopsie. But Robertson—like so many of his cultural brothers and sisters back in Fifth Ward—was never fully satisfied just doing zydeco. He dreamed also of playing and singing his own songs in the Texas blues style he preferred, heavy on the electric guitar. So, after returning to the blues via a brief road gig playing behind Third Ward product and star Johnny Copeland, Robertson set a new course for himself, turning his back on zydeco despite the steady work it offered.

Forming his own band and aggressively marketing himself, Robertson landed slots at some U.S. and European festivals and clubs, catching the attention of veteran British blues-rock producer Mike Vernon in the process. Two Vernon-produced CDs, *I'm the Man* (1994) and *Here and Now* (1995), followed—both on the Code Blue imprint distributed by industry giant Atlantic Records. The first of these earned Robertson a W. C. Handy Award nomination and established him as a widely recognized blues artist. Then, in 1998, he teamed with California-based producer Joe Harley to record *Going Back Home* for the stereophile label AudioQuest Music—the first recording that fully utilized Robertson's talents as songwriter as well as singing guitar slinger.

These days, though he still lives in Houston and spends lots of time at his mama's house back

Sherman Robertson, Continental Zydeco, Fifth Ward, 1998.

in Frenchtown, Robertson continues to tour internationally and make plans for the next recording. When not on the road, he shows up now and then at low-key blues jams in small clubs around town, and he occasionally might even sit in with a zydeco band. But Robertson's focus, despite his Creole heritage and impressive credentials as a zydeco player, is locked mainly on the blues scene well beyond his longtime home base. And in terms of his professional status at the start of a new millennium, he reigns as one of the higher-profile blues artists to emerge from Frenchtown.

black Creoles, past and present, have generally come to Houston for the same reason as everyone else (regardless of race): employment, a chance to make money. And for much of the twentieth century, greater Fifth Ward offered all blacks—those with and without French ancestry—a fairly good place to do that. Its numerous and affordable residences lay in close proximity to jobs in local industries (especially along the ship channel and in the railroad yards) as well as to many black-owned businesses and institutions. Despite the fact that poor people, starting with those emancipated slaves who originally settled the land, have always been part of the ward's demographic profile, Fifth Ward has often symbolized a place of progress and achievement for African Americans of the upper Gulf Coast region.

But, perhaps more than any other in the city, this ward has experienced bipolar extremes of socioeconomic prosperity and despair. For much of the twentieth century, it was home to a thriving business and entertainment district (just south of Frenchtown) along Lyons Avenue, a thoroughfare once rivaled only by Third Ward's Dowling Street as a center of African American life in Houston. Diana Kleiner points out that by 1925, there were already over forty black-owned businesses operating on Lyons Avenue alone, and by 1927, the nearby Phillis Wheatley High School ranked as "one of the largest black high schools in America," with a faculty of sixty teachers and a student body of over 2,600. Later, in the late 1940s, the music-business entrepreneur Don Robey would base his operations out of an office at 4104 Lyons Avenue, the original home of Peacock Records.

But following the decentralizing effects of desegregation—and the concomitant negative impact on many black-owned establishments and institutions—that once proud street became so impoverished and dangerous that Houston bluesman Weldon "Juke Boy" Bonner warned, in the title of a song, "Stay Off Lyons Avenue" (c.f. Arhoolie CD 375). His lyrics go on to describe the violent crime commonly found there, with special emphasis on the perils of venturing around Lyons and Jensen, an intersection near a place he calls "Blood Alley" (more popularly referred to, well into the 1990s, as "Pearl Harbor"—because of the large number of men who suddenly lost their lives there).

Indeed, for the last three decades or so of the twentieth century, Fifth Ward was widely perceived, by insiders and others, as uncommonly dangerous urban turf. According to the *Houston Chronicle* writer Rebecca Mowbray, it was once dubbed "the most vicious quarter in Texas" by *Texas Monthly* magazine. And in the minds of many Houstonians who've never even ventured there, this ward is somehow known as a place to avoid, unless you're seeking to be a target for trouble. During the 1980s and 1990s, that menacing public image was likely amplified, for some, by the rise of hard-core *gangsta* rap produced by Fifth Ward–based Rap-a-Lot Records and its best-selling groups, such as the Geto Boys. But the violent reputation fostered in the media can be misleading.

Today Lyons Avenue and the surrounding area are experiencing a true socioeconomic renaissance, triggered by construction projects sponsored by Habitat for Humanity and, since 1990, especially by the ongoing efforts of the Fifth Ward Community Redevelopment Corporation co-founded by Reverend Harvey Clemons, pastor of the historic Pleasant Hill Baptist Church. New apartment complexes, single-family dwellings, banks, restaurants, and businesses are gradually staking claim to a landscape that, until recently, was characterized by weedy lots and abandoned or neglected properties, such as the shell of the boarded-up Deluxe Theater.

In an earlier time, the Deluxe might have been one of the finest black-owned-and-operated movie houses in the South, located near the relatively upscale Crystal Hotel and the famous Club Matinee (neither of which survives). Decades later, the Deluxe had become an empty and massive target for vandals, the dominant eyesore on the block. But by 2001 its front walls had been decorated with beautifully painted murals (including one titled "The Ghosts of the Matinee," depicting silhouettes of performing musicians against a deep blue background) created by art students from Wheatley High School. And the old building is scheduled to be demolished eventually and replaced by new construction, including a community arts center. Lyons Avenue, the ward's defining thoroughfare, is coming back, even if it will never again be the music-rich entertainment district it once was.

As saxophonist Grady Gaines says with a sigh, "I've seen Fifth Ward go through a lot of changes." Like many other current or former residents, Gaines recalls with special pride that his old neighborhood—home to the likes of the esteemed U.S. Congresswoman Barbara Jordan (1936–1996), the heavyweight boxing champion George Foreman (b. 1949), and myriad great musicians such as the jazz artists Illinois Jacquet and Joe Sample (b. 1939)—was once a business and cultural center for thousands of Houston's blacks.

I was in third grade when we moved to Houston. We moved straight to Fifth Ward, off of Liberty Road. . . . Lyons Avenue was the biggest thing we'd ever seen in a black area—businesses and people all up and down. . . . You see, Fifth Ward used to be where all the big name acts would stay when they came to Houston—like Louis Jordan, T-Bone Walker—all the action stayed there in Fifth Ward at the Crystal Hotel, and they'd play at the fabulous Club Matinee. . . . That was the top name place in town.

As Gaines and other players of his generation know, along with Third Ward's Eldorado Ballroom, the Club Matinee is one of the most significant venues for classic blues and R&B in Houston history. As one veteran California-based recording artist reminisced backstage at a local tribute concert in June of 2000 for the late Ervin Charles (1931–2000) of Beaumont: "Houston was one of the biggest blues towns anywhere, back in the fifties. It was heavy blues here. And this is where you wanted to play—especially at the Club Matinee or at the Eldorado Ballroom."

The musician, former record producer, and educator Henry Hayes concurs about the central importance of Fifth Ward's most popular nightclub:

> That one on Lyons Avenue, yeah, Club Matinee, that's the one! That's where the big attractions used to come. This guy that owned that, he had a big cab stand and everything there. It was a really nice club. But most of them others were just small joints. Being over in the Frenchtown area, you had some good bands over there, but the other clubs wasn't that large.

As Hayes hints, the Club Matinee owner, Louis Dickerson, had developed quite an impressive empire there on Lyons Avenue. In addition to the nightclub and taxicab operations, he also owned the adjacent 115-room Crystal Hotel, the finest African American–owned lodging establishment in the city at the time. Such investments proved profitable enough that—according to Jim Fisher (a media archivist of local history and Senior Producer at KUHT, Houston's PBS television affiliate)—*Ebony* magazine profiled Dickerson in an October 1957 article about "Negro millionaires in Texas."

Former Bobby Bland road manager and blues promoter John Green explains that the segregationist practices of the era caused the majority of prominent black visitors to Houston to stay at the Crystal Hotel, which only added to the aura of excitement and nightlife generated by the nearby club.

> Club Matinee—oh yeah, that was the jumping-off place. That's where all the bands would come to stay, next door at the Crystal Hotel. Before integration, that's where all the entertainers, music or not, would go to stay, at the Crystal Hotel. Club Matinee stayed open twenty-four hours a day. You could get food there twenty-four hours, and you could get you a bottle of booze after hours [laughs], all night long. . . . All the guys brought the girls there.

Whatever illegal activities may have occurred there after hours, Club Matinee's always-open restaurant also served as one of Fifth Ward's most popular eateries, patronized by people of all ages. Fifth Ward–born blues and zydeco promoter Ed Berry, whose father used to front a local band known as the Harlem Music Makers, has told me stories about going there regularly as a child to eat breakfast in the restaurant. And the club, like its Third Ward counterpart the Eldorado

Ballroom, also frequently hosted afternoon talent shows on weekends, big events that attracted scores of Houston-area youngsters looking to break into show business.

Unlike the Eldorado Ballroom, however, Club Matinee's role as a twenty-four-hour gathering place for off-duty musicians also provided them with a comfortable and important venue for networking for gigs. For instance, having already reached the pinnacle of local achievement for a blues player—performing in the house band at the Eldorado Ballroom for three years straight—Calvin Owens' ascension as a professional ultimately depended on bandleader Pluma Davis' recommendation. And the opportunity for him to offer it to the right people depended on the milieu provided by Club Matinee. Owens relates the story, which takes place in 1953:

> Pluma Davis . . . he knew Bill Harvey, who had the backup band behind B.B. [King] at the time. And Pluma Davis was a cat that—see the Club Matinee was where all the cats would meet, where all the bands that would come to town would stay [i.e., next door at the Crystal Hotel]. And Pluma Davis only lived right around the corner from Club Matinee. So he was the kind of a cat that mingled with all these people.
>
> Anyway, by me working in his band, somehow I became a pretty good trumpet player, as far as the professional music scene. . . . So when anybody needed a trumpet player—for recording sessions or whatever—they would usually ask Pluma, and I would usually get those calls. So when Bill Harvey needed a trumpet player for the backup band behind B.B., they called me. Well, I knew Bill Harvey. I had met him. I used to go by the Club Matinee too and hang out with those guys sometimes. And so I got the gig. And I went on the road with B.B. King. Yeah, buddy!

Bass player Hamp Simmons (1937–2000), a longtime stalwart of the Bobby Bland band, also recalls the Lyons Avenue establishment as a type of home base and travel depot for working musicians. "The Club Matinee, it was a point to meet. Bobby would stay there, at the Crystal Hotel," he says. "And we would meet up there, in the parking lot of the Matinee, to leave town. And when we'd come in, we'd come in to the Matinee. That was always the gathering spot for us—because they had that restaurant open all the time."

In short, the sprawling Club Matinee complex served a variety of functions as one of the highest-profile general entertainment centers in Fifth Ward. As Grady Gaines explains, its layout could change, depending on the type of function:

> Club Matinee was actually both a restaurant and a club. And it had another room off to the side was called the Anchor Room. And the Anchor Room would have a band every weekend. But if you played in the whole Club Matinee, the full club, they would open the thing up, and I guess it would hold about five or six hundred people.

Gaines also affirms that the club, despite being a venue for famous touring acts and regional head-liners, was also a place where a beginner could take the stage and make a name for himself or herself.

> King Bee, Clifton Smith [1928–1985], a DJ on KCOH, used to broadcast over there from Club Mati-nee. And they used to have big jam sessions and talent shows too. That's where Trummie Cain's talent show was held, and the great Joe Tex was discovered from being on one of those talent shows, when he was still a boy.

That versatile Southern-style soul performer ultimately known to the world as Joe Tex (1935–1982) was born Joe Arrington Jr. in the Central Texas town of Rogers. But it was after his family's move to Baytown, just southeast of Houston, that the precocious adolescent crossed paths with a public school teacher—and music insider—who would introduce him to the Club Matinee and start him down the path to stardom. That person was former Fifth Ward resident and accomplished keyboard artist Richie Dell Thomas (1922–2001).

The proud daughter of "the man who brought black education to Baytown, Texas," Thomas made music for most of her nearly eighty years. As a pianist and organist, she played professionally with a diverse range of artists, including Big Joe Turner, Clarence "Gatemouth" Brown, Calvin Owens, Buddy Hiles, Clarence Green, Conrad Johnson, and many others. She also was a close friend and colleague of other Houston-area blues pianists of her era—most notably Amos Milburn and Charles Brown. Yet she persuasively told me that none of these experiences could compare with the ultimate professional satisfaction she achieved as a public school educator, a gig she maintained for thirty-two years before retiring in 1981.

Born in nearby Groveton to parents who were schoolteachers in Baytown, Thomas was raised by her grandmother in Fifth Ward. She started taking piano lessons (at twenty-five cents each) at age five, an experience that soon triggered an insight: "I realized that this is what I wanted to do—to be connected with music." She credits her ability to fulfill that dream to supportive parents, especially her mother:

> Most people didn't have phonographs in Fifth Ward at that time. Well, there was a place across the street, and the people used to play the nickelodeon, we called it, loud! So whenever I heard something I would tell my mother, when she was at home during the summertime, I'd say, "Mama, go over and put a nickel on that song." I remember it very well. . . . And she would go and put the nickel. Now she was a very religious woman who never walked into a joint as such, but she would do that for me. And she put a lot of nickels in there. . . . And I could hear the music—at our house across the street—where this old piano was.

Along with the formal lessons, these listening experiences introduced Thomas to the blues and ultimately prepared her for her first public performances: playing at neighborhood parties and, later, in her collegiate dining hall while still a teenager.

After receiving her Bachelor's degree in music from Prairie View A&M, Thomas made a tenuous commitment to teaching at first.

> I taught school my first year out of college in Port Arthur, Texas. . . . And I got my dad to give [fellow Prairie View graduate] Charles Brown a job—because my father was the principal of Carver High School in Baytown. So Charles went to Baytown and I went to Port Arthur. And after one year, I said, never again. It was a disaster—no music, no support, just horrible. Anyway, we decided, we made a pact between us, Charles and I, that we were going to Los Angeles where there's some music. And we did—that summer—we both resigned our jobs and went to Los Angeles . . . in 1943.

Nevertheless, after a seven-year span there that included lots of late-night sets in nightclubs, additional studies at the University of Southern California, a marriage, the birth of her three children, and a divorce, Thomas decided to return home to the relative stability of teaching and an eventual master's degree from Texas Southern University.

The California years may have been a detour in Thomas's career path as an educator, but they marked a key period in her development as a professional musician, as they have for various other Houstonians. Arriving there together in the midst of World War II, she and Brown—who had been close friends since meeting as twelve-year-olds in a scholastic competition—first scrambled for jobs, then joined the musicians' union, and eventually found work worthy of their talents. For Thomas, the initial big break came playing piano in a show called "Sweet and Hot with Dorothy Dandridge" with a roster of performers that included Joe Liggins (1916–1987). Thomas also met Ivie Anderson (1904–1949) and began playing at the legendary Ivie's Chicken Shack, a job that lasted for about five years. During this period, Thomas continued to be a sister figure for Brown, whom she remembers working on his biggest hits, "Driftin' Blues" and "Merry Christmas Baby," in her L.A. apartment, and she vicariously assisted in and enjoyed his emergence as a major recording star.

Once back in Houston, the highlight of her career in education was the quarter of a century that she taught voice and choir at Fidelity Manor High School in the suburb of Galena Park. "Teaching music in high school, that was my joy. . . . Out of that bunch of children, I got a lot of music teachers, performers."

The most famous of these was Joe Arrington Jr., whom she actually met during a three-year stint teaching English (her college minor) at her father's school—before the music position opened

Richie Dell Thomas, at home, 1997.

up for her in Galena Park. "Joe Tex was one of the people I worked with. He was in my seventh-grade class in Baytown. I was not his music teacher; I just saw his talent." During this time, Thomas was also playing regularly at Club Matinee, so she took her student there to perform in one of the talent shows, which he promptly won. "He sang 'I Know I'll Go from Rags to Riches' and wore an old tuxedo that Charles Brown had left at my house," she recalls with a big smile.

From that start, the dynamic young Tex went on to acquire his first professional work as a singer, eventually breaking out of his home state to record numerous popular R&B hits, including "Hold What You've Got," "Show Me," "Skinny Legs and All," and others. By the time he released the smash single "I Gotcha" in 1972, he had achieved the rarefied status of a genuine crossover star, appealing to young fans black and white all over the nation. As such, he's likely not only Thomas's most famous former pupil but also the biggest commercial success ever to emerge from the old Club Matinee talent shows.

Recollecting the good old days of that Lyons Avenue establishment, the elegant and petite Thomas notes the ironically disruptive effect on the black community triggered by desegregation:

> Today Houston, and especially black Houston, has spread out everywhere, so now you just don't know where anything's going on. But it was actually a lot of fun during those years when it was all compacted together because of segregation. You know, we knew where we could go to hear some dynamite music on a Sunday evening, there at Club Matinee. You know, we knew where to go to hear it. I didn't know so much about Third Ward because I lived in Fifth Ward, but it was good down there too. . . . Today it's not the same.

Veteran musician Texas Johnny Brown also remembers Sunday evenings at Club Matinee as a special time for Houston's indigenous blues people:

> We used to have guitar sessions, guitar battles on Sundays out there at Club Matinee. And there'd be about four or five of us in there, and man, guitars would be ringing like everything! It was wild! It would be myself, it would be Goree Carter, it would be Joe Bell [b. 1930], and Grady Gaines' brother, Roy Gaines, and Clarence Hollimon. Those were the real guitar players around here then, and we'd all be together there at the Matinee, Sunday nights, actually getting started in the afternoon. And all the people would love it—the end of the weekend, and everyone digging the blues.

Roy Gaines, one of the hotshot guitarists Brown remembers from those jams, is unabashedly angry and outspoken over how and why Fifth Ward's major business and entertainment district changed in the late 1960s. As he bluntly told me in a 1998 interview,

Texas Johnny Brown, Big Easy, 1996.

We lost all of that great movement on Lyons Avenue and such to the move that was made when Martin Luther King came in and everything was desegregated. He made good solid speeches that led people to believe that desegregation was a good and wonderful thing, but I always thought that we lost everything that we gained from slavery after Martin Luther King got his thoughts to work on the masses. Blues, gospel, and jazz were struck severely. . . .We lost everything that we gained from slavery . . . when our grandmas crawled on their knees.Whatever hard times are, they suffered [them]; they were trying to get a community.And they were praying and hoping for a community where they could have their own hotels and their own cafes and their own banks and everything, their own theaters, places like barbershops and salons, and the nightclubs.And they had that. Strangely enough, that's what they had at the time desegregation became a big issue.

. . .That makes me think, what we were looking for, we had. And what we were thinking we were going to better ourselves with actually put ourselves way back.

In subsequent discussions, Gaines has explained that he does not seek to defend the segregationist practices once common in the Bayou City and throughout the South, and he has assured me that he does not mean to disrespect Martin Luther King Jr. He instead provocatively calls into question certain standard absolutist assumptions about social history, emphasizing his point that "progress" has come at a price. Ultimately, Gaines has mixed feelings, perceiving in retrospect that segregation ironically fostered racial solidarity, a necessary self-reliance that stimulated the black economy in ways that once made Lyons Avenue the proudest showcase of a relatively prosperous Fifth Ward. To him, the visible decline of that central thoroughfare symbolizes an unfortunate loss of culture. And his candid comments are echoed, albeit usually less stridently, by others who also miss not so much the food or even the music but the unity once shared at the Club Matinee.

as are other houston wards, the Fifth is actually made up of a series of smaller neighborhoods that collectively define the larger community.The Creole presence, originally concentrated in Frenchtown, is found throughout the area, but especially so in enclaves such as the Settegast Addition and Sawdust Alley, both home to numerous other blues and jazz musicians who've shared their stories with me.

One of those people was Eugene Carrier, a college-educated keyboard artist of great wit and insight, and a special friend to me. Carrier could talk in depth about blues, not only from extensive professional experience but also (unlike most of the players I've met) from extensive reading and analysis of history.The son of two Creoles, John Walden Carrier from southwestern Louisiana and MaryTheresa Byoune from EastTexas, he was raised in the Settegast Addition and was strongly influenced by his maternal grandfather. "Poppu," as the elder was known, ran the only general store in the neighborhood, a place that functioned as the community social center. According to Carrier's own account, his informal training as a storyteller, jokester, and oral historian began there in Poppu's establishment. It continued at another Settegast institution, the nearby C & L Shoe Shop, where he shined shoes and further educated himself musically by spending his nickels playing tunes on a jukebox the shopkeeper maintained.

Growing up in Fifth Ward, Carrier was naturally immersed in zydeco and blues culture from his earliest memories, and he soon took up his first instrument, the drums. As a teenager, he also became fascinated by the piano and began to explore the thriving Third Ward music scene south of his home turf, often riding the city bus across town to see a show at the Eldorado Ballroom or catch a jam session at Shady's Playhouse. It was at the latter that he first met his major early influence as a pianist, Charles Brown. After graduating from Wheatley High School, Carrier formally studied jazz at North Texas State University and went on to tour or record with numerous stars of the genre, including fellow Fifth Ward natives Joe Sample and Eddie "Cleanhead" Vinson, and Third Ward's Arnett Cobb. But Carrier always considered himself a bluesman too.

No wonder: He's best known for his long stint playing piano and organ with the B.B. King band, which he joined in 1979 upon the recommendation of Sawdust Alley native Calvin Owens, who was then King's trumpeter and bandleader. Carrier recorded and toured widely with King through 1988, appearing behind him on albums such as *Live at San Quentin* and *Live at the Apollo,* on television shows such as *Austin City Limits* and the Grammy Awards, and in the film *Rattle and Hum* with the Irish rock band U2.

Over the course of his career, Carrier also worked from time to time with many other famous blues musicians based beyond Houston, including John Lee Hooker (1917–2001), Albert King (1923–1992), and Matt "Guitar" Murphy (b. 1929). After departing B.B. King's band to spend more time with his family, Carrier temporarily relocated (with his wife, Naomi, and two sons) to New Orleans, where he enjoyed five years of steady employment playing in the French Quarter. Then in 1994 he returned to Houston and played with various bands, including those led by Texas Johnny Brown, Grady Gaines, Pete Mayes, Jerry Lightfoot (b. 1951), Leonard "Low Down" Brown (b. 1949), and others. Through most of 1996 Carrier also performed on Tuesday nights with I. J. Gosey at C. Davis Bar-B-Q. His final major gig was a European tour with Joe "Guitar" Hughes in November and·December of that year.

Though he had traveled widely and could "play everything from Beau Jocque to Bartok" (as he once told me), Carrier remained vitally connected to his roots in Fifth Ward's Settegast Addition. I remember him once saying that no academic course he mastered or book he studied had ever taught him as much as he had absorbed just hanging around Poppu's store. He revered them both— lofty intellectual pursuits and folklife—and it showed in his ability to create powerful music, whether based on complex jazz arrangements or gut-bucket blues.

Eugene Carrier, at home, 1996.

Like his former colleague and fellow Fifth Ward native Carrier, trumpeter Calvin Owens has admittedly "straddled the fence musically," moving freely between jazz and blues, content to be playing what he simply defines as "our music." Raised in the area known as Sawdust Alley, Owens first performed professionally in the forties, ballyhooing with a traveling minstrel show at a time when trumpet players, not guitarists, were still the "natural" blues soloists and bandleaders. In fact, it wasn't until 1953, when he joined the Bill Harvey band backing B.B. King, that Owens played regularly with a featured guitarist. Before then he had worked in a number of blues combos and big bands producing such powerful horn-based music that amplification was generally necessary only for vocalists. Thus, Owens is a living link to a Texas urban blues tradition that reaches back to an era before the emergence of the electric guitar—a tradition expansive enough to include brassy jazz stylings and densely textured arrangements. And as the new millennium begins, Owens is focused on taking his big blue sound right into the twenty-first century—not as some relic of a bygone era but as an ever vital force, rooted in tradition but open to new musical possibilities.

In his 1996 autobiography, B.B. King says Owens "has the respect of all the master musicians. Calvin's a master himself." The genre's defining megastar surely knows of what he speaks, for in addition to touring and recording with Owens during two key phases of his career (1953–1957 and 1978–1984), he also won a Grammy Award for an album—*Blues 'n' Jazz* (MCA, 1983)—for which Owens wrote all the arrangements. King's high opinion of Owens is echoed by the popular blues artist known as "Little Milton" (Milton Campbell, b. 1934), who said in a 1998 radio interview in Houston, "Calvin has always impressed me as, like, one of the *main maestros,* with that big sound." Indeed, Owens' grand horn work has been utilized not only by King but—at various times over the past half century—by the likes of T-Bone Walker, Amos Milburn, Big Joe Turner, Junior Parker, and Arnett Cobb, to name just a few examples.

Not bad for a guy whose beginnings were so humble, even by Fifth Ward standards. But as Owens tells it, what his home neighborhood may have lacked financially or materially it more than compensated for in terms of social support.

Sawdust Alley—I guess I moved there when I was about ten years old. We first lived on a street called Deschaumes, which is off part of Sawdust Alley, kind of a housing project. . . . And it was a real friendly community. . . . Sawdust Alley was this little place between a street called Sumpter and the tracks. . . . It was my mother and me. We didn't have much, but what we had she would share with other people. . . . That was really a great time. That's when we, my mom and I, stopped rooming with people and living in other people's houses. So we finally had our own place.

The modest home that Owens remembers so fondly was located in an unusual neighborhood that actually came by its name literally—thanks in part perhaps to Houston's anti-zoning policy (a legacy that's given rise to numerous areas in which industries and residences exist next door to each other, especially within the central wards). As Owens further relates:

> Sawdust Alley was a place where there had been a sawmill way back when, so over the years sawdust had accumulated as tall as this [two-story] house. And the owner never removed the sawdust; he just spread it throughout the neighborhood. The mill was not in operation when we moved back in the area, but guys would still gamble out there every day like they did when the mill was running. . . . In Sawdust Alley, when you wanted to get water, you had to take a Bull Durham tobacco sack and stretch it over the faucet to filter out the sawdust in the old water tank. It tasted fine, the greatest water there was, 'cause you didn't know—you hadn't tasted any other.

Whatever the quality of the ambient physical environment in Sawdust Alley, Owens remembers it especially fondly because it functioned like a little village that supported its own.

> I stayed there, man, until after I was married to my first wife. My first children were born there. Sawdust Alley was really a great place in some ways. . . . The guy that took care of all the houses, he never really put nobody out. If you didn't have any money to pay, he might stand there and joke with you, but you'd pay him eventually and everything was cool.
>
> My last year of high school I was married. And after I got married . . . the preacher built the house for my wife and me, a little two-room shotgun house. We had to use the toilet on my mother-in-law's back porch and so on . . . but that was the kind of community it was. They built a house for us so we could have a place of our own.

Though his professional achievements would eventually enable him to move out and afford a succession of much nicer residential accommodations—on prominent Southmore Street in Third Ward as well as in Brussels, Belgium, where he lived for twelve years—Owens has never forgotten the place that he believes most significantly influenced his life. In fact, after leaving his job directing B.B. King's band and moving to Europe in 1984, he eventually created his own production company and record label, proudly naming them both after the old neighborhood in Fifth Ward. Today, overseeing and starring for Sawdust Alley Productions keeps Owens, a spry septuagenarian, actively engaged in making music. In fact, given its small size and independent status, it's fair to say the company and its founder have been rather prolific.

Assuming the mantle of headlining artist with the Calvin Owens Blues Orchestra while still in Belgium, Owens first produced and released two CDs on Sawdust Alley Records, *True Blue* (1993) and *That's Your Booty* (1996), both of which feature numerous guest artists (including B.B. King, Johnny Copeland, David "Fathead" Newman [b. 1933], Otis Clay [b. 1941], and Archie Bell [b. 1941]).

Calvin Owens, Sawdust Alley, Fifth Ward, 1997.

Then, in January 1997, Owens and his Belgium-born wife, Sarah Send, permanently resettled back in Houston. Among the highlights of his homecoming was a stunning performance by the new, Texas-based version of the Calvin Owens Blues Orchestra at the Twenty-first Annual SumArts Juneteenth Blues Festival. The return to his hometown also led to a third—and absolutely unique—Sawdust Alley recording project featuring Houston singer Norma Zenteno backed by Owens' big band on a CD entitled *Es Tu Booty* (1998)—a remake in Spanish translation of several tracks from *That's Your Booty,* combined with some new tunes by Owens, Zenteno, and a Hispanic rapper called Valdemar. By 1999 Owens was pursuing a different musical direction with the release of his own "pure" jazz album *Another Concept,* an all-instrumental disk except for one impressive collaboration with Houston playwright and poet Thomas Meloncon, a track called "Listen to My Song."

The year 2000 brought the debut of the fifth Sawdust Alley Records production, *Stop Lying in My Face,* another CD highlighting Owens' skills as lead trumpeter, singer, and bandleader—and featuring a variety of guest blues artists, including two Fifth Ward–born vocalists, Trudy Lynn (b. 1947) and Gloria Edwards, as well as Texas guitar legend Pete Mayes and one of the masters of Chicago-style harmonica, James Cotton (b. 1935). Additionally, this far-reaching disk includes progressive contributions from young rappers such as Big Snap and Valdemar, as well as one track with zydeco accordionist Chubby Carrier. "I kind of like to mix things up like that," Owens says of the production, "so I can have different colors, different concepts. It's like a big show, or a musical stew." In fact, Owens has since released a "fused music" version of *Stop Lying in My Face* on which he collaborates with rappers on every track, including the Houston-based Latino star known as "South Park Mexican" or simply "SPM" (Carlos Coy).

Invigorated by the healthy lifestyle he adopted in Belgium and by the reception he has experienced since returning to Houston, Owens maintains a level of excitement and energy unusual among musicians half his age. And despite ongoing creative innovations—such as his potent blending of bluesy big-band arrangements with Spanish lyrics, Latin rhythms, zydeco, funk, and even rap—Owens' Sawdust Alley Productions still evokes an older era in Texas music, a time when the trumpet was the truest and bluest voice of them all.

As for the challenge of classifying his productions in a single stylistic category, Owens seems oblivious to industry genre labels. In fact, like Houston bandleader Milt Larkin before him, he seems intent on creatively blurring the perceived line between jazz and blues, even while assimilating other influences. "Jazz and blues are the same to me. People think of the trumpet as being a jazz instrument, and it is. But it's blues too," he says, citing W. C. Handy (1873–1958) and Louis Armstrong (a favorite of his Creole mother) as forerunners. He articulates a vision of his African American musical heritage as a single source, not a dichotomy. "So even when I do jazz, it's still the blues. I like to just think of myself as a musician."

The same might be said for many of Owens' recent collaborators, including Fifth Ward products Gloria Edwards and Trudy Lynn. The former, who grew up just around the corner from Sawdust Alley, has remained based in Houston throughout a career that started out in gospel, then took a secular focus in the late 1950s, when she began singing with a number of Houston-based artists, including Clarence Green, Clifton Chenier, Lavelle White (b. 1929), and Texas Johnny Brown. Some of the solo recordings Edwards did decades ago for the controversial producer Huey Meaux have recently been reissued on CD on a British label as *The Soul Queen of Texas* (Edsel Records, 1999). The assertion of royal status might be overstated, but the title nonetheless aptly classifies the fundamental quality of her singing.

When she performs today, as a frequently featured guest with the Calvin Owens Blues Orchestra or fronting her own small combo, Edwards draws from a deep blues and soul foundation (even when she's interpreting contemporary R&B, funk, or jazz standards), a musical legacy that she inherited from a family long at home in Fifth Ward. Asked to categorize her sound and where it originates, she says:

> *Fifth Ward, Texas—lot of soul in there. . . . I lived across the street from some musicians. . . . I remember their parties, kind of my introduction to the blues.*
>
> *I don't separate the kinds of music I do. Whatever I do, I always keep my blues and my gospel roots in there. Because that's me. That's how I feel. The blues is a tremendous overwhelming feeling of either happiness or sadness or pleasure. You know, you put those three things together into a song, and that's when you come out with the blues. The blues is a feeling.*
>
> *How I first started: My mother was a blues singer. She used to sing with Big Walter [Price]. . . . He used to play downstairs at the Little Red Rooster, down from my grandmother's house, and I could see him, you know, [I'd] go down there and look in through the back door and watch them, but I never did sing with him then. . . . I used to see my mother singing with him though.*
>
> *And she worked with Calvin Owens. He was just like a daddy to me. And one of my grandmothers, she used to sing and dance in the minstrels. And my great-uncle played blues and ragtime piano up on Jensen [Street] at the old Roxy Theater, when I was a little girl. So I used to go watch him and sing, you know, "Limehouse Blues" and things like that with him, without my grandmother knowing. I was eight, maybe nine years old then.*

Given that background, it's not surprising that Edwards "really had this dream of being a blues lady" since girlhood. However, any open pursuit of that possibility was forbidden by the grandmother who raised her. So it took the passage of several years—and some chance occurrences down on Lyons Avenue—to prompt her seriously to consider a career in secular music. Under her grandmother's strict direction, she was being groomed as a young gospel diva. But the church (Lyons Unity Missionary Baptist) she attended just happened to be located "right across the street from the Club Matinee."

One evening, while a teenaged Edwards was earnestly vocalizing a religious number in the youth center, she looked up to see the popular blues singers Bobby Bland and Junior Parker standing just beyond the open doorway staring at her. As she recalls it, "Little Junior Parker came to the door, and he's looking in the door. And he waved, and I waved. And so when I got finished . . . I went outside to talk with him." At first, not sure of the star's intentions, Edwards half expected him to try to pick her up for a quick date. (She'd often been warned by her grandmother to stay away from such men.) But Edwards soon sensed that Parker was sincerely motivated by honest intentions, speaking to her as one vocalist to another. "He asked me if I had ever tried to sing anything else other than spirituals. And I said, 'Yeah, I sing lot of blues, been singing blues all my life—without my grandmother knowing it.'"

After gaining his encouragement and advice, Edwards began to strategize about singing the blues in public. And soon the popular talent competitions at the big club across the street—and the cash prizes to be had there—became too much to resist. She continues:

> Then this girlfriend of mine at church went over, and she started being on the talent show, you know, over there at the [Club] Matinee, . . . and she got paid real money! Sure thing, and I ain't never heard of this before, you know, like being paid real money—because I would go and sing in churches all over Texas, especially for conventions and so on, and nobody even mentioned the word "pay." [Laughs heartily]
>
> So I went over there. My brother took me, helped me get out of the house. And we were supposed to been going to a basketball game, and we didn't go to a basketball game. We went over to the Matinee. So I listened the first time I went over there. Patience Valentine was on the show, Luvenia Lewis, . . . Wilma Davis, and lots of others. It was just, just total heaven, you know, so I started slipping out, going every opportunity I could get to get away.
>
> So I finally got up enough nerve, you know, to audition. . . . See, they auditioned you like right before the show. . . . Everybody who wanted to be on it, they would take you in the back room and let you sing a couple of songs. Then someone would say, "Well, yeah, you're good enough to go out there." And so I went out and I did "My Man's an Undertaker, He's Got Coffins Just Your Size." And I won. And I did that every time, and I won and I won and I won.
>
> And so they hired me—Mr. Dixon hired me—to sing there all the time. And he gave me a regular job. I was making eight dollars a night. . . . But then my grandmother found out about it, so everything had to come to a halt.

Refocused, willingly or not, on her gospel career, Edwards eventually left home to attend Mary Allen Baptist Seminary in nearby Crockett, where she was assigned a roommate who happened to be the sister of Joe "Guitar" Hughes. The two freshmen soon became close friends, a seminary affiliation that ironically would lead Edwards away from the Bible college and more deeply into the blues scene.

> I would come home and stay overnight with her whenever I had a chance to hear Joe and Johnny Clyde [Copeland] and all the guys that would come over there and play. And I had a real case of singing the blues then, you know. So Joe asked me would I be interested in singing with him sometimes. And I say, "Yeah, like maybe when I come home during the summer."
>
> So that first summer I came home, I went to work with Joe Hughes and Clarence Green. Blues for Two was the name of the band. Joe and Clarence was working together then. . . . This was about '57 or '58.

Over the next few years Edwards would go on to perform with numerous other groups on the local and regional circuit, establishing a reputation as a passionate blues singer in the process. But after she married, she soon discovered that her commitment to her chosen vocation was seriously challenged by her spouse's notions about what was proper and improper behavior for a wife and mother.

> I had married my first husband then, and so every gig my first husband would come and cry on so and make me go home. He didn't want me to sing, so I finally just had to quit. So I quit for, oh, I'd say about four or five years, after I had started having children and everything, so I stopped for a while. . . . It [singing the blues] was always in my mind, but no peace at home.

Following a divorce and a second marriage, Edwards reemerged on the scene, first performing mainly with jazz ensembles to please her new husband, a serious keyboard player who tended to look down on the blues as unsophisticated and demeaning music. But Fifth Ward native that she was, Edwards knew where to retreat to when she felt the urge to return to the music of her upbringing: "I sometimes worked on Sundays during that time, to keep my soul and my roots together, over at the Silver Slipper," she confides. "That was how I kept my soul together! And that was like blues, classic R&B, and a little zydeco stuff."

Over the course of subsequent decades and additional marital changes, Edwards has always found a way to maintain her blues connection. In fact, in the late 1990s, she became actively involved in creating her own blues education projects directed toward the younger generations.

Gloria Edwards, Embassy Ballroom, 1996.

Her efforts have now included a series of programs produced in collaboration with the Houston Blues Society at the Children's Museum and other local venues, as well as independent productions of blues-consciousness-raising events and in-school appearances around the city. In the summer of 2000, Edwards' work in this field was formally recognized by her multiple appearances—as a presenter, respondent, and musical performer—at the International Conference on the Blues Tradition (subtitled Memory, Criticism, and Pedagogy) hosted by Penn State University at the Paul Robeson Cultural Center.

Like Edwards (and, in fact, numerous other African American female vocalists), Fifth Ward's Trudy Lynn worked early in her professional singing career under the tutelage of bandleader and former Duke-Peacock guitarist Clarence Green. Born in Mont Belvieu, just east of the city, Green, the oldest son of a Creole mother, had grown up in Frenchtown. He had first started making music on homemade string instruments devised in collaboration with his brother Cal Green, who years later would become the lead guitarist for Hank Ballard and the Midnighters, moving permanently to California in the process. Clarence, however, stayed in Houston all his life, doing session work and recording singles under his own name at various studios (including Don Robey's), and backing major players such as Fats Domino on regional tours. By the mid-1960s his group the Rhythmaires had emerged as a Bayou City favorite, mixing blues, jazz, and soul music—and playing at all manner of venues, from the funkiest little all-black clubs to ritzy all-white corporate affairs downtown and in private mansions.

During the more than three decades that Green fronted that band, he was known not only for his precisely swinging sound laced with exuberant solo romps on the electric guitar, but also for featuring a succession of brilliant lady singers: B. B. Carter (who later also moved to California), Luvenia Lewis (who married Cal Green but did not follow him to the West Coast), Lavelle White, Gloria Edwards, Trudy Lynn, Iola Broussard (b. 1941), Faye Robinson, Vanessa Gatlin, and others.

Of all these talented women, several of whom remain active on the Houston scene at the turn of the century, one of the more commercially successful is surely Trudy Lynn. Born Lee Audrey Nelms in 1947, she was already using the stage name Trudy Lynn by the time she joined the Rhythmaires in the late 1960s. But she had started out earlier performing in her home neighborhood with another Houston guitarist, as she recalls:

> The first time I was onstage was a couple of years before I got out of high school. There used to be a club on Lockwood, in Fifth Ward, called Walter's Lounge. Albert Collins was the first person I got on the stage with, right there. . . . He had a group with a saxophone player and a vocalist named Big Tiny. . . . And Albert Collins was one of the headliners on the show. That was during the time that he first put out "The Freeze" and, baby, that was a Houston song there! The people were just going crazy at Albert's shows! So I was jumping right into the fire, and I loved it.

Clarence Green, at home, 1996.

Following her initial stints with Collins and her subsequent tenure as a featured female vocalist with Green, Trudy Lynn—a spirited performer with an uncanny capacity to evoke audience fervor—naturally gravitated toward booking herself as the main act in local venues.

In the seventies I started going out on my own, working in the clubs [as a headliner]. I knew all the basic tunes. During that time, there was just some blues tunes you had to know, you know. So I was working in Houston clubs, sometimes doing two or three jobs a night. You know—do a show here, another show over here, and then go and do a show over there, all right here in Houston. . . . If you could sing those blues, mixing in some soul tunes too, you could work those joints.

Eventually she would graduate from the home-turf proving grounds and begin to tour regionally, then later abroad—attracting the attention of Ichiban Records (an overseas label with a U.S. headquarters in Atlanta), which launched her recording career. Now a multiple W. C. Handy Award nominee with numerous acclaimed solo CDs to her credit (including six with Ichiban between 1988 and 1996, plus her 1999 release, *U Don't Know What Time It Is,* on Germany's Ruf Records), Lynn still acknowledges Green as her ultimate mentor. "I feel like he schooled me on everything I know," she told the French writer Sebastian Danchin in an interview published in 1996. Five years later, when I asked her to explain how she cultivated her distinctive stage persona, the same theme resurfaced:

A lot of it comes by instinct, and a lot of it comes through working with Clarence Green. He put so much in me, you know—understanding about stage presence and how you look and how you're supposed to work with a band. He was really a teacher to me. I used to bug him, and I'd talk about him—you know, being young. . . . And he'd fine me for making mistakes, not just onstage but, like, putting powder on my face out in a club before the show—because the ladies' room was too crowded. Well, he taught me, you don't do that. . . . But I don't regret nothing that he taught me.

Lynn also points to the band's female vocalist immediately preceding her as a primary inspiration. In fact, she says that before launching her own career, she would often attend Rhythmaires shows specifically to study the technique of Luvenia Lewis. "Oh yes, Luvenia Lewis was a role model for me," she says. "I think she was one for all of us—I mean, us that came up behind her. Because she came through with Clarence, she was one that I really looked up to—her and also Lavelle White." Lewis, who sings only gospel today, confirms the recollection: "I remember before Trudy Lynn ever sang, she used to come and watch me." Today Lewis rightly considers the younger soul-blues singer her protégé, adding proudly, "She's very successful now, and she deserves it."

After temporarily relocating to Atlanta for a few years in the mid-1990s to be closer to her record label and management, Lynn (who frequently visited her hometown during the interim to see her family) officially moved back to Houston in 1998. And though she's played the finest venues and the major festivals, and toured as far away as Turkey—earning accolades all over the globe for her high-energy, roof-raising singing (and her skillful songwriting as well)—she's still a significant presence on the local circuit.

From time to time she stages her own show at an area nightclub (sometimes opened by one of her own protégés, such as the good-natured blues growler Donna "Lady D" McIntyre, b. 1946). And she's headlined a variety of big events in the Bayou City, such as the Twentieth Annual SumArts Juneteenth Blues Festival, which honored her as its 1996 Blues Artist of the Year. But it's her frequent, often unannounced, guest appearances at jam sessions and gigs around town that make Lynn such a Houston favorite. When they occur, they inevitably create a sensation, usually triggered as soon as Lynn walks through the door. All it takes is one glance at the shapely woman with those unbelievably long and meticulously lacquered fingernails—the one decked out in colorful regalia befitting a star known as "the First Lady of Soul"—and even those patrons who've never before heard her sing realize immediately that she's someone extra special. And when she wraps those curving nails around a microphone, her charisma infuses the room and compels the full attention of those in it—whether she's shouting out a rocking blues shuffle or poignantly interpreting a smooth ballad.

But these days, for all the times Lynn does appear on Houston stages, both large and small, rarely does she get the chance to perform back in the old neighborhood where she began: Fifth Ward. At the turn of the century, there just aren't too many clubs that feature blues still operating in the area folks call "the Nickel." One of the few exceptions (in addition to the Silver Slipper) is an establishment called Mr. A's, located on Cavalcade just a few blocks north and a mile or so east of the Silver Slipper. There you're apt to find a mix of musical styles from night to night, sometimes including blues singers such as Eugene Moody (except for Sundays when he's back in Third Ward at El Nedo Cafe) or his friend and occasional collaborator Faye Robinson, another vocalist formerly featured with Clarence Green and the Rhythmaires.

Robinson, a powerful singer (and ersatz onstage comic who weaves risqué jokes and humorous stories into almost every set she plays), was born in Louisiana but grew up in the Scenic Woods neighborhood just beyond Fifth Ward. By chance, her family settled on the same street where Luvenia Lewis lived, a coincidence that played a key role in Robinson's development. As Lewis told me in a 1996 interview:

> There's another singer, Faye Robinson. Now she's a lot younger than me—in the age bracket with my oldest daughter—between thirty and forty, something like that. But anyway, she used to live across

Trudy Lynn, 1996.

Faye Robinson, Silver Slipper, Fifth Ward, 1997.

the street from me, and I heard her singing. She was doing something out in her yard one day, and I heard her, and I went "Golly, that girl can sing!"

So I went and asked her mother could I take her to be on this talent show that Clarence Green was playing. She was kind of reluctant, but she let her go with me, because she knew me. So I took her, and she won that night, and she started singing with Clarence Green right after that. That's how she began singing the blues. . . . A wonderful voice!

By the late 1990s, Robinson was a single mother of a teenaged daughter, making a living singing five to six days per week at a wide spectrum of venues all over the city. She often scheduled multiple performances back-to-back: doing a Happy Hour gig here, quickly driving across town to fill the midevening slot somewhere else, and sometimes capping it off with a late-night set at yet another location. Out of necessity, Robinson's repertoire today extends well beyond blues to include a wide range of popular material—especially for one long-standing job she once had singing in a hotel lounge. But on those late-night shows when she's back in Fifth Ward, playing to an almost exclusively black audience at Mr. A's, Robinson can still lay down some satisfying blues— and with as much vocal finesse and personal conviction as anyone in town. By her own account, on nights such as these, she's coming home.

Fifth ward used to be home not only to large numbers of blues performers but also to a multitude of related venues, from large-scale professional operations such as Club Matinee to more obscure and laid-back mom-and-pop enterprises. Of the scores of examples of the latter, one in particular stands out in the early-career memories of Calvin Owens:

The Casino was a place in Fifth Ward; it was owned by Creole people . . . a beer joint where people would go to eat gumbo and stuff. . . . It was a place where we would play every Friday and Saturday, and Miss Grace would pay us six dollars a man. . . . I worked in that joint off and on—well, I could always work there when I didn't have nothing else to do, for a long time. It was my home spot. . . . I knew the people on a one-to-one basis. My mother knew the people; they were in the neighborhood, that kind of thing. . . . It was just a family situation. You know, once you worked there, anybody, if you had another gig somewhere else paying more money, no problem. But when you were not working, on that particular night, you could always go into the Casino and make that six dollars.

Reflecting on the easy-going ambience of performing at this little club, Owens adds, "You know, I sure wish I could find me a home spot like that today."

But the chances of him ever again doing so back in his neighborhood of origin seem slim. As popular musical styles changed and the economic fortunes of Fifth Ward cratered in the 1970s, 1980s, and early 1990s, not only did the old blues clubs (large and small) close down, but in most cases the very structures that housed them were demolished. During a personally guided tour of his native turf in 1997, Owens repeatedly pointed out to me razed or reconstructed lots where some of his favorite music venues used to stand. After one particularly rapid sequence of such observations, he eventually exclaimed, "Man, they're all gone, *all* gone . . . even the buildings, not a trace."

But as another Fifth Ward native, guitarist extraordinaire Clarence Hollimon, once told me, "There's still one building up there, you know, that's got a lot of history behind it, over on Erastus Street." The edifice that he refers to, though now transformed for other uses, was formerly the home of a Fifth Ward nightclub ultimately more noteworthy than even the Club Matinee, an establishment that would evolve into the home office and studio for one of the most significant independent record companies in American music history: Duke-Peacock Records.

Clarence Hollimon, I. J. Gosey, and Texas Johnny Brown, former site of Duke-Peacock Records, Fifth Ward, 2000.

CHAPTER 5

the duke-peacock legacy

Taking It to the World

from the 5500 block of lyons avenue, head north about a dozen blocks or so on Lockwood Drive till you cross an overpass spanning an immense railroad and trucking yard. This industrial complex—defined by lots full of large shipping containers, eighteen-wheelers, and rows of dusty tracks crowded with boxcars and flatbeds—is easily surveyed from the elevated portion of the roadway. Once clear of that bridge, turn immediately to your left and into the northwestern quadrant formed by the intersection of two Fifth Ward thoroughfares, Liberty Road and Lockwood. A couple of blocks beyond that right angle, you'll find the little backstreet called Erastus.

On the west side of that street—still within sight of all those parked or slowly shuffling train cars—you'll see a rectangular one-story building sporting a rather austere façade of whitewashed stucco. Its most distinctive architectural feature is a wing-shaped crest jutting up from the roof line and centered over the main entrance. These days that skyward-pointing flourish is emblazoned with the words "Charity Baptist Church." Slightly smaller characters below specify further "F. W.

McIlveen Educational Building," so as to distinguish this structure from the main sanctuary located around the corner and facing Liberty Road. Floating gently above the lettering is a traditional Christian icon: the image of a snow white dove.

But that prominent space above the front door was once graced by a neon-illuminated caricature of a very different bird, a fowl considerably more colorful and flamboyant. Color this one *bronze,* as in the skin tone of many African Americans (especially among the Creoles so numerous in Fifth Ward), and forget the humble profile of the dove; make this one a stylish *peacock* in full strut. For this building—decades before it ever hosted a Sunday school class or a Bible study group—is the place that gave rise to the ultimate symbol of Houston's postwar blues culture, a symbol that encompassed a legendary performance venue, a unique record company, and a distinctive sound.

For countless black Houstonians among whom that sound survives today (both in memory and performance), the simple term "Peacock" evokes it all. The lingering power of that word dates back over half a century to 1945, when Fifth Ward–born entrepreneur and self-professed gambler Don Deadric Robey founded an establishment formally known as the Bronze Peacock Dinner Club. There at 2809 Erastus Street the new building imposed an exciting presence, housing arguably the most sophisticated African American–owned-and-operated nightclub in the South during the 1940s and early 1950s. It hired only the most prestigious chefs and offered an extensive menu of fine food and drink. Its roomy stage hosted productions featuring the leading "uptown" musical acts of the era, from the suave blues star T-Bone Walker to the clown prince of jive Louis Jordan (1908–1975) to the early R&B diva Ruth Brown (b. 1928) to the jazz master Lionel Hampton. And unlike somewhat similar "high-class joints" such as the Eldorado Ballroom in Third Ward or the Club Matinee down on Lyons Avenue, Robey's place never hosted afternoon talent shows for precocious youngsters or remote broadcasts from popular radio DJs. Instead, it catered exclusively to an adult clientele with relatively exquisite tastes in music, food, and fashion—people with money to spend and a desire to do so in high style.

As recalled by Evelyn Johnson, a remarkable woman whose business acumen would prove invaluable to Robey through all of his Peacock-related enterprises, "The Bronze Peacock was something. We had everything but the chorus line in there!" And anecdotal evidence suggests that her assertion is not much of an exaggeration. Reportedly there was even a special "gaming room" where patrons could discreetly retreat for high-stakes gambling with cards and dice. Such activities were illegal, of course, but because of the club's upper-class ambience and its owner's considerable political and economic clout around the city (including alleged ties to the underworld), such backroom operations were generally ignored by local authorities, at least up to a point. In fact, the writer James M. Salem, in his 1999 biography of Johnny Ace, devotes a whole chapter to the plush scene at the Bronze Peacock, dubbing it "Las Vegas in Houston."

But despite its incomparable status as *the* entertainment venue of choice for well-heeled blacks pursuing a ritzy night on the town, the Bronze Peacock would remain in operation only eight years, gradually becoming less and less the dominant focus of Robey's ever expanding business interests. In some ways, its value to the owner logically diminished in direct proportion to his successful pursuits of other ventures in the entertainment industry—new and profitable schemes that would extend Robey's influence far beyond the Bayou City or even the Gulf Coast, and ultimately to the world at large.

In another sense, the Bronze Peacock Dinner Club was simply a unique phenomenon at a particular moment in Houston's social history, and as such, it fell victim to its own success as times changed. Its sensational reputation and increasing popularity would eventually compel unwanted attention in the form of gambling raids and related hassles by law-enforcement agencies. Moreover, as word spread about the quality of nightlife the place offered—and as long established social attitudes gradually began to change in the prosperous postwar years—Robey's club would inadvertently violate Southern codes of racial segregation by drawing some curious visitors from beyond the black community. According to Johnson, the resulting tensions and conflicts over black-white integration at the establishment went beyond issues of race alone; they pivoted, she claims, on perceptions of socioeconomic class.

> *You see, the whites had started coming to the Bronze Peacock. And as long as it was [well-to-do individuals from] the Duncan Coffee Company and the Finger Furniture Company and folk like that who were coming there, that was fine. But when just the regular white people in general started coming, well, then that didn't land too well. So they started upping the price. [Houston Police Department officers] also started hanging around and turning them around at the door. And then they upped the cab fare on the blacks too. It became just a whole lot of irritation and agitation.*

Such difficult situations, coming at a time when the owner was increasingly distracted by new entrepreneurial opportunities, would ultimately lead him to close the club in November of 1953. But the demise of the Bronze Peacock was not a defeat for Robey. He had a daring new plan for that Erastus Street building, the fruition of a dream he had embraced several years earlier when he had impulsively decided to enter the business of managing, booking, and later even recording people who sang the blues. And by the time that plan would play itself out (some twenty years after closing the Bronze Peacock), Robey had launched the careers of some of the biggest names in blues, R&B, and gospel while establishing himself as the first black businessman to achieve big-time success as a modern music industry mogul. At his retirement in 1973, his related company holdings—which would be sold outright to the Los Angeles and New York–based ABC/Dunhill concern for an undisclosed sum—included not only five record labels but also a catalogue of close to 2,700 song copyrights, reportedly 2,000 unreleased masters, and contracts with over 100 artists. For Robey, the Bronze Peacock had left behind a nest full of golden eggs.

accounts of how Robey came to discover Clarence "Gatemouth" Brown—the first artistic talent he would manage, as well as the stimulus for the creation of both Peacock Records and the Buffalo Booking Agency—vary in the impressions they convey. Brown himself has widely propagated a narrative in which he boldly ascended the Bronze Peacock stage one night from his anonymous seat in the audience (implicitly without permission or foreknowledge by the ownership or management) during a lengthy break while a suddenly ailing T-Bone Walker retreated to the dressing room. According to this version, Brown just walked up and grabbed Walker's guitar, turned it on, started improvising, and drove the audience wild with a driving boogie. As a result, he triggered Walker's anger, evident when the established star rushed back to the stage, indignantly snatched his instrument, and shooed away the brash upstart. This anecdote typically concludes with Brown being immediately signed to a management contract by an impressed Robey, who was astonished by the showmanship and musical talent displayed by this previously unknown customer.

But other evidence suggests that Robey was well aware of Brown before the night when he introduced himself so abruptly onstage at the Bronze Peacock. In fact, contrary to the impression created by the often-repeated vignette summarized above, it seems Robey actually may have invited Brown to come to Houston. In a 1996 piece Brown himself wrote and published (with unedited misspellings) in a glossy New Orleans magazine called *Tribe,* he acknowledges that while performing as a drummer and a singer in a San Antonio club, he had previously met Robey, who "gave me one of his card [*sic*]. And said if you ever come to Houston stop in and se [*sic*] me." This version corresponds with what Brown told me backstage at Miller Outdoor Theater during the 1996 Juneteenth Blues Festival, while reminiscing about his old roommate Big Walter "the Thunderbird" Price: "Yeah, I lived in his aunt's house for a long time. She was a nice lady," he said, adding, "I was living there when I left San Antonio and came to Houston, after Don Robey saw me at Don Albert's Keyhole Club and told me to come over." In the *Tribe* article, Brown claims that he hitchhiked to Houston and just showed up at Robey's club, where "nobody knew I played guitar"—at least not until later that night, when he supposedly stole the show from T-Bone Walker.

But some of Robey's closest associates recall the start of his business relationship with Brown in far different terms—though all parties agree that this affiliation directly inspired the beginning of Peacock Records and the Buffalo Booking Agency. One of those associates was John Green, who served Robey's interests in a number of capacities, especially in the role of road manager for top acts. "I've known Don Robey since I was a little kid. I've been knowing him all my life, ever since

Clarence "Gatemouth" Brown, 1992.

I was two or three years old," Green told me in a 1997 interview. "Back in the thirties, my uncle [Morris Merritt, d. 1982] and Don Robey had the Harlem Grill out in Fifth Ward," he explains, "before Robey even thought about starting the Bronze Peacock." When the subject turns to Brown's first appearance in a Robey-owned club, Green is quick to assert, "Robey had sent for Gatemouth to come play the Peacock, back when T-Bone took sick."

This view is confirmed by Evelyn Johnson, who recalls the circumstances in some detail:

> What happened was, T-Bone Walker was playing at the Bronze Peacock . . . and he became ill. So the doctor told him he would have to go to bed, quit working for a while. And T-Bone said [She imitates the voice], "There's a little guy down there"—T-Bone talked real cocky—"in San Antonio and he can play a guitar all around me." So then, that's when we sent for him—to play T-Bone's vacancy at the Bronze Peacock. That was the beginning of Gatemouth Brown, right here in Houston. . . . And Gatemouth Brown was the reason for Buffalo Booking Agency. That's why I applied for the license.

Not only does Johnson suggest that Brown's appearance at the Bronze Peacock was by specific request (as opposed to being a complete surprise to the management), she also says that Brown actually may have auditioned—on guitar—for Robey before he ever took the stage in the club. She continues:

> At any rate, we brought him there, and I was in the office, making out the payroll, this and that. And Robey says, "Come here, come here. You want to hear something?"
>
> I said "I don't want to hear him," thinking that was T-Bone I heard out there playing. I said, "What is he doing out there in the first place?" Because I had told him—you see, the doctor had told him to go to bed—and I told him that if he came to work he was going to be fined a hundred dollars. . . . So I said, "What is he doing out there?"
>
> And he [Robey] said, "Come on, I want you to hear something." . . . And there was Gatemouth out there: plunk-plunka-plunk, just like T-Bone.
>
> I said, "Oh, please." [Laughs] And we started with him right then, working at the club.

In reviewing this account, Green opines that this audition may have occurred *after* Brown had briefly usurped Walker onstage, but Green also admits he was not present for either episode. He also speculates that Robey may have actually set up that little drama by encouraging the newcomer to seize Walker's guitar and play, thereby creating a sensational pretext for Brown's replacement of the ailing headliner over the weeks to come. But Johnson insists that Robey knew in advance that Brown could play electric guitar and had invited him to come to the Bronze Peacock specifically for that purpose, based on Walker's recommendation.

Whatever the particulars—whether Brown had emerged unexpectedly from the audience (as he's often claimed) or had shrewdly been recruited and set up by management to substitute for Walker during a planned sick leave—there's a universal consensus that Brown's initial appearance at the Bronze Peacock made a huge impact. The audience enthusiastically received him, showering him with cash tips and begging for more. Trusting his instincts and ignoring his own lack of experience in the field, Robey signed Brown to an artist-management contract right away. Convinced of the potential value of his first such client, Robey also wasted no time and spared no expense in preparing the young man for celebrity, promptly buying him a new Gibson L-5 guitar (just like Walker's) and a wardrobe worthy of a major entertainer. Regarding the latter, Johnson recalls, "So Robey took him to Jeff the tailor, took him and had him made tuxes, made him some tails. Every color—red, green, black—with top hats to match!" Green adds, "Gatemouth would play that big guitar and had those tails, and they'd be just swinging. Everybody'd say, 'Lord, have mercy!'"

Robey—seeking to capitalize, via increased media exposure, on his fashionably color-coordinated star-in-the-making—soon also secured him a contract with a California record label. But following the production of a few lackluster singles that failed to cause much of a stir in the music industry, the Bronze Peacock founder quickly grew disillusioned with the willingness and ability of white-owned Aladdin Records to promote his bright new discovery among black music fans. His solution was to start his own record company, and then—to support the artists it featured—a booking agency. Forget that Robey knew little, if anything, about how to create and properly cultivate such professional enterprises. Thanks to the phenomenal success of his Fifth Ward nightclub, he had cash and confidence aplenty. But he needed something, or rather someone, else—and he had her too. Accomplishing (and ultimately surpassing) these initial goals would have been all but impossible if not for the ingenuity and reliability of perhaps the most important Houston woman in modern music history.

though she doesn't sing, play a musical instrument, or write songs, Evelyn Johnson is a crucial figure in the evolution of blues and its various popular offspring during the late 1940s through the 1960s. Her work is of special significance to the careers of not only numerous Texas artists but also some of the greatest Memphis performers of that era. The fact that Johnson's not that well known may have something to do with gender. But it's also because the multifaceted role she played in the evolution of black music was generally executed well behind the scenes, where she served as Robey's discreet and proficient enabler.

As the business manager of the Bronze Peacock and later the main person in charge of daily operations at the Buffalo Booking Agency as well as the Peacock, Duke, Songbird, Back Beat, and Sure-Shot record labels, this college-educated black female collaborated with Robey to record, manage, or promote a number of hugely influential artists during the era when they first established themselves as national stars.

For instance, in addition to Brown and various other well-known performers, one of her longtime clients at the Buffalo Booking Agency was a fellow called B.B. King—who went on, following his nine-year affiliation with that Houston-based organization, to become the world's most recognized blues figure. It seems safe to assume that if anyone is qualified to recognize superlative achievement in the field of black music, it must be King, and he acknowledges Johnson as simply one of the best. Commenting on the woman who first helped book and promote his performances beyond his native Delta region, he tells the interviewer Alan Govenar in *Meeting the Blues,* "Evelyn Johnson is a remarkable lady, one of the great women of her time. I don't think she gets enough recognition, because to me she was one of the pioneers. She helped lots of people, not only in the blues field, but in jazz, soul, and rock as well." However, beyond her groundbreaking work with the Buffalo Booking Agency, which played an enormous role in the development of the so-called chitlin' circuit west of the Mississippi River, Johnson is also of major significance to the recording industry.

Of course, it's her boss, the older moneyman Robey, who is generally and understandably perceived as the force behind the booking agency, the Lion Publishing Company, and the various record labels. Nelson George, in his provocative 1988 book *The Death of Rhythm and Blues,* marvels that "Don Robey built an empire worth millions in a city far removed from the main line of entertainment." But according to many firsthand observers (including several former Duke-Peacock insiders from whom I've personally collected oral histories), Johnson was the true genius overseeing an enterprise that developed into the largest and most influential African American–owned-and-operated record conglomerate in the world during the 1950s and early 1960s.

As Johnson has told me (and others have confirmed, including a previously published account by James M. Salem), Robey mainly possessed two things: "guts and money." And both were surely necessary ingredients for the success of all the entities generally lumped under the expansive "Peacock" umbrella, dating back to the famous dinner club that first used that name. But equally crucial were the professional skills, ingenuity, and personal savvy Johnson brought to the table, or at least developed via on-the-spot experience. This woman, who was born in 1920 and never had children, found some of her personal fulfillment instead in using Robey's considerable financial resources to start several music-related businesses from scratch, then nurture them into major conduits of both culture and cash (which didn't necessarily flow back and forth in equal measures).

By and large, Johnson—who frequently refers to herself as a "triple minority" when reflecting on her years in the music business—realizes that issues of gender, race, and age may have obscured her achievement. Yet even early on, some folks in the know recognized this young lady's capacity for greatness. For instance, as Salem points out, a 1954 article in the *Pittsburgh Courier* paid her the following tribute: "An astute business woman, Miss Johnson's combination of beauty and brains has captured a gigantic hold on the nation's rhythm and blues range from deep in the heart of Texas."

But though she indeed operated from the largest city in Texas, Johnson's ultimate impact on American music owes much also to the largest city in the Mississippi River Delta region to the east—Memphis. Through her collaboration with Robey, for over twenty years Johnson facilitated an important (and commercially viable) cultural exchange specifically between these two urban centers. And that interplay of artistic personnel and musical styles ultimately had a major impact on the evolution of blues into a classic R&B sound, the forerunner of rock and roll.

Peacock Records, the first of the labels, drew much of its talent from a readily available pool of Texas-based performers such as Gatemouth Brown, Marie Adams, Big Walter "the Thunderbird" Price, Mildred Jones (b. 1928), and Elmore Nixon, to name just a few examples. But Robey's 1952 acquisition of the Duke label from David James Mattis, then the program director for Memphis radio station WDIA, created a fresh fusion of Texas talent with that from Beale Street—with Bobby "Blue" Bland, "Johnny Ace" (John Alexander, 1929–1955), Junior Parker, Roscoe Gordon, and Earl Forest (b. 1926), for instance. The synthesis achieved via this commercially triggered dialectic of performers from the Delta and the Lone Star state resulted in some of the most potent blues, and especially rhythm and blues, of the fifties and sixties—including the first major R&B "crossover" star, Johnny Ace.

From Johnson's perspective, "The musicians at Duke and Peacock invented rock and roll. Definitely, laid the ground for it, right here." And even if Elvis Presley had never covered Big Mama Thornton's "Houndog" (the 1953 Peacock single 1612), such a claim merits respect, given the far-ranging influence of the two labels, nationwide and overseas. And as other insiders have testified, that phenomenon would not have been possible without Johnson's direction and oversight. For instance, John Green, a confirmed Robey loyalist, insists, "Evelyn Johnson, she was the backbone and the brains behind everything Robey accomplished in the music business."

Though her intelligence, professional skills, and articulate nature had almost everything to do with Johnson's pivotal role in music history, many musicians who worked with her acknowledge, directly or indirectly, that the fact that she was a woman also played a key part in her ability to get things done. For example, in *Meeting the Blues,* Gatemouth Brown tells Govenar that he had considered Johnson to be "a mother figure of mine in business," someone he could trust to look after his best interests. And for many of us who personally know Gatemouth Brown—and have sampled firsthand his often ornery penchant for artistic independence and defiant self-reliance—such a statement seems remarkable in its implicit intimacy. Johnson herself concurs regarding her relationship with her clients, saying in Govenar's *Early Years of Rhythm and Blues* that she functioned as

Evelyn Johnson, 1998.

"mother, confessor, lawyer, doctor, sister, financier, mother superior, the whole nine yards. What they needed they asked for, and what they asked for they got."

So who was this woman who played such varying and invaluable roles in the lives of some of the world's seminal blues and R&B artists? How did she end up in the position to do so in the first place? What training or life experiences had prepared her to do what she did? And looking back, how does she now view her accomplishments in the music business? I've been fortunate to be able, on more than one occasion, to pose such questions directly to Johnson, who's always been kind and patient in her explanations to me—even while convalescing from cancer treatments during the spring of 2000. Her biographical responses reveal a woman of unique character and experience—a survivor who embodies both the nurturer and the visionary.

Born to a Creole family in the south Louisiana town of Thibodeaux, as a preschool child, Johnson moved with her mother to Houston. They naturally settled in Fifth Ward, where she would later graduate with honors from Phillis Wheatley High School. Soon after that milestone, she found employment doing what then seemed like fairly prestigious work for a black female: serving as an X-ray technician at Houston's Memorial Hospital. It turned out to be an experience that would significantly enhance her professional persona, as she daily dealt with doctors, nurses, and administrators—most of whom were white people who otherwise lived in a totally segregated world. But this job would also ultimately threaten her physical health, due to radiation exposure and institutional neglect. Unfortunately, it would also introduce her to the cultural barriers facing a so-called triple minority at the time. As Johnson explains:

> The medical work was immediately out of high school. I walked out of high school into a doctor's office—and to what was Houston College for Negroes [forerunner of Texas Southern University]. . . . In my earlier years, I worked with nothing but doctors, and that was good training for me in itself. . . . But I never received the type of professional training I needed to advance in my chosen career [as a radiologist]. There was a school for it. However, I was not permitted to take the state board in Austin. It was the same old thing: number one, I was too young, too dark, and too female. . . . Actually, while I was working in the medical field, I was in school in the business field. So I was working on a business education too, just in case.

This ambitious young woman, blocked by the system in her attempt to achieve professional certification in radiology, was nonetheless required by her employer to operate dangerous X-ray equipment—having been briefly trained to do so, she reports, by a sales representative for the equipment company. Due to the lax protection standards of the era (and perhaps the nonchalance of hospital administrators about exposing a young African American female to job-related health risks), Johnson eventually suffered, both physically and financially. She continues:

But while I was in the hospital, with overexposure to those X rays and all, I had experienced a thirty-point drop in my hemoglobin, so I was put on leave. That was from Memorial Hospital. And had I gone back when I got well, then I would have gone back and picked up a three-month paycheck that I was due—which wasn't a whole lot of money, but . . . [her voice trails off]. They didn't pay me before. They would have paid me only after I returned to the same job that made me sick, but since there was no after, I didn't get paid.

Following her disillusionment in being physically exploited and shabbily treated by an employer that evidently wished her to return to the same sickening conditions, Johnson decided to pursue a different path. She says, "So I came back and went full-time into the business part. And that's how I got involved with the Bronze Peacock and this and that."

The Bronze Peacock was, of course, already one of the premiere black entertainment venues in the nation. But Johnson was drawn to a new career opportunity managing the establishment not so much by her love of the music or the nightlife as by her instinct for putting herself where the action was—in a financial sense. As she asserts, "No, I wasn't really a music fan, per se. I was at large. [*Laughs*] I liked everything. But my first interest was medicine. . . . and that didn't work out for me. So I turned to business, and that business just turned out to be music."

Working for Robey as the managerial and bookkeeping whiz behind the daily operations of the highly successful club, Johnson was directly involved in orchestrating the situation that would lead to the formation of Peacock Records in 1949. Robey and Johnson had begun their first experiment with artist management in 1947—back when Gatemouth Brown had debuted at the Bronze Peacock—with no thoughts at the time of going into the record business, a field in which neither of them had any training. But that would all change as they collaborated to develop Brown's career. As Johnson's oral history continues:

Then Eddie Mesner [of California-based Aladdin Records] was here all of the time because he was scouting talent. So then he saw Gatemouth and signed him to a recording contract. I think Robey got four cents royalties for Gate. That was unheard of! Nat [King] Cole wasn't getting four cents royalties. Anyway, Mesner recorded four sides. The contract was a year, with an option. If the contract would have expired, or was to have been picked up on option, on the 30th, he released the second two sides on the 29th. . . . We didn't like that. . . . Then he signed [Houston-born pianist] Amos Milburn, who went on to have a big record, and he did not pick up the option on Gatemouth Brown.

Faced with the problem of managing a burgeoning young blues star who now had no record company to popularize his work, Robey and Johnson improvised their own solution—or rather Robey put Johnson in the position to do so herself. Johnson explains:

So Robey said, "We don't need Eddie to put out records on Gatemouth. We can put them out ourselves."

I said, "Oh, we can?"

He said, "Yes."

I said, "How do you make a record?"

He said, "Hell, I don't know. That's for you to find out." And those are the minutes of origin for Peacock Records.

So how did she do it? How did she figure out not only how to make records but how to transform that effort into the force that the Peacock enterprise would eventually become? In her own words:

I had a coworker, Loreen Williams . . . and she was working at the Bronze Peacock office too. So we get busy, trying to find out how you go about making a record. [Laughs] So there we went! And so much of the information—we would just call on the telephone, like, the Library of Congress—knowing that they did not have anything in this life to do with the information we were looking for. But we were talking to breathing human beings at that time. And they were so genuine and so for real. They'd say, "You know, we don't handle that. Perhaps you should call thus and so, and this and that. And here is the number. Why don't you call them?" [Laughs] And that's where we'd get our information.

Possessing college-trained skills in basic research and understanding intuitively how to utilize the telephone in a professional manner paid off for Johnson as she learned about contracts, copyrights, creating a recording studio and pressing plant, and such. Johnson says she knew how to be inquisitive in a courteous manner that prompted strangers on the other end of a long-distance telephone line to offer useful tips and advice—in contrast to the brash speaking style and impatiently demanding nature for which Robey is often not so fondly remembered. She also suspects that cultural conditioning about gender may possibly have given her an edge in extracting valuable data from cold-call queries: "Maybe people were just more inclined to help a woman," she says.

So as the record business began to evolve into a legitimately profitable enterprise—especially following Marie Adams' 1952 hit "I'm Gonna Play the Honky-Tonks"—Robey, with Johnson's encouragement, decided to close the famous Bronze Peacock nightclub. Their logic was simple: First, they could do without the legal and social headaches that the dinner club was provoking at the time; moreover, Peacock Records and Buffalo Booking Agency desperately needed more space. So they moved those operations from the original office located at 4104 Lyons Avenue (which later would become the site of a medical practice for the owner's son, Dr. Louis Robey), and expanded into the remodeled and roomy Erastus Street building that formerly housed the club.

John Green summarizes the transformation:

They took it and converted it to the recording studio and the booking office. So Buffalo was there too. And they had a pressing plant in the back, and pressed the records right there. In '53 the Bronze Peacock was still open, and then in late '53 is when they converted it. . . . And that building was the base for all of Peacock until they sold out in '73.

Soon after they began the business of making records, Robey and Johnson almost concurrently founded the Buffalo Booking Agency, named after Buffalo Bayou, the major waterway slicing through central Houston (in fact, the bayou on which the city had been founded in 1836). Significantly, the new booking agency was legally registered not in Robey's name but in Johnson's. As she recalls:

Buffalo Booking Agency was created because those [Peacock] artists didn't have anybody to represent them. It all started off with Gatemouth Brown. There was nobody to book him, really. So I applied for a franchise from the American Federation of Musicians. And [AFM president James C.] Petrillo was stupid enough to send me one. And that's how it all got started. I didn't know up from down.

Time and again, Johnson's explanations reflect a simple pattern: She and Robey would analyze a situation and determine a need—for a record label, a pressing plant, a management company, a booking agency, whatever. Then he would provide the funds while she provided the brains to figure out how to meet that need without having to turn to other already established companies (which Robey generally distrusted). In this way, Johnson was the key behind-the-scenes figure in laying the groundwork for Robey's independent empire.

The multiple roles that Johnson played in managing, booking, and recording performers such as Gatemouth Brown put her squarely in the middle of "a conflict of interest," as she now freely admits. Yet her holistic focus on promoting the artists seemed also to earn Johnson their trust, as they respected her efforts to make each of them a star. As Salem observes, "For artists signed to the Duke and Peacock labels, Evelyn Johnson had created by 1952 perhaps the most efficient system for arranging personal appearances of any independent label in America." As a result, in addition to the already hot Gatemouth Brown, other Peacock talent (such as Willie Mae "Big Mama" Thornton, for example) emerged from relative obscurity to become blues sensations during the early years of the enterprise.

But the success of Peacock Records would ultimately be topped by the acquisition of the Duke label, a Memphis-based company founded by a radio station program director who—only three months after creating it—brought in the cash-rich Don Robey as a partner. Although this transaction turned out to be a bad deal for financially strapped Duke owner David Mattis, it paid huge dividends for Robey. As Johnson recalls:

David Mattis, who was at WDIA in Memphis, Tennessee, recorded "My Song" and about three other sides on Johnny Ace. See, he was dealing with the Beale Streeters. Now the Beale Streeters were [Earl] Forest and Roscoe Gordon—who all eventually did a little something on their own—and Johnny Ace. And B.B. [King] became a part of it, Bobby Bland—that whole crew.

Anyway, David couldn't get the records to going too well. And he could not get anybody in Memphis to supply him with money. He was just the station manager at WDIA, you know. So what he did, he contacted Robey, and they got together.

Of course, given the phenomenal success of the Peacock label, Robey had all the money Mattis needed. And within another four months, Robey had shrewdly manipulated his resources to buy out Mattis, dissolve the partnership, and make the Duke label his own.

Whatever the ugly realities of capitalism at work, Robey's acquisition had important cultural results, forging a link between Houston and Memphis—uniting postwar urban sounds from the Texas Gulf Coast and the Delta. Foremost, it established Houston as the professional base from which Memphis artists such as Johnny Ace, Bobby Bland, Junior Parker, and many others would operate during the defining era of their careers. It also brought them together with a host of distinctive Texas sidemen and collaborators: musicians, songwriters, singers, and arrangers such as Joe Scott, Pluma Davis, Clarence Hollimon, Teddy Reynolds, Hamp Simmons, Grady Gaines, Roy Gaines, Texas Johnny Brown, Calvin Owens, Pete Mayes, Lavelle White, Luvenia Lewis, Clarence Green, Joe Medwick, Joe Hughes, Oscar Perry—just to list some of the names.

Thus, many of the best players from Houston's premiere blues districts, places such as Third Ward and Fifth Ward, merged with the brightest young stars of Memphis' vibrant Beale Street. Together they toured in widely popular musical revues. Together they created numerous essential early R&B records—including masterpiece albums such as Bobby Bland's classic *Two Steps from the Blues* (Duke LP 74) or Junior Parker's *Driving Wheel* (Duke LP 76). They also developed a sound that would go on to inspire countless members of the predominantly white rock-and-roll generation (with artists such as Elvis Presley, the Grateful Dead, Eric Clapton, Stevie Ray Vaughan, J. Geils Band, and many others eventually remaking songs from the Duke-Peacock catalogue).

The consolidation of the Duke and Peacock talent rosters under one production facility and the creative intermingling of personnel that ensued brought new musical influences to Houston. As Johnson explains:

Actually, Memphis had all that Mississippi sound, and all of those areas, that Deep South sound, where they really came from. And then they had the Nashville connection. See, there you would get a leakover of the country music and the blues. So those things, those are the basis for great music

Bobby "Blue" Bland, 2000.

anyway. . . . This influence was really good for the Texas artists we were already producing—and, in reverse, it was probably good for those Memphis artists too, that Texas swing.

Calvin Owens—a former Duke-Peacock session player and producer (as well as a B.B. King cohort)—traces the roots of the Houston-Memphis hybrid to a core group of players who teamed with bandleader Bill Harvey to provide musical backing, both in the studio and on the road, for Robey's artists.

It's where all this really came from—the connection with the individual musicians of Houston and Memphis. And that came because of Don Robey and Evelyn Johnson. Don Robey was starting to record a lot of Memphis people. So, like, you had Houston musicians going out on the road with the musicians from Memphis. That's what was happening in my case. The cats in the band was around here [Houston] almost all the time . . . because of the Bill Harvey band. Everyone was hooked up with Buffalo Booking and the Duke-Peacock recording thing too. . . . Bill Harvey came out first with the Gatemouth Brown band. And Bill Harvey was from Memphis. And Don Robey was dealing with Sunbeam in Memphis and that kind of thing.

Sunbeam was a cat named [Andrew] Mitchell, but everybody called him Sunbeam. He was like one of the booking agents there. He also had this club [Club Paradise, located in the Mitchell Hotel on Beale Street] where the musicians stayed. And some would play the night, and the ones that didn't play waited tables. Cats were rehearsing there all the time. It was really a music training grounds. . . .

So that's how that Houston-Memphis thing came about. With the recording of Bill Harvey, coming down and recording with Gatemouth Brown, going out on the road with Gatemouth Brown, putting Houston cats in the band. Then came B.[B. King], and then Bill Harvey was working with B.B. right here in Houston, and it just all came together.

Hamp Simmons, a longtime Duke-Peacock bass player, confirms the importance of this Houston-Memphis connection. From firsthand experience he points out:

Bobby [Bland] actually never did have that many musicians from Memphis, because he came here when he was in the service in Austin, and he came to stay here. So he recruited most of his musicians from Houston. B.B. had quite a few from Memphis, but plenty of Texas guys too. . . . We all learned from each other.

And in comments Bland made onstage at Miller Outdoor Theater in 1997 during the Twenty-first Annual SumArts Juneteenth Blues Festival, he acknowledged his special connection to the Bayou City: "When I come back here to Houston, it's like coming home," he said. "The Eldorado and Club Matinee, Duke and Peacock, oh yes—a lot of good memories here."

This link between Houston and Memphis ultimately became so established that Owens says numerous musicians from the two cities—not just Bland—came to view both places as home base. He adds:

> *If we were closer to Houston when we had days off, we'd all come to Houston. And if we were closer to Memphis, everybody'd go to Memphis. Memphis was like a second home for the Houston guys, and for the Memphis guys, Houston was like a second home to them also. It was great. For some of us, that connection still exists today. This is where all this comes from.*

This comfortable and mutually beneficial working relationship between musicians in Texas and the Delta would likely never have occurred if not for the behind-the-scenes business acumen and peacekeeping of a rare woman, an anomaly in an era of male dominance in the workplace. And Johnson strongly believes that her gender was both an asset and a liability as she represented the record company or the booking agency in business negotiations. As she explains:

> *To be perfectly frank with you, being that kind of minority was really something. You had to be gutsy. Talking with people—so far as booking is concerned. Not only the people who did the one-nighters. We had what we would call promoters, who would buy a group of dates in a state, playing from one city to another. It was difficult because there you were, in a man's world, and trying to talk to them. Now if he started cussing, you could not accept that as being an insult to you—because you were in his territory. So there were instances where, when I talked to certain people, I learned how to cuss. [Laughs] . . . You know, when in Rome, act as the Romans.*

But Johnson ultimately sees her distinct individuality, more so than her gender identity, as the key to her success in music. "At the risk of sounding egotistic, I think my personality carried me a long way. Because I mention the cussing in passing, but I was being facetious there. There was not that much of that—because *I was respected*," she says emphatically, pausing between each of the last three words. "Intelligence, general personality, and attitude—I think that made the difference. And then, too, whenever I was talking to somebody, I knew what I was talking about . . . or I didn't talk about it. I think it was that measure that really got me over."

Being knowledgeable and self-confident about business matters was essential for Johnson's success, but so was that maternal instinct noted earlier by Gatemouth Brown. For many of the musicians (and perhaps especially so among those artists who had relocated to Houston from the region around Memphis, leaving their families of origin behind), Johnson assumed the role of the dependable matriarch, a responsible and capable female in an industry full of cutthroat males. For her, these clients and associates were like family. She explains:

I worked hard and I cared. Because there we were, all in this together. You take, for instance, Bobby and B.B. and all, we were like—when one child [of theirs] was being born, the other woman was in labor. I had to be mother, sister superior, confidante, and financier—and I had no money myself. [Laughs] But you have to be these things, to them. . . . [The musicians] did not trust men. . . .

As a matter of fact, many times I had to convey; I had to be the one between. They couldn't even discuss it together, the men. It was, many times, a conflict of interest for me.

. . . So many times I had to be the go-between. There were times when they would not sign that record contract unless I presented it to them. That's the truth.

As one might infer, Johnson's role as the conciliatory go-between was often necessitated in particular by Robey's run-ins with artists. For a company owner who was reported occasionally to have brandished both firearms and fists in dealing with his artists, Robey certainly must have depended heavily on Johnson's considerable charms and skills, given the commercial and cultural success of his music-related enterprises. Summing up the situation, Johnson comments via a telling metaphor on how she served the interests of Duke-Peacock and Buffalo Booking, working in the background to keep operations smoothly functioning:

There was a disc jockey in New Orleans, he called me a scavenger. . . . A couple of guys took an attitude about it and said, "Why do you call her a scavenger?"

He said, "Because Robey goes around slinging s-h-i-t [she spells out the word] in people's face, and she goes around with a clean towel wiping it off."

Recollecting that anecdote, Johnson heartily laughs, obviously enjoying the symbolism—which renders her again as a special sort of mother figure, the all too familiar image of the dutiful female cleaning up after the slovenly and ill-tempered man of the house.

Her good humor regarding the invaluable work she did for Robey and his artists is based, Johnson says, on the fact that all in all, she enjoyed the Duke-Peacock and Buffalo years. As she explains, "It was very satisfying to prove we could do it." And perhaps she found other rewards too. For this woman, biologically childless yet a matriarch to many, ultimately sums up her professional identity by joking that the contracts she managed often turned out to be more like "adoption papers." Johnson brought a feminized stability, intelligence, and grace—both professional and personal—to the far-reaching music business interests Robey bankrolled. With all of her special qualities, she is a unique figure in the Houston-based evolution of postwar blues and R&B.

not surprisingly, Evelyn Johnson is deeply respected by most of the surviving Duke-Peacock players, and I've directly witnessed displays of their affection for her. For instance, in January of 1998, as part of the project for this book, a large contingent of local blues people were invited to gather for a group photograph. I was overjoyed, relieved, and honored when this previously reticent lady showed up at the designated site. And so were many musicians who had formerly worked with her, as evidenced when they rushed to greet her, warmly exchanged memories and updates, and buzzed among themselves that "Ms. Johnson is here!" Fully mature men and women hovered around her like schoolchildren flocking to a favorite teacher. It was a spontaneous and impressive moment communicating a depth of collective goodwill.

However, the sentiments among former Duke-Peacock players are not so unified when the subject shifts to Don Robey, a man some people vilify and others revere. Granted, it's practically become a Houston bluesman's cliché to claim that "Robey cheated me." But it's often a charge for which the details turn out to be vague and inconsistent, more often a feeling than a documentable fact. And in most cases, musicians ultimately acknowledge making unwise decisions that legally permitted Robey's exploitation of their work.

Certainly Robey's reportedly gruff and swaggering personality alienated some of his former employees, just as his financial success (and apparent tendency to flaunt it) bred some deep and lingering resentments. And it seems clear that the shrewd entertainment mogul regularly seized any advantage he could find in negotiations or transactions, especially if the opposing party was naive or confused about such matters. But hard evidence of specific cases of Robey illegally profiting from Duke-Peacock-affiliated talent seems rare, as researchers before me have discovered.

One of the more commonly heard accusations against Robey is that he ripped off songwriters—purchasing a composition outright for "chump change," then copyrighting it under his own name or that of his frequently invoked alias in the song-publishing field, "Deadric Malone." Later he could score big on royalties if the song was eventually recorded and sold well, as was the case with many, though not all.

Numerous people cite the name of Third Ward native singer-songwriter Joe Medwick (aka Joe Veasey) as the most frequent victim of such dealings. But oral history from people who knew Medwick, as well as his own testimony, suggests that this prolific composer was aware of both the short-term benefits and the long-term drawbacks of selling his compositions outright for quick cash (as opposed to copyrighting them himself and retaining an interest in royalties that might or might not follow).

Many songs that supposedly came from Medwick's pen—by general acclamation of local blues culture if not by legally filed copyright—did turn out to be major hits, occasionally not only for Duke-Peacock but also for different labels when other artists recorded cover versions. Examples include Bobby Bland singles such as "Farther Up the Road" (which was later covered by rock superstar Eric Clapton, among others), the authorship of which is officially credited to Don Robey and Joe Veasey; on this one, Medwick, via his own pseudonym, is at least partially acknowledged as the creator. But the long list of songs that insiders ascribe to Medwick's creativity includes titles such as "I Pity the Fool," "Cry, Cry, Cry," "Yield Not to Temptation," and numerous others that more frequently formally identify the writer only as Don Robey or his alias, Deadric Malone (a combination of Robey's middle name and his second wife's surname, a camouflage he supposedly invented in response to industry criticism). And there's the root of the controversy.

Scanning various Duke-Peacock singles and LPs, as well as CD reissue booklets, one commonly finds the Robey name or pseudonym among composition credits. For instance, it's listed on eleven of the sixteen tracks included on the CD *Greatest Hits, Volume One: The Duke Recordings* by Bobby Bland (MCAD 10666, 1992). Remarkably, that number accounts for almost 70 percent of the songwriting on this album, a retrospective showcasing some of Bland's biggest Duke sellers. Likewise, in the CD compilation *Hound Dog: The Peacock Recordings* by Big Mama Thornton (MCAD 10668, 1992), composition of nine of the eighteen tracks is credited, at least in part, to Robey or Malone. Perhaps the finest song ever written by Texas Johnny Brown, the elegant "Two Steps from the Blues" (released as the title track of a classic Duke LP by Bobby Bland), officially documents the fictitious Malone as co-writer (and therefore recipient of half of all songwriting royalties). And these are just a few examples, for, as author James M. Salem has pointed out, Robey ultimately registered BMI writer credit for himself (or his alias) on approximately 1,200 song titles—making him appear to be one of the most prolific songwriters in the history of popular music.

Yet over several years of talking directly to Duke-Peacock alumni such as Brown, I've never met anybody who believes that Don Robey actually wrote or co-wrote any song, much less classic numbers such as these. Except for those instances when the legitimate songwriter is acknowledged with a share of the credit, such compositions are often credited (by local insiders) to Medwick or to one of his friends for whom he reportedly served as song broker in dealings with the Duke-Peacock proprietor. Such perceptions are what has fueled the general opinion that Robey profited immensely from the work of some creative but careless people who never made much money off their talents. And, understandably, some people believe that's just not fair.

In fact, Robey seems regularly to have purchased full claim (or, when the writer held out, half claim) to such songs and thus had the right—as defined by law, if not by morality—to call them his own. Such a right existed because Medwick and others often readily peddled their work, and their share of royalties, for instant money. It seems they did so mainly because Robey would present such freelancers with a false dilemma—the *either/or* fallacy that illogically limits options to only one of two extremes—and they typically did not challenge it, at least not with much effectiveness.

In short, Robey manipulated their impatience. His usual offer was either to buy uncopyrighted material outright for a small sum of cash or to pay nothing at all while taking copyrighted material, leaving the creator to wait and wonder whether the song would ever be recorded and thereby earn any royalties. Apparently, few if any songwriters questioned the assumption that it had to be one or the other extreme. Of course, Robey could have paid a cash advance against future royalties *and* granted (at least partial) credit to the actual songwriter, as is usually the case. But when cash-starved writers such as Medwick accepted the false dilemma that Robey constructed, he could legally exploit them—mercilessly, some would say.

Surprisingly, however, in a 1990 *Houston Chronicle* article by Rick Mitchell, a candidly reflective Joe Medwick is quoted as saying, "Don't write nothing bad about Don Robey. . . . If you came to him meaning business, he'd treat you like business. If you came to him wanting $30, he'd treat you like a $30 person. He got a bad name, but he was a man with a soft heart." In fact, fair or not, Robey's ways of dealing with songwriters were actually common business practices at the time—at least in the blues and R&B industry. Salem cites numerous specific cases of other record-company owners of the era keeping song-publishing or record royalties for themselves, and he quotes Evelyn Johnson as saying, "This was just normal business." Apparently, even among the songwriters who ultimately surrendered potential royalty earnings for so little cash, that attitude prevailed.

In such a context, making what then seemed like quick money for dreaming up a song became part of a live-for-the-moment lifestyle that some of the musicians simply, but obviously unwisely, embraced. One of Medwick's closest friends and frequent collaborators was Teddy Reynolds, who often provided musical ideas to complement the lyrics. He describes the typical songwriting scenario, which usually started out down in Third Ward at Shady's Playhouse before traveling by bus up to the Erastus Street headquarters:

> You'd see Joe down like this [he imitates the posture of someone engaged in intensely focused penmanship] all the time. Writing, all the time! Then, "Come on, Teddy, let's go."
>
> "I ain't got no bus fare, man."
>
> "Come on, I've got some bus fare for me and you." I'll never forget that, boy. Bless his heart. Bus fare to go up to Peacock, to Don Robey's. We'd get up to Fifth Ward, didn't know how we was going to get back. See, Mr. Robey could've turned the tunes down, and there we is out there with no bus fare or nothing. But then, he never did. We always had hits. Ain't that something? We always had hits!
>
> And, boy, I'd say, "I know we're going to have some money tonight." Joe would have seventy-five dollars and I would have twenty-five, and boy, that was some big money back then. Oooh, that was big money, boy. I'm telling you the truth, that was big money!
>
> So cats'd be asking, "Where [are] Joe Medwick and Teddy and them?"
>
> "They're over there at the studio putting some tapes on."

"Uh-oh, I know we're going to have a good time tonight!" [Laughs] . . . And they'd all be waiting for us when we got back. . . . Time to party!

Later, when we'd run out of the money, we'd just write some new songs and do it all over again.

The story Reynolds tells here doesn't ring of victimization, and his demeanor was typically happy, even proud, when we talked about his days of collaborating with Medwick to peddle songs to Robey. Looking back as an older and smarter man, he certainly regretted that in his youth he had opted for the sure thing—the quick cash that he calls "big money"—as opposed to making a long-term investment in his own songwriting skills. He understandably believes that Robey took advantage of him. But Reynolds doesn't claim that Robey actually broke any law by openly buying full rights to songs that he and Medwick co-authored.

Robey's business associate John Green offers further insight into the lopsided relationship between the Duke-Peacock boss and some of his most productive ghostwriters:

I was in the Army with Joe Medwick. . . . And Joe got out [of] the service, and I don't know when he got the idea that he was writing songs—but he could write 'em. And he would go out there, and sometimes Robey would make him sit around there all day long. And then say, "All right, Joe. What you got, man?" And Joe would have these songs. You remember these Big Chief [writing paper] tablets? Well, he'd have a Big Chief tablet full of songs, a lot of songs. And Robey would look through them and say, "Joe, I'll give you twenty dollars, or whatever, for all this."

And he'd say, "Man, give me the twenty, and let me get out of here. I've been here all day long!" [Laughs] And then he'd go back down on Dowling Street, and they would party.

Green understood the shrewd leverage Robey wielded in such a negotiation, especially after (possibly deliberately) frustrating the writer by making him wait in the office for hours.

The thing was, the guys wanted some money that day. So Robey'd say, "Now how do you want to do this? Do you want to sell it outright, or do you want to give it to the company and wait for your royalties to come?" Now you know how long it takes royalties to come? Two years. [Laughs]

So they would tell him, say, "Man, I have my light bill that's due," or "I've got to have some gas for my car," or "My wife is at home and I ain't got no food in the house. So just give me ten dollars and take the song."

Given this firsthand witness account of the rhetoric Robey typically employed in negotiations with cash-desperate songwriters, it's easy to imagine how someone like Reynolds, an elementary school dropout, might have then assumed that the *only* way to get royalties for a song was to "give it to the company and wait." Robey evidently never first proposed that a writer might sell it to the company and still receive some fair portion of any royalties that might accrue. Obviously, people such as Medwick or Reynolds didn't travel across town just to *give* anything to Robey; they wanted some immediate compensation. So Robey perceived the situation and manipulated his adversary's understanding of possible options to fabricate the *either/or* dilemma.

Green's additional explanations underscore the retrospective impression that Duke-Peacock production insiders placed higher value on the arranging that took place within the walls of Robey's headquarters and undervalued the freelance composing that often necessarily preceded it beyond those walls. For various reasons—perhaps including issues of class and ego—Duke-Peacock staffers may have been inclined to ignore the simple fact that without the original songwriting there would be nothing to arrange or produce.

> *To them [songwriters such as Medwick and Reynolds], it wasn't nothing but some words on paper at the time. And [Robey] would take it and develop it, get with [in-house bandleader, arranger, and producer] Joe Scott and tell Joe, say, "Man, look at this." And Joe would take it, change it around, and write [i.e., transcribe and arrange] the music to it, do everything! And that's how a lot of that stuff was done.*
>
> *And Teddy [Reynolds] and Joe Medwick and them, like I said, they liked to drink wine. They would just be hustling that wine money.*

Green's insider attitude, which clearly demeans the value of original concepts and lyrics by linking their existence to mere "hustling" for drinks, makes the songwriters sound more like panhandlers than creative artists. And such notions may also have prevailed among Robey and his office staff, who evidently considered themselves far more sophisticated and talented than those ragtag song peddlers. In an interview quoted by Salem, Evelyn Johnson belittles the "so-called songwriters" (in particular identifying Joe Medwick) who sold roughly developed song material. In turn, she credits much of Duke-Peacock's success to the fact that it had in-house staff members "like Joe Scott and different musicians to write scores, and they were either paid scale for the job or they were salaried people."

Such views reinforce the old class-based dichotomy between the upscale and the down-home in postwar American culture at large, and in Houston blues culture in particular. On the one hand, professionals such as Robey, Scott, Green, and Johnson had a socioeconomic perspective perhaps best symbolized by the urbane milieu of the old Bronze Peacock; on the other, free-spirited songwriters such as Medwick and Reynolds identified mainly with the gritty subculture of Shady's Playhouse. Is it really any surprise that here, as often elsewhere in human enterprises, the established power structure may have openly manipulated the economically disadvantaged, making fun of them in the process and demeaning the value of their contributions?

Green's view of how some capable but financially desperate songwriters foolishly were led to focus only on immediate gratification is confirmed by other sources who regularly witnessed transactions involving freshly penned compositions. And many of those who directly observed those dealings find fault not so much with Robey—who was admittedly taking a gambler's risk (though a minor one, given his financial status) on any raw song material he might purchase—but with the individuals who so cheaply prostituted their ability to create lyrics and tunes. In general, the insiders tend to view many of those quick-fix-seeking song peddlers as willing participants in their own degradation—and therefore spare them no sympathy. For example, Calvin Owens bluntly denounces the impromptu songwriters who claim to have been victimized by Robey:

> A lot of people say, like, he'd mess 'em out of their songs and so forth. But it was always the writers that was always trying to [screw] him. Because they'd jump in a cab in Third Ward and write ten songs—I might be a little exaggerating—but write some songs from Third to Fifth Ward, just for their money for their drinks or whatever they needed for the moment. Mostly it was drinks. And Robey would always be a cat who said, "Well, do you want to sell it now, or do you want to wait and let me give you a contract on it?" Now their purpose on going out there was to get money—cash in the pocket . . . so they'd just sell and run.
>
> Then when Joe Scott would take those songs and really develop those things into a great piece of music, then a cat would jump up and say, "Ow, he done stole my song."

Another then young songwriter who sometimes assisted Duke-Peacock interests by developing material Robey had purchased was Oscar Perry, who also went on to compose fully credited hits for Bobby Bland and record as a solo artist under his own name. Directly familiar with the label owner's way of dealing with freelance composers, Perry's view of such matters repeats the basic theme:

> A lot of people say that he cheated them out of money, but that's not the truth. What would happen is these guys would write songs, and they would try to sell the songs to Robey. So he would tell them that they ain't nothing but some words, and they would sell it. After he'd buy it from them, sometimes he would give the words to me and tell me to make a melody to it. And we'd record it with Bobby Bland or somebody. Then [the original songwriters] would say it's been stolen. But I don't think he did it—because they didn't have to sell it. They could have put it on contract. They wanted quick money.

One constant among various accounts of the song-development process at Duke-Peacock is the key role played by Texarkana-born trumpeter Joe Scott. Sometimes collaborating with protégés such as Perry, sometimes working solo, he served as the primary arranger and producer, transforming what admittedly may sometimes have been relatively simple song ideas into vibrant blues and R&B. In short, both the vagabond songwriters and their detractors concur that Scott was the studio genius whose musical skills were as necessary as Evelyn Johnson's business skills in making Duke-Peacock the mighty force it was. In the words of former Peacock artist Big Walter "the Thunderbird" Price, Scott was "a wizard . . . the brains behind it all, you know, musically, that is."

Hamp Simmons, who played bass on many of Scott's most critically acclaimed productions for Bobby Bland, also praises the producer, singling him out as a unique motivator and an especially effective in-house teacher:

> Joe Scott was so good. Say, like, if you had nothing, no ideas, just zero-zero, and he would ask for that nothing, you would give it to him. You know, even if you had nothing to give, but if he asked you, you just had to give it to him. He was so good, you just wanted to give him whatever he needed, musically speaking. . . . He taught me a lot of stuff, taught me how to read charts real good, how to collaborate with other musicians too.

Such testimony is common from those who worked on Duke-Peacock productions under Scott—not only in the Fifth Ward studio that served as label headquarters but also beyond. As Simmons, who spent almost a decade touring and recording with Bland, goes on to explain:

> And then there were plenty of times that Joe Scott came out on the road with us—and would start writing and arranging for the band and everything. We got more sessions like that, and we stopped recording exclusively here in Houston. We started also recording in Nashville and Chicago and Los Angeles—out there where we were making the rounds on the road. A lot of those songs, the actual recording came out of Chicago or Nashville—the ones that made the big, big, big money. But it was always the Houston musicians out there doing them. . . .
>
> I. J. [Gosey, bass player] and Johnny Brown [guitarist] and them would do some demos for Bobby [in Houston] and send them out to Bobby wherever we were on the road. . . . Joe Scott would bring those demos and tell us what he wanted. And wherever we were on the road at that particular time, we'd go into a studio and make that record. So whether it was in Houston or somewhere else, it was usually always Joe Scott calling the shots on our music.

Among insiders and fans, Scott seems universally esteemed for the way he called those shots. His swinging, tightly crafted, brass-heavy productions came to epitomize the signature sophistication of Duke-Peacock blues—a hybrid sound whose evolution may initially have been defined by bandleaders such as Bill Harvey and Pluma Davis but which came to maturity in the late 1950s and 1960s, mainly under Scott's tasteful direction. It's a sound that runs counter to the raw black folk

Hamp Simmons, 1998.

Oscar Perry, Big Easy, 1996.

music of the old South and the rough-edged electric blues of postwar Chicago (styles that were generally favored by most in the younger generation of new white fans during the late 1960s and beyond). But it's a sound that survives today among Houston blues figures such as Perry, a deep-voiced singer and sweet-toned guitarist who worked with Scott not only as a collaborating songwriter but also later as a featured artist on Robey's Back Beat label, a Duke-Peacock subsidiary.

Now a record producer and independent label owner (TSOT and Perry-Tone) in his own right, Perry creates intelligent urban blues and R&B—"smooth blues," he calls it—in the polished, mellow style he learned from his mentor. On a number of excellent self-produced CDs (especially *Still Blue, Brand New Man,* and *When Love Is Gone*), as well as in his regularly scheduled nightclub performances around the city, Perry's work sometimes evokes, for me at least, a sense of what new Joe Scott productions might have sounded like, had they continued into the 1990s. It's a quality Perry is proud to claim: "[Scott] showed me how to write for strings. When he had an arrangement and needed somebody to do a melody, he would come get me. We had a pretty close relationship."

Significantly, Perry's positive feelings for this widely respected Duke-Peacock A&R (Artists & Repertoire) man extend also to the often maligned boss who employed them both. "I personally liked Don Robey, and I think he liked me," he asserts. Thus, he's at odds with those people who reflexively condemn the company owner (sometimes with good reason perhaps and sometimes, it seems fair to say, only on the basis of hearsay and local tradition).

Granted, there are various accounts of how Robey ruthlessly sought to dominate the Houston music market via intimidation of his competitors. For example, the founder of short-lived Kangaroo Records, Henry Hayes, angrily insists that one of his best productions of Albert Collins (the first version of "The Freeze") never got much attention because Robey "just killed that record." His rationale is that the Duke-Peacock kingpin controlled "all the black disc jockeys . . . had all of them paid off and everything," and ordered them never to play the Kangaroo single—a Collins original that reportedly was being well received during live performances in local clubs. Asked why he never obtained legal recourse for a host of wrongs he alleges that Robey committed against him, Hayes offers the following anecdote:

> So I decided, "Man we've got to do something about that," and got a lawyer. And this lawyer had everything for us to sue Robey. And after he got all the work done and everything, he told me, "Naw, man, I'm afraid to sue Robey. You know, Robey's known as a gangster man, and I'm afraid."
> . . . And this lawyer didn't want to file it because one of the shareholders in Robey's company at that time was a very influential man, you know what I mean. . . . So [the lawyer] said, "This is everything y'all need to get your money. But just get somebody else to file it." But the lawyer didn't want to do anything about it, so that was the end of that. . . . You see, they didn't want to offend the big man.

Could this account from Hayes have merit? Absolutely. And it's bolstered by the fact (called to my attention by Dick Shurman) that Duke Records shortly thereafter in 1958 recorded Fenton Robinson (b. 1935) doing a cover of "The Freeze" (single 190) in an apparent attempt to overshadow the Hayes-produced recording of Collins. But two key points remain: First, whatever the explanation, Robey was never charged or convicted of any of the various crimes that Hayes and others allege against him; and second, in contrast to those who still denounce Robey, there are many others, such as Oscar Perry, who praise him.

Perhaps the most vocal among those in the latter group is Calvin Owens, never one to suppress his opinions. During a lengthy 1997 interview session, when I passingly referred to Robey as "the man that Houston blues musicians love to hate," Owens immediately responded: "Don Robey's a *great* man and I love him very much, and he's nothing like what people say he is, as far as I'm concerned. May be the first time you ever heard anyone say anything good about Robey, but Robey was a great man."

And to some degree Owens' point must ultimately be acknowledged by all. For no matter how heartlessly Robey took advantage of needy songwriters, and no matter what level of innuendo persists against his character, the magnitude of Robey's business achievement cannot be denied. And though some observers might quantify the range of the Duke-Peacock empire only in numerical terms, it must also be appreciated as a cultural phenomenon. In the forties, fifties, and sixties, Robey's music-business interests—and especially his and Joe Scott's stylistic preference for an urbane, smooth blues sound—impacted the nation at large, profoundly changing black Houston in the process.

And the legacy of that distinctive Duke-Peacock sound has proven both a blessing and a curse for the local community. On the one hand, its evolution once made Fifth Ward a recording center for some greatly influential music, involving hundreds of Houston residents in the creative and commercial processes and, in many cases, still binding them together today. Yet, on the other, since that relatively sophisticated R&B-style blues differed so significantly from the coarser modes popularized during the mainstream baby-boomer blues revival of the 1960s, its defining characteristics also virtually ensured the subsequent anonymity of many of its veteran players. For better or for worse, the Duke-Peacock experience transformed the lives and destinies of numerous talented individuals who, despite remaining largely unknown to mass audiences, have continued making music and calling the Bayou City home.

of all the duke-peacock alumni still performing at the end of the twentieth century, no one's reputation for instrumental excellence surpasses that of Clarence Hollimon. So when the sixty-two-year-old Fifth Ward native died on Easter Sunday of the year 2000, local blues and jazz culture lost more than just another gifted musician. It lost the player countless insiders consider to be the greatest all-around guitarist ever to emerge from any of the city's wards. Given that those old neighborhoods have been home to a long list of six-string heavyweights, that's quite a reputation. And it's one that was first documented at 2809 Erastus Street, not far from the wood-frame house where the guy that friends called "Gristle" was raised.

Over the last seventeen years of his life, Hollimon served as one-half of what may have been the most widely traveled and recorded husband-and-wife blues duo in contemporary history—Houston's for sure. That partnership was formed with vocalist Carol Fran (b. 1933) following their 1983 common-law marriage. Billed as Fran & Hollimon, they annually played marquee concert halls in numerous European cities, as well as big festivals and special events nationwide (including a performance at the 1996 Olympics in Atlanta). The duo remained Hollimon's proudest musical affiliation. And this from a guy who'd performed extensively with some of Robey's most well known artists, such as Bobby Bland, Junior Parker, O. V. Wright, Joe Hinton, Buddy Ace, and many others. Not only that: Beyond the Duke-Peacock circle, he also had logged meaningful time as lead guitarist with Charles Brown, Dionne Warwick, the original Jazz Crusaders, Arnett Cobb, and a wide range of stars of black popular music from the 1950s through the 1990s.

But collaborating with his wife, the woman he affectionately dubbed "Blabs," was his ultimate joy. As a team they recorded *Soul Sensation* (1992) and *See There!* (1994) for the Black Top label, as well as a rare live concert performance briefly available only in Germany. In January 2000, they made what would be their final CD as a duo, *It's About Time,* on the British label JSP. But all in all, Hollimon's tenure in recording studios stretched back across more than four decades.

He had gone pro early in life, dropping out of high school in 1954 (at the age of seventeen) to play guitar with the Bill Harvey Orchestra, backing Clarence "Gatemouth" Brown and Willie Mae "Big Mama" Thornton on Buffalo Booking Agency–sponsored road tours. This work eventually led him to Robey's Duke-Peacock studio, where from 1957 to 1962 Hollimon proved to be a brilliant session guitarist complementing the musical efforts of various blues, soul, and gospel artists. As he once told *Living Blues* about his tenure there, "I was just like the house band."

Despite being one of the most respected players for the major black-owned record company of his youth, Hollimon remained a quiet and humble man. His ego-to-talent ratio was more lop-sided than most people had ever witnessed elsewhere. It was minuscule bits of the former, and gracious, ever expanding heapings of the latter—making him the ideal sideman. Great vocalists especially loved to work with him, for Hollimon's genius wasn't conveyed via show-stealing extended solos or fretboard histrionics but through economical and respectful collaboration.

That distinctive technique was reportedly influenced by his close listening to piano players, more so than other guitar players, in his youth. As it evolved, it became a signature sound. Calvin Owens calls Hollimon "one of the most unique guitarists of my time." He goes on to explain, "I mean, his guitar playing was different from anybody else's. Very modern, whether it was blues, jazz, whatever it was. . . . So that you go anywhere and hear it and immediately say, 'That's Clarence.'"

Reflecting on their work together in Robey's studio, Owens recalls a defining moment that illustrates how the younger Hollimon's genius influenced the evolution of a jazzier, more progressive element in the music:

> I became aware of Clarence while working at Duke and Peacock. Clarence was doing most of the guitar work out there. Clarence was like on staff. . . . One of the classic stories I know about Clarence, out at Peacock, we were recording some blues. And Clarence was playing a solo on this, and he went up a half-tone in his solo and came back down—you know, that kind of jazz thing. And man, Don Robey must have had ten hemorrhages! [Laughs] "What is that boy doing?" he yelled. But that record became a hit. [Laughs] That was something that he did that was outrageous. I mean, you just didn't do nothing like that—mixing jazz concepts with the blues—but Clarence did it. And it worked. And he did that with all his stuff, man.

In more recent years, Hollimon elected to do studio work for a wide variety of artists, including his former Duke-Peacock colleague Lavelle White, who featured him prominently on her well-received CDs *Miss Lavelle* (Antone's, 1994) and *It Haven't Been Easy* (Discovery, 1996). On those tracks, as elsewhere, he distinguishes himself as an amazingly fluent guitarist whose style is characterized not by bombast or speed but by intelligence and diversity—by those same musical instincts Owens had first witnessed in action long ago.

Like Hollimon, White had first emerged as a professional recording artist as part of Robey's deep roster of talent. Back in the years between 1958 and 1964, she recorded a series of fourteen tracks that Duke released on singles under the stage name "Miss La-Vell." A Louisiana native who lived in Houston for much of her adult life (before relocating for a while to Chicago, then more recently to Austin), White is part of that tradition of talented female vocalists previously affiliated with Clarence Green and the Rhythmaires. Over the years of her primary development she also worked locally with bands led by Johnny Copeland, Texas Johnny Brown, Albert Collins, Houston's "Guitar Slim" (Rayfield Jackson), and several other guitarists.

But from her earliest recordings to the present, White stands out as a rarity among contemporary Bayou City blues women (along with Trudy Lynn) in that she wrote many of her own songs, including classics such as "Stop Those Teardrops" (Duke single 307). White even composed one number that became a hit for Bobby Bland, the gospel-spiced ballad "Lead Me On" (Duke single 318; also featured on Bland's LP *Two Steps from the Blues*). But following the pattern of some of her male counterparts, she had unwisely sold that song outright to Robey, who published it as yet another of his Deadric Malone compositions. Hence, her experience makes it clear that, in some

Clarence Hollimon, 1994.

Lavelle White, Big Easy, 1996.

ways at least, the Duke-Peacock owner did not discriminate based on gender. (He also shared presumably undeserved songwriting credits for numbers composed by other women artists, such as Marie Adams and Willie Mae "Big Mama" Thornton).

But whatever the confusing realities regarding copyrights and authorship, Robey's Erastus Street studio served as a place where—just as Hollimon had done—many Houston women gained valuable experience and professional identity as recording artists. Other examples include hometown singers such as Mildred Jones (who recorded several Peacock singles and toured with B.B. King) and Luvenia Lewis (who recorded Duke singles under the name "Lovey Lewis," a moniker she now says she disliked but accepted at Robey's insistence). But apart from featured acts whose names actually appear on the records, Robey also offered some relatively anonymous females the opportunity to work as session players and background vocalists. Though never in the spotlight, such women are part of Duke-Peacock history, and it, in turn, is a key part of their own.

One of these backup singers is Third Ward native Mickie Moseley, a powerful singer whose current repertoire has evolved to focus almost exclusively on music best classified as a gospel-jazz hybrid. But as a younger woman, she first learned about vocal technique and the inner workings of the recording business among blues and R&B players. "Iola Broussard and myself and a few others, we used to do backup music behind some of the artists who came through Duke and Peacock," Moseley recalls. "I remember Bobby 'Blue' Bland was one of them, and Joe Hinton, who did that song 'Funny (How Time Slips Away)' [Back Beat single 541, recorded in 1962]." Looking back on the start of a career that eventually led to her opening for jazz greats such as Dizzy Gillespie before turning to a Christian music ministry, Moseley considers herself "blessed" and "educated" by this early experience.

So, too, does Galveston native Iola Broussard, who worked as both an instrumentalist and a backing vocalist under the direction of studio producers such as Joe Scott. The daughter of a blues pianist, she had first moved to Houston in 1961 to attend Texas Southern University. Not long after that, she started working with the respected local bandleader Leo Baxter (1930–1980), performing in both his regionally prominent big-band orchestra and in his group called the Baxterettes (which featured a rotating cast of female singers, sometimes including Broussard and Moseley, among others). It was a key time in Broussard's life, an era when she was gradually discovering that the music she had long loved to play could possibly lead to a real career. As she tells it:

Word got around, and then I started doing recording work for Duke and Peacock Records. I was the piano player and doing a lot of the background vocal for a lot of the hit records that were cut then. . . . There was Bobby "Blue" Bland, Little Junior Parker, Ernie K-Doe, and the other one, with the white hair, Buddy Ace. Yes, I was playing piano for them. And if they needed background vocals on some of the songs, I was doubling, doing both.

Luvenia Lewis, at home, 2001.

As someone who had mastered a popular instrument as well as her own fine alto voice, Broussard proved to be a particularly useful session artist—a reality that led to her deeper-than-usual immersion in a domain dominated by men. "At that time, I was just the only one," she says regarding women instrumentalists in the studio. Over the course of several years Broussard went on to collaborate with established sidemen such as Hollimon and Texas Johnny Brown, earning their respect and creating her own niche as a Duke-Peacock side*woman* in the process. "Just whenever they needed a piano player with some of the blues recordings, I was available," she recalls. "I've worked with all of them. At one time we've all been—maybe not just on a job, but through the recording studio—we've all been connected one way or the other."

As the lone female on various recording sessions or gigs, Broussard would seem to have been a likely candidate for special treatment, positive or negative, based on gender. But she disputes such assumptions as irrelevant to her own experience.

> *As for being a woman in the music business, I think it's all in the way a woman presents herself. . . . I mean, I've always been treated like one of the boys—because that's the way I wanted to be treated. And I think it's just equal opportunity for both—you know, if you can play. If you have something to present, it doesn't matter if you're a man or a woman.*

Moseley concurs that the music ultimately mattered far more than gender roles, both at Duke-Peacock and onstage. And though she acknowledges that sexual tension sometimes arose, she downplays its significance, implying that it was never a threat to someone who took herself seriously as an artist.

> *I was the only woman in various bands, but I never really thought of it that way—I guess because the music was the thing that turned me on so. I was just in it, you know, so I never thought about being the only female in the group. I never focused that way. I was always focusing on, How does that go? or Why did you do this? How can you do this? You know, just amazed at how the cats could play. And some of them had just talents, that never went to school or anything, just tremendous energy and stuff. That fascinated me, I guess.*
>
>   *I wasn't mistreated—at the early parts, I wasn't anyway. Nobody ever even thought about it. The guys were very nice with me, I guess because they were older than I was, and you know, had a thing going already. Every now and then one or two would come in and try to hit on me or something, but it never did pan out, you know, because I understood musicians. [Laughs]*

For women such as Moseley and Broussard, the Duke-Peacock experience seems to represent a positive initiation. Inadvertently or not, it introduced them to the possibility that professional

Iola Broussard, 1996.

Mickie Moseley, 1996.

merit could trump gender and sexuality in defining workplace identity. Despite never having been among Robey's stars, they surely saw themselves, their skills, and their futures somewhat differently following their session work for the labels. Having started there quite young, they grew and matured into savvy pros.

And, of course, they were not alone in experiencing life-changing transformations as a result of their affiliation with Robey's studio. For numerous men and women, that building up on Erastus Street marks the site of a key turning point in their personal history and their self-image, if not their financial fortunes. From songwriters to session players to featured entertainers, making records at Duke-Peacock was sometimes a way of remaking their lives.

Perhaps no better illustration of that phenomenon exists than Big Walter "the Thunderbird" Price. Born in rural Gonzales County in 1914 (a date often previously, and apparently incorrectly, reported as 1917), this legendary Texas piano player is perhaps the oldest living Duke-Peacock artist that I've come to know personally. Now the elder statesman of Houston's blues culture, Big Walter (who actually prefers not to be called by his last name) maintains a charmingly idiosyncratic persona that was first cultivated and popularized during his tenure under contract to Robey in the mid-1950s.

Following the earlier example of his former roommate Clarence "Gatemouth" Brown, the man born Walter Travis Price first came to the Bayou City at Robey's invitation, around 1955. Previously, he had worked menial jobs in cotton fields and on railroad lines—that is, before breaking out as a gospel singer, then learning how to play barrelhouse-style piano and switching to blues and boogie. He initially got Robey's attention after recording a few singles for TNT Records, a small San Antonio–based label; the most popular of these was the talking blues "Calling Margie" (TNT 8005).

Once signed to Peacock, Big Walter and His Thunderbirds (a newly formed group that included Fifth Ward sax man Grady Gaines) released a total of five singles over the next two years, beginning with the swamp blues–flavored hit "Shirley Jean" (1661) and including his most well known number, the rollicking "Pack Fair and Square" (1666). This latter song would eventually be covered by the Boston-based rock group J. Geils Band on two different LPs for Atlantic Records—the self-titled 1970 debut album and the 1972 live recording *Full House*—popularizing it with a whole new generation.

Following the stint with Peacock, Big Walter recorded on a variety of other independent labels (including Goldband, Myrl, Jet Stream, and Tear Drop). But for his fans as well as himself, it is the identity that was first widely popularized during his Peacock years that best defines the man, even now at the start of the twenty-first century.

A large part of the Big Walter persona is intertwined with the nickname he adopted and shared with his backing band—starting with his initial recordings in Houston and continuing to this day.

Inspired by Robey's Peacock logo, he selected the name of another proud bird, one already established in the Native American mythology of the southwest and then popularized with the debut of the Ford Thunderbird automobile. Not only did he begin to call himself "the Thunderbird" and refer to his supporting players as the Thunderbirds, but he also "wrote a slogan behind it," as he says. Though these days the details can shift along with his moods and memory, the version he delivered for me during a 1995 interview is true to the basic content and spirit of the "slogan," which he recites in a type of gleeful rap:

> I am Big Walter the Thunderbird, the bird that flies so swift from coast to coast. No matter where you may go, no matter where you may be, you can always find Big Walter. If you're in Kingston, Jamaica; Norway; Czechoslovakia; France; Australia; or Belgium; Holland; Hobbs, New Mexico; England; China; USA; Houston; Pasadena; Mobile, Alabama; Nashville, Tennessee; New York; Hollywood; or Japan—it is Big Walter the Thunderbird!

This grandiose self-image, replete with a hodgepodge of apparently random global references, epitomizes the Big Walter I've come to know and love.

Sure, he's a person whose childhood worldview was sadly defined by the boundaries of a cotton field, where he labored under the critical eye of the reportedly abusive aunt who raised him. He's a person who never received much formal education—mainly because by the time his aunt moved into San Antonio from her impoverished farm, the then nine-year-old boy was deemed too old and too physically large to start in first grade (so he was placed at a higher level, where he struggled and eventually dropped out). He's a person who can tell painfully detailed stories of life as a poor black man in Texas in the 1920s, 1930s, and 1940s—accounts vivid with the realities of class consciousness and racism. But in his own mind and those of local fans and friends who revere the elderly gent, Walter Travis Price is also someone else, someone dynamic and unique: "The bird that flies so swift from coast to coast."

A heightened sense of self is, in many ways, the real legacy of Duke-Peacock, not only for "the Thunderbird" but also for numerous other less colorfully named musicians still present (and in many cases still active) in the Houston blues community. Whether their work there encompassed scores of recording sessions or only a few, these people generally are quite proud to have been affiliated with one of the great independent record labels in U.S. music history. Whatever their feelings about Robey, they consider the African American–owned-and-operated enterprise that was Duke-Peacock to be culturally significant—a defining presence not merely in their own lives but also in those of their people, locally and beyond. And though there may be some lingering bitterness based on personal experience with (or perception of) Robey's empire, they deeply regret the absence of the enterprise. As Calvin Owens once explained, "Robey told all the musi-

Big Walter "the Thunderbird" Price, at home, 1995.

cians, he said, 'You know, if I close these doors, you're going to miss it. I mean, you think that you're going to do better?' . . . So we don't have that anymore. We really don't." But even though the company formally folded in 1973, its heritage survives, influencing some people's sense of who and what they are, onstage or off.

Most performances these days featuring Big Walter "the Thunderbird" don't occur on a stage but in the privacy of his northeast Houston home, a small, government-subsidized apartment he calls "the dugout." Perched there on a piano bench beneath a gold-framed Peacock Records publicity photo of himself, this joyously eccentric bluesman can still deliver quite a show, at least when his arthritis subsides. On those good days when the gnarly fingers limber up a bit, he seems perpetually fascinated with the creative possibilities of his Yamaha keyboard. It's a newfangled machine that can synthesize any sound, from gospel-style B3 organ to the lonesome wail of a train whistle to the rhythmic creeping of a string bass to the classic piano tones of his old recordings. He'll doodle with the switches and keys for a while, then burst into a soulful, gut-wrenching rendition of one of his signature songs, numbers such as "Blood Stains on the Wall," "If the Blues Were Money (I'd Be a Millionaire)," or "Shirley Jean." Sometimes he'll improvise a tune and lyrics based on what's happening in his life at the moment or who's present with him in the room. Whatever the case, when Big Walter sits down to play, "the Thunderbird" does fly again. And for a moment—here, as elsewhere around the city when certain others perform—the ghost of the Peacock arises and resumes its noble strut.

I. J. Gosey, C. Davis Bar-B-Q, Sunnyside, 1995.

CHAPTER 6

beyond the wards

Yesterday and Today

it's 5:00 o'clock on a Sunday afternoon in December of 1999, and both the blues and barbecue are really cooking. In a deep southeast Houston establishment that epitomizes the organic link between this sound and this food, a woman named Rena Singleton is seated at her regular table. And, in her own words, she's "as close to heaven" as she hopes to get in this world. While sweetly piercing electric guitar notes ring out over sustained chords on an organ, the diminutive elderly lady slowly stands up and lowers her head, rolling it hypnotically from side to side. Lacking a proper dance floor or partner is no hindrance to her. Without moving from the cramped space in front of her chair, she gyrates her hips in a deep bass groove. Eyes closed, lips pursed, and elbows gently swaying, she's right where she wants to be: C. Davis Bar-B-Q.

There beneath a glitter-bespeckled banner announcing their common identity as the "Golden Girls," Singleton shows up each week with her closest friends to savor the blues. She's been doing so

Dancers, C. Davis Bar-B-Q, Sunnyside, 2000.

without fail for nearly a quarter of a century. And for her—as for most of the other black women who make up her neighborhood social organization—that enjoyment is no passive experience.

"It's like a soul-searching music, the way I. J. plays the guitar," she says. "I just love it and need to hear it." She adds that many people "say they like my style of dancing and enjoying the music." Indeed, observing the elegant funk of Singleton's expressive body language—and that of her friends—is an essential complement to the first-class musical performances regularly served up in this rustic eatery. It's part of the real-deal ambience that has prompted I. J. Gosey, his fellow players, and fans of local blues to gather there for years.

Located beyond the 610 Loop due south of Third Ward in an area known as Sunnyside, C. Davis Bar-B-Q announces itself on Reed Road only via hand-painted letters on a sheet of plywood nailed above the corrugated metal roof of its front porch. Despite the ramshackle exterior of the maroon-colored building, thickly wafting smoke promises sumptuous food inside. But there is no visual clue whatsoever—other than the typically packed gravel parking lot—that every Sunday afternoon and Tuesday night this family-run restaurant hosts some of the city's top blues musicians.

Gosey has presided over those musical gatherings since 1973. On the bandstand, he consistently pleases regular patrons and newcomers alike with his versatile grace on guitar. "He can really work that instrument," Singleton says. "And he plays it right—right from his heart, right from his soul." Beyond the fine fretwork, he also brings an unpretentious passion to his singing and good humor to the occasional storytelling between songs.

Performing an eclectic mix of jazz standards, instrumental versions of old pop hits, and lots of fifties- and sixties-era blues and R&B, the former Duke-Peacock studio musician obviously enjoys his sessions at C. Davis Bar-B-Q, which he calls "just the most comfortable place in the world." The folks who've religiously attended those gatherings over the years obviously agree. "I love the music here," says Singleton. "It's like family and good friends. When you come, you meet people, and you're never a stranger here again."

Verta Mae Evans, who's lived in Sunnyside for most of her life and has frequented the Bar-B-Q since the day it opened, concurs: "The musicians here are really something special. Sometimes I'll bring my tambourine and play right along with them." Evans, in fact, has participated in jam sessions and concerts throughout the city, working that instrument alongside a variety of professional players. She's been doing it for almost fifty years—so long and so well that she's generally recognized as a musician herself. But her home base for several decades has been this little barbecue joint, and the rapport she shares with the regular performers there is especially tight. As a result, this former drum majorette (for Third Ward's Yates High School marching band) often improvises some impressive percussive accompaniment from her seat in the snugly packed room whenever she catches the inspiration. "They don't mind 'cause it's all about having fun—and I do know how to shake a tambourine," she says.

Indeed, Gosey and his band originally took the C. Davis gig in the name of freedom and fun. When restaurant founder (and amateur harmonica player) Clarence Davis first invited them to work at the modest little smokehouse, they jumped at the opportunity despite the meager pay they'd earn there. As Gosey recalls:

> They asked, "Can we play just what we want to play there?"
> I told them, "You can play any damn thing you want!"
> And man, look-a-here, they said, "Go get it!" So I took this gig for my band. And C. Davis Bar-B-Q became something very special to us all right away.

Located near the southern edge of a suburban working-class community that still retains some rural ambience, this restaurant offers music sessions that draw a mix of appreciative folks. Most are middle-aged to elderly regulars who compensate for what they might lack in disposable entertainment income with an intense passion for the performances and repertoire that make this one of the city's best authentic blues venues beyond the wards.

Morgan Bouldin (b. 1960), a generation younger than Gosey, fronts his own "groove jazz" combo around town most of the time, but for several years he was also the Sunday-afternoon house keyboardist at C. Davis. "It's just a big happy party every Sunday," he once told me. "We run our own show. I. J. is so cool, you know. We ain't under no pressure to play no certain kind of music. I mean, we've got to get down to the blues, but we can take that any direction we want. No big egos, just music."

In addition to the regular members of Gosey's four-piece combo, another three to ten guest vocalists, guitarists, horn men, or keyboard players may contribute their talents each session. Some of these are veterans whose professional credentials rival the bandleader's; others are simply gifted amateurs. Regardless, if they merit a space on this small stage, you can be sure they can play.

Among the many impressive impromptu guest performances I've personally observed there, several stand out. I especially remember the day when vocalist Martha Turner returned to sing at C. Davis for the first time in years. A Louisiana native and a fixture on the Houston scene since 1962, she had grown up in blues culture but, capitalizing on her versatility and charm, had migrated to better-paying jobs in private supper clubs and upscale lounges over the past two decades. As a result, in public she rarely concentrated on the music that launched her professional career back in the late 1950s, when she first performed as a seventeen-year-old supporting vocalist on tour with the blues icon Jimmy Reed. In the late 1990s, between working the mainstream music gigs on weekends and—in stunning contrast—holding down her weekday job as an independent school-bus driver, Turner rarely has had much inclination to revisit old blues haunts. But one Sunday afternoon in 1997 she showed up unannounced at C. Davis, and it was something special.

I. J. Gosey, on his birthday, C. Davis Bar-B-Q, Sunnyside, 1995.

Martha Turner, C. Davis Bar-B-Q, Sunnyside, 1997.

Despite her lengthy absence from the venue, Turner obviously still had many friends and admirers among the regular customers. Gratefully surprised men and women rushed forward to greet her, hug her, joke with her, and reminisce. By the time she had made her way to a stage-side table (which had been quickly cleared and offered to her), Turner had a large wad of dollar bills in one hand and a drink in the other—spontaneous tokens of appreciation from the crowd.

An hour or so later she would finally step onstage and give them what they had been anticipating, reasserting her status as one of Sunnyside's favorite singers in the process. Her interchange with the audience was direct—the glistening eye contact and vivid body language, the witty banter between, even during, songs. She sang three numbers in a jazzy style, sometimes employing a mellow scat technique to improvise vocal riffs and punctuate a lyric. But thanks to her emotive delivery, she simultaneously conveyed a depth of primal passion, holding notes and shouting out key lines. And for Turner, that's the legacy of her roots holding true.

"I love the blues. It's a feeling," she explains. "You got to *feel* a song, you know. When a person comes into a club to see you, they enjoy your expression, not so much as what you're singing. They watch your face." In truth, during this particular homecoming performance at C. Davis, Turner's face and ample figure held the complete focus of the audience, triggering murmurs and shouts of approval with every nuance of expression. Veteran that she is, she intuitively grasps the psychology of vicarious experience. "You watch this person sing a song, and it's almost like you're doing it yourself. Know what I'm talking about? You enjoy that blues," she explains. "The blues is something you can identify with."

Another Sunnyside resident who shares Turner's insight and has also occasionally graced the C. Davis stage is Carolyn Blanchard. "Blessed with the gift of voice," as she says, she first sang blues as a child on the playground at St. Nicholas Catholic School, causing a disconcerted priest to summon her grandmother. But blessed also with a supportive family environment, including a mother who "had a blues [record] collection and a jazz collection out of this world," this distinctive, meticulous singer has performed the music for most of her life—in grand halls as far away as Italy as well as in little joints back home. Like Turner, she embodies a sophisticated elegance that initially seems out of place in the tin-roofed, concrete-floor establishment out on Reed Road. But surrounded by lifelong friends and the fundamental music of her upbringing, she readily embraces the blues—cutting loose with sassy interpretations of numbers such as "Ain't Nobody's Business If I Do."

Like so many of her Bayou City peers, Blanchard first formally took the stage as a teenager competing in talent shows at the old Club Ebony and Eldorado Ballroom in her native Third Ward. By age sixteen, she was also gigging at the once mighty Cinder Club further to the southeast. A few years later, she began touring in big bands led by Leo Baxter and Arnett Cobb, two of the most highly esteemed cultivators of local talent. "These were the blues masters in Houston," she says.

Carolyn Blanchard, 1997.

"They taught us and supported us so much!" As a result, Blanchard has traveled widely, ultimately performing in high-class jazz or blues revues "in forty-four different states, plus Europe" over the course of her career (a feat she mentions with obvious pride).

But these days she only occasionally ventures far from home or plays big concerts, the exceptions being appearances with Conrad Johnson and the Big Blue Sound in Houston or as a featured solo artist at the annual jazz festival down the coast in Corpus Christi. Yet when the mood would strike her, she could leave the fancy evening gowns in the closet, find a ride to nearby C. Davis Bar-B-Q, and sit in with Gosey and the band—no pretense, no dress code, just the straightforward music she craves. "Blues is a full-fledged feeling of emotion," she explains, "a gut feeling of life." And like many other musicians, Blanchard fondly recalls a special place in Sunnyside where everybody else understood.

One of the great (but largely unrecognized) Houston blues bands of the 1990s owed its very existence to the consistently cool music scene cultivated by Gosey at the old Reed Road eatery. The eight-piece group known as Mac & Company was the brainchild of saxophonist Wilbur McFarland (1937–1999), an Alabama native who came to Houston in 1962 and soon joined—on the bandstand and in the recording studio—Clarence Green and the Rhythmaires. After leaving Green in 1969, McFarland formed a fifteen-year affiliation with Gosey in a group that is most remembered for having featured a young Trudy Lynn on vocals. But all of that was merely the preface to his fulfillment of a personal dream nurtured during jam sessions at C. Davis.

In 1988, after decades of working for others, and encouraged by Gosey's advice, the gentlemanly giant of a sax man finally formed his own band. From the start, Mac & Company was an unapologetically horn-driven outfit, heavy on the brass (led by trumpeter Vurn Ollison) and reeds. But it also featured former gospel singer Joe Halliburton (b. 1940) on vocals. Teamed together, McFarland and Halliburton shaped that group into one of the most potent, crowd-pleasing ensembles in Houston, though it never played the mainstream venues or received the attention it merited from local media. The band's appeal was due in large part to its ability to balance apparently contradictory styles—from funky, muscular instrumentation with fierce blasts of horns and pulsating rhythms to tenderly soulful ballads and slow blues. Mac & Company could play it hard or soft.

This dualism was reflected in McFarland himself, a towering fellow who thrilled at honking his sax for frenzied late-night club audiences but who maintained a straight-laced, conservative lifestyle off stage. As this publicly "wild" man once confided to me with a sheepish grin during a 1997 interview, "All the years I've played, you know I have never drank, smoked, or did drugs in my life. Right now I'm sixty years old, and I don't even know how to hold a pool stick."

Like his mentor Gosey, McFarland was mainly interested in the music, not in the distractions readily available in the social scene that typically surrounds it. So even after formally parting from

Wilbur McFarland, C. Davis Bar-B-Q, Sunnyside, 1997.

Joe Halliburton, at home, Sunnyside, 1997.

Gosey to form his own band, he continued to show up at C. Davis Bar-B-Q to absorb new lessons. As he once explained about his friend and teacher:

> I've learned more with I. J., and he inspired me more than anybody I've ever played with. Because I. J., if it's on the chart, anywhere, he know it! He's a jazz-oriented guitar player, and the things that he's doing now, blues guitar players don't do any more. . . . He had more influence on me studying my horn and learning my horn than any musician I've played with, because he knew. And you can't teach anybody something you don't know.

Not only did Gosey push McFarland to greater mastery of his instrument, he also introduced him to Halliburton, the West Texas–born singer who would become an essential element of Mac & Company. After starting out as someone equally at home with both gospel and blues, Halliburton had abandoned the secular stage in the mid-1960s in deference to a wife who did not condone "singing in beer joints." So when that marriage ended in divorce in 1975, he found it difficult to establish himself on the local scene, despite his powerful tenor voice and impressive capacity for emotionally wrenching storytelling via song. "I had hell getting in this circuit when I first got started back," he admits. His eventual emergence depended on Gosey and the little barbecue place located not far from Halliburton's own Sunnyside residence.

"I. J. gave me the first chance," the singer gratefully recalls. "I'd go down there on Sundays, and I. J. would let me sit in, come up and do two numbers. He was the onliest guy that would do that. He took partial to me." It was during such jam sessions that McFarland first took notice of the spirited stranger crooning and raving into the microphone. "And then Wilbur'd come by, and we got to play together and know each other's styles," Halliburton says. "So when Wilbur got ready to step out and get his own band, he asked me if I'd be his lead vocalist."

Through the 1990s, Mac & Company performed occasionally on the regional nightclub circuit and sometimes opened shows for touring artists such as Bobby Bland, Tyrone Davis, Johnnie Taylor, Denise LaSalle, Marvin Sease, and others. But mainly the group appeared in venues obscure to most of Houston—places like the old Evening Shadows near Third Ward or the Silver Eagle, a spacious hall located on Reed Road not far from the smokehouse restaurant where McFarland and Halliburton first met.

The story of Mac & Company is just one example of how C. Davis Bar-B-Q—though it was located outside the historic inner-city wards where Houston blues originated—played a key role in the evolution of the local culture during the final quarter of the twentieth century, right up until it closed in May of 2001. Echoing the memories of McFarland and Halliburton, numerous other artists credit this makeshift music venue as the place where they got started or learned, the place

Little Joe Washington, C. Davis Bar-B-Q, Sunnyside, 1997.

Charles "C.C." Colson, C. Davis Bar-B-Q, Sunnyside, 1996.

where they met a crucial musical associate, or at least the place to which they often strategically retreated for a fresh infusion of the old blues spirit.

Some of them, such as Louisiana-born singer and pianist Charles "C.C." Carlson, made visits to Gosey's jam session an established part of their schedule of activities for many years. "Oh yeah, man, I've got to make it by here and see my people every week," he explained in 1996. "Sometimes I play and sometimes I just listen. But if I'm able, I'm usually here." The same could pretty much be said for numerous other musicians.

Big-voiced contralto Diunna Greenleaf, who is young enough to be one of Gosey's children, utilized a few impromptu appearances at C. Davis in the late 1990s to help establish her now rock-solid reputation among local blues veterans and fans. A Houston native, she reports she had never sung secular music in public until 1975, when, as an international exchange high school student in Denmark, she was coaxed (by the boyfriend of her host) to sing some blues and old-style R&B in a Danish band. Having been raised in a religiously devout family (her father was a founding member of the Spiritual Gospel Singers of Houston, Texas), Greenleaf returned to the United States inspired by her European debut as a blues singer but unwilling to disappoint her family. So she went to college (ultimately obtaining a degree in educational counseling), took a day job, and collected and studied blues records on the side.

Many years later, Greenleaf determined to pursue her long-simmering blues vision at last. Encouraged by the late Teddy Reynolds and others, she eventually began to make the rounds of local jam sessions. At C. Davis Bar-B-Q, she met Gosey and relished the guidance he had to offer as an experienced and unusually compassionate professional. Following a few enthusiastically received guest appearances on his stage at the restaurant, Greenleaf was motivated to assemble musicians and create her own band. By late 1998, a group billing itself as Diunna Greenleaf and Blue Mercy was performing in local venues, and in 1999 it represented the Houston Blues Society at an international talent competition in Memphis. Today Greenleaf's band works steadily on the local circuit, showcasing her powerful vocal delivery and wide-ranging repertoire of blues styles.

Greenleaf is just one of several younger performers who directly benefited from the musical environment created by the impeccable Gosey during his impressive twenty-eight-year tenure at C. Davis Bar-B-Q. Another is vocalist Roger Valentine (b. 1958), son of the late Houston singer Patience Valentine. Gosey has also welcomed numerous nonblack players as well, such as the youthful guitar phenomenon Brad McCool or the keyboard whiz Mike Stone. "Mr. Gosey's just so nice, and he's just so smooth. He's awesome, anything he does, oh yes," Greenleaf exclaims, adding, "He's taught me so much." And the Duke-Peacock veteran clearly enjoys the role he's assumed as a respected mentor to a whole new generation of blues performers.

But what makes Gosey treasure the memory of C. Davis Bar-B-Q the most is the uncommonly devoted fan base he discovered there. "I've been a lot of places, played a lot of clubs, but I haven't

Diunna Greenleaf, 1999.

played nowhere with the atmosphere and clientele that this place has," he told me in 1999. "These people *live* for Sundays and Tuesdays!" Though the weekend performance usually commenced after 4 P.M., "people'll be in here at one o'clock in the daytime," says an awestruck Gosey. "They come in here, get their tables, and sit and wait for us."

Most prominent in the standing-room-only Sunday crowd were the ladies' clubs from the surrounding neighborhood. In addition to the "Golden Girls," there were also the "Wonderful Ladies" and the "Golden Angels"—all of whom proudly hung paper banners staking claim to certain tables. "This is our place to hang out and socialize, especially on Sundays," one elderly woman told me in 1995. These unofficial sororities functioned like grateful pep squads for the blues.

For instance, I recall a scene from late 1999: As Gosey tears into a juicy instrumental improvisation, the women simultaneously raise hands toward the ceiling and ecstatically sway in unison, dancing without even standing up. During an especially earthy string-bender, several of them squeal intense encouragement. The guitarist smiles and shouts back, "Don't rush me now. Let me take my time. Ain't nothing good if you rush."

They all laugh together as he drops the tempo, then raises it back to a frenzy before nodding to the keyboardist, who unleashes an organ solo that fills the room with a crescendo of pulsing riffs. Finally, Gosey brings the moment to its teasingly delayed climax with his vocal exhortation to "Love me or leave me, either way you want to do"—a line that triggers an approving roar from the audience as the free-form jam segues back into a song.

Moments such as those made it clear that C. Davis Bar-B-Q served up something that the city's more popular (and cunningly marketed) mainstream blues-themed restaurants can never replicate: a palpable sense of community, a place where food and music and life are one.

beyond the old wards where Houston blues took root are various other venues of cultural significance, past and present. Veterans tell stories of great music and wild times at former edge-of-town establishments such as Sid's Ranch, where pianist Amos Milburn frequently performed in the late 1940s (before departing for California and stardom), or the Double Bar Ranch, noted by many musicians as an "after-hours place" to gather and play following an evening's work elsewhere around town. According to singer Luvenia Lewis, who performed there for eighteen years, "I'd get new life when I got through with the last gig and would go to the Double Bar Ranch." Her friend and fellow vocalist Big Robert Smith recalls that it was located "in the country," on a sandy road off of South Main, past the city limits sign. "We'd stay there until seven o'clock in the morning," Lewis adds.

During the same era, the north-side community of Trinity Gardens was home to the legendary Whispering Pines Night Club, which advertised itself as "Houston's Famous Dance House" and

Golden Angels, C. Davis Bar-B-Q, Sunnyside, 2001.

Sunday afternoon, C. Davis Bar-B-Q, Sunnyside, 1996.

featured a kitchen "specializing in Creole dishes." That's where notable guitarists such as Milton Hopkins and Roy Gaines first got started as young teenagers. They followed in the wake of Whispering Pines alumnus Lester Williams, later known as the composer and performer of the 1949 and 1951 nationwide hits "Wintertime Blues" (single 5000-B on the Macy's label) and "I Can't Lose with the Stuff I Use" (single 422 for the Specialty label). These successes earned the lifelong Houstonian the 1952 title "King of the Blues" in a newspaper poll and, starting that same year, a series of dates at Carnegie Hall sharing the bill with Dinah Washington (1924–1963).

By the 1970s most of the older establishments such as the Whispering Pines had closed down, but throughout the metropolitan area different venues appeared (and disappeared) as hot spots for live blues during the final third of the twentieth century. Some of these are well-known nightclubs in fashionable locations. But others, like much of the Houston scene, are less obvious.

For instance, since the May 2001 closing of C. Davis Bar-B-Q, Gosey and friends have carried on the tradition of gathering for Sunday-afternoon and Tuesday-night music sessions by relocating to the south-side joint known as Mr. Gino's. Though some of the band personnel has now changed, Gosey's group performs there with much the same gusto they once displayed inside the old smokehouse on Reed Road. And though some of the former C. Davis Bar-B-Q customers may have been unwilling or unable to make the transition to this replacement venue, many of the old regulars, and scores of new fans too, now seem right at home with Gosey at Mr. Gino's. Located in an old houselike structure on Cullen Blvd. just inside the 610 Loop South, this establishment— part down-home juke joint and part run-down urban disco—features a long bar, a raised bandstand with a dance floor, and significant spaciousness among the many nooks and crannies of the L-shaped wing and adjoining rooms that open into the primary performance area. And drawing larger crowds than could have ever fit into the cramped space at C. Davis Bar-B-Q, Mr. Gino's now functions as a major place for folks to congregate to hear blues, zydeco, jazz, and R&B—especially on Sundays when Gosey and company cut loose.

Meanwhile, just to the south back in Sunnyside, the old Ponderosa Club has sporadically functioned since the early 1960s as another out-of-the-way performance space for musicians such as Leo Morris (b. 1933), Oscar O'Bear, and Andy "Too Hard" Williams (b. 1932). Owned and operated for years by a black man who always wore a big cowboy hat and identified himself only as "Boss Cartwright," this spacious back-street club (replete with gaudy western décor) hardly looks like a haven for wide-open blues and old-school soul music. But on and off over recent years, it has truly been just that. The booking policy there has sometimes extended to female headliners such as versatile vocalist Faye Robinson, but more often than not it has featured gritty male guitarists, as exemplified by the trio mentioned above.

One person for whom the Ponderosa long functioned as a sort of second home is the obscure but talented Morris, a lanky former gospel singer who began playing blues guitar after moving to

Sunday afternoon, Mr. Gino's, 2001.

"Boss" Cartwright, Ponderosa Club, Sunnyside, 1999.

Houston from south Louisiana in 1953. Over the next two decades, he worked professionally backing the likes of Peppermint Harris, Earl Forest, and Big Walter "the Thunderbird" Price, as well as various others. In 1960, he recorded a couple of original singles under his own name for the small but important Ivory Records, the Houston label created by Ivory Lee Semien. But in a city full of players with ties to blues history, Morris is largely unrecognized today, even by the most serious fans. His primary identity among many folks on the south side of town is simply that of proprietor and lead mechanic at M&M Motors, an auto repair shop he's operated since the mid-1970s. On the other hand, to Ponderosa regulars such as O'Bear, who has frequently accompanied Morris onstage and credits him as a teacher of advanced guitar techniques, he is as respected a musician as any bluesman in town.

During my 1998 visit to his residence in Sunnyside, Morris warmed up a wobbly turntable and played his cuts "I Want to Know How You Feel" and "I Don't Need You" from an original 45 RPM Ivory disc that he keeps wrapped in plastic on a living-room shelf. While each side of that scratchy record spun, he sat on the couch, shut his eyes, and patted a large open palm against one thigh, keeping time with the music—and seemingly blissfully remembering another era. Later that weekend, at my request, he reprised the first of these numbers live onstage at the Ponderosa. Clearly enjoying the opportunity to give me a history lesson, Morris worked biting solos on his Gibson 335 guitar and bellowed lyrics over a rousing Texas shuffle groove, his sudden blast of energy compelling a swarm of dancers onto the large wooden floor near the raised stage. For that moment, he sang and played the blues with as much passion and precision as anyone in the city. Yet given his age, his weekday commitment to M&M Motors, and his comfort in playing mainly only on Sunday evenings at this neighborhood club, I realized he would likely never seek or find higher-profile gigs—and thus would remain unknown to most of the contemporary local audience for blues. Nevertheless, at the Ponderosa, he was a star.

The club's clientele, at least during my visits there in the late 1990s, consisted mainly of middle-aged to older African Americans, a sizable number of whom shared Boss Cartwright's self-identification with cowboy culture, obviously signified by the style of hats, belts, and boots they wore. Of course, there were exceptions—and some of the customers exuded a distinctly urban fashion sensibility, visually disavowing any connection to the mythic Old West. But, as is the norm at several black-owned-and-operated blues venues around Houston, a segment of the audience typically arrived decked out in attire worthy of Roy Rogers. Such is the case with some performers too, including another common presence on the Ponderosa stage, Andy "Too Hard" Williams.

This Andy Williams—obviously not to be confused with the similarly named pop singer and television personality—often appeared at the Ponderosa (and elsewhere) in regalia ranging from ten-gallon headgear to western vest to huge silver belt buckle and pointed-toe boots, sometimes even sporting a ring featuring a cluster of diamonds arranged in the shape of a horseshoe. Yet his

Leo Morris, at home, Sunnyside, 1998.

music is strictly electric blues and traditional R&B devoid of any country-and-western references. For him, as indeed for most of the similarly dressed black people around the city, the cowboy fashion aesthetic is not necessarily an indicator of any particular musical preference. Maybe, consciously or not, it's a sartorial tribute to their Texas heritage—or merely the consequence of some impulse to look cool. Whatever the case, to the casual observer, Williams probably sounds different than he looks, a reminder not to judge merely by appearance or label.

Yet, as his nickname suggests, there is something *hard* about the way Williams plays the blues. The amiable left-hander came by his distinctive moniker the honest way. That is, he didn't invent it himself (as performers tend to do) but had it bestowed on him by an acute observer—Marty Racine, a former *Houston Chronicle* music writer who critiqued Williams' fierce and chunky flat-picking style as being "too hard"—and the label just stuck. But the fact that he received any notice whatsoever from a journalist with the city's major daily newspaper emphasizes a key difference between Williams and Leo Morris, who are otherwise two equals on the Ponderosa stage.

Morris has gigged professionally in Houston for almost fifty years, but he's usually played in all-black bands in black-owned clubs in parts of town that remain largely invisible to the nonblack population. On the other hand, Williams—who spent eighteen years on the West Coast before returning to Houston in 1977—has often sought and found work, whether leading his own band or backing other artists, not only in the black-owned establishments but also in venues that draw large numbers of whites. For instance, he used to play second guitar and sing in a racially integrated band (the Essentials) led by Jerry Lightfoot, one of the most popular, accomplished, and respected white blues-rockers in the city's history. This work has introduced and established Williams on a certain segment of the local music circuit that Morris will never know. Yet Williams is also clearly at home in places like the Ponderosa. The point is, he's just as apt to be found, in the audience or on the stage, in either type of venue—the white-owned clubs in the major entertainment districts or the black-owned joints in the old neighborhoods.

This fundamental difference between the two men illustrates perhaps the primary dividing line between all contemporary African American blues interpreters in Houston. With a variety of motives and results, some have sought and found opportunity, employment, and hence an audience beyond the black community, beyond the culture where the music originated. However, for an infinite number of possible reasons, others have not. Does that distinction make one of these two groups more authentic than the other? More professional? More culturally significant? More satisfied? Not necessarily—for such qualities are better assessed in individuals than in sweeping generalizations. Moreover, integrity (and its opposite) is to be found among people on both sides of this basic divide. These days, whether or not an African American musician plays the blues for audiences predominantly of his own race seems to depend largely on opportunity, nothing more. Now, how he or she plays the blues—the manner in which the tradition is interpreted—may be another matter altogether. But when it comes to the business of music, obviously the wider the range of exposure, the better a performer's chance for recognition and economic reward. Ultimately, it's the musician's choice where and among whom to perform. Most seize whatever opportunities they can.

At any rate, though Williams has hardly gotten rich playing blues all over Houston, he has been successful enough to self-produce a CD, appropriately titled *Left Hand Soul* (Dal-Segno Records), as well as to establish himself on the list of "name" players on the Lone Star scene. In 1996, this reputation secured him an invitation to the Long Beach Blues Festival in California, where he shared the stage with Clarence "Gatemouth" Brown, Lowell Fulson, Cal Green, and some of the other finest Texas pickers in a grand finale "Tribute to T-Bone Walker." But for the most part, Williams is just a fixture on the local circuit, playing gigs and jam sessions at a wide variety of clubs, whatever the racial demographic. In short, like many of Houston's African American blues players at the dawn of the twenty-first century, he's comfortable going it both ways. He just wants to play.

One other-end-of-the-cultural-spectrum performing environment where an open-minded bluesman such as Williams might now venture is located north of White Oak Bayou in the Heights, a historic (formerly predominantly white) neighborhood long noted for its namesake boulevard graced with grand Victorian-era houses. In its northeastern quadrant, on a residential street lined with large trees and sturdy working-class bungalows, there stands a dingy and sprawling wood-frame building fronted by a pot-hole-prevalent gravel parking lot. Whatever functions it may have served in previous years (including, reportedly, once housing a popular Italian restaurant), in its current incarnation (dating back to 1988), it's one of Houston's strangest places to hear the blues: Dan Electro's Guitar Bar.

Inside, the wood-paneled walls are covered with scores of vintage guitars of all types, each hanging vertically, headstock up. Apart from the impressive display of stringed instruments, the typical neon-lit beer sign appears here and there amid scattered forms of psychedelic artwork—surreal and colorful hand-painted images that clue the first-time visitor to the essential hippie ambience permeating the place. A triangular stage straddles the main corner of the large L-shaped room; the immediate background and bandstand are covered with black-light-activated paper featuring a pattern of eerily glowing star shapes. The people who take the stage there can range from long-haired roots rockers to African American blues and soul traditionalists to bizarrely conceptual performance artists. Apart from the occasional benefit fund-raiser or special event, the key mixing time for such disparate factions is the long-running weekly blues jam. Though it started out as a Monday-night ritual, this event shifted to Thursdays years ago under the leadership of guitarists such as Teri Greene. Since then, it's become a showcase and a proving ground for large numbers of local players, professionals and amateurs, old style and progressive, black and white and other.

Andy "Too Hard" Williams, Dan Electro's Guitar Bar, The Heights, 2001.

Although the focus on straight blues performance may typically be limited to only one evening per week at Dan Electro's, it's the almost nightly norm at the southwest-side establishment called the Big Easy, a perennial winner in the annual *Houston Press* Music Awards in the category of "Best Blues Venue." Located on a major thoroughfare, Kirby Drive, near the upscale Rice Village shopping district, it enjoys unusually high visibility for an independently owned blues club, obviously a contributing factor in its success. But there are other reasons adults of various ages and races consistently flock to this casual mid-sized joint.

For starters, though the name and decorative theme (including a purple and gold façade) reveal founder Pete Selin's fascination with all things in a New Orleans style, the booking policy almost exclusively celebrates the strength and diversity of the contemporary Houston blues scene. Selin had come to appreciate the rich pool of available local talent while previously operating two high-profile establishments: Club Hey Hey (1987–1990) and Pat & Pete's Bonton Room (1990–1993), both of which had focused primarily on regional and national touring acts, and only secondarily on Bayou City musicians. But since its opening in 1994, the Big Easy has featured practically every major blues player in town—regardless of race—and many of those on a regular basis. This emphasis became even more pronounced after Selin sold out to partner Tom McLendon, a capable harmonica player who occasionally sits in with the bands that grace his stage. Live blues performances happen every Tuesday through Saturday—featuring established veteran units such as Texas Johnny Brown and the Quality Blues Band as well as relatively younger groups such as Tommy Dardar and the Sheetrockers—and live zydeco each Sunday. Perhaps most importantly, with the exception of the rare show by a regional touring artist (which happens usually no more than two or three times per year), there is never a cover charge.

The Big Easy has also been home base for a wide variety of successful midweek jam sessions hosted by an established cast of savvy male and female players from various backgrounds. For most of the late 1990s, the Tuesday-night shows were anchored by African American guitarist Leonard "Low Down" Brown, a native of Indiana who worked first in gospel, soul, and pop before moving to Houston in 1981 and settling into a Texas blues groove. Conversely, during that same era, the Wednesday-night jams were led by guitarist Rick Lee (b. 1955), a lifelong Houstonian of Asian ancestry who regularly entertains audiences with table-walking renditions of his signature song, "Can a Chinese Man Play the Blues?" Those who've preceded or followed Brown and Lee in such roles at the Big Easy include bassist Allison Fisher, retro fingerpicker "Harlem Slim" (the performing name for Gary Pisarelli), and many others. Since 1995, on the last Thursday of each month, the club has also staged a special program sponsored by the Houston Blues Society that features a paid set by a highlighted artist followed by an open jam. This event has triggered some of the most heavily attended and impressive musical interchanges among the different segments of the greater Houston blues community—bridging gaps of race, age, style, and experience.

Leonard "Low Down" Brown, 1997.

But for photographer James Fraher and me, the Big Easy has also been an especially important place because of our opportunity to conduct some of our fieldwork in its side room; nominally an office, the space previously housed McLendon's short-lived CD shop, Yeah You Right Records. Thanks to the owner's standing invitation, on several occasions over almost three years we were able to utilize that area (located in the northern front corner of the one-story building) as a designated meeting site for interviews and photograph sessions with certain blues artists. Those we worked with there range from female singers such as Lavelle White and Pearl Murray to keyboard players such as Earl Gilliam to numerous guitarists, including Jimmy "Louisiana" Dotson (b. 1934), Oscar Perry, and others. An easily accessible sanctuary from most club noise and intrusion, this spacious office proved an amenable setting for documentary work and good-spirited conversations with a wide variety of blues people.

Among the many memorable interchanges we experienced there, perhaps the most surprising occurred the evening we had an appointment with drummer/pianist/singer and former record-company owner and producer Ivory Lee Semien, also known as "King" Ivory Lee. Like so many other Louisiana Creoles, Semien had migrated to Houston years ago, settling here in 1949 and immersing himself in the Fifth Ward and Third Ward music scenes. Unlike most of them, however, he not only succeeded as a professional musician (playing in the 1950s with stars such as the original "Guitar Slim" as well as Houston lap-steel guitar ace Harding "Hop" Wilson); he also established himself as a maverick entrepreneur on various levels of the independent record business. In 1960, Ivory Records was created; its logo featured a simple drawing of an elephant with gigantic tusks. By then, Semien already owned a music store and TV repair shop called Top Ten Records, located on Lyons Avenue, Fifth Ward's main drag. He had previously recorded on the Alameda label in 1954. But it was with his namesake company that Semien ultimately made his major mark—especially after performing on and releasing the Wilson original "My Woman Has Got a Black Cat Bone" (Ivory 127), a regional hit that was later reprised in a duet by Johnny Copeland and Albert Collins on the Grammy-nominated 1985 album *Showdown!* on Alligator (AL 4743). In addition to songs by Wilson, Ivory Records produced and issued singles by D. C. Bender (aka Bobby Dee, b. 1919), zydeco accordionist Lonnie Mitchell, Leo Morris, Semien himself, and various other Bayou City bluesmen, even the great Lightnin' Hopkins.

By the mid-1970s, however, Semien seems to have abandoned the music business and devoted himself to other interests, breaking contacts with many members of the local blues community in the process. Among some former associates, there were unsubstantiated rumors and innuendoes speculating about his involvement in various inappropriate activities. Other people simply presumed that Semien, long absent from the scene, was dead. Then in 1995, under the name "King Ivory," he unexpectedly released a new batch of recordings on a CD called *The Bitch Done Quit Me* on the Home Cooking/Collectables label (COL 5562). Semien's apparent reemergence in music might have been cause for some excitement among fans; however, most of the initial enthusiasm was soon tempered as folks became aware of his public affiliation with an unusually notorious figure.

The producer for Semien's new disc was the Home Cooking label founder, Roy C. Ames (b. 1937)—a one-time minor employee of Duke-Peacock Records who went on to be a controversial early manager for Texas-born blues-rock guitarist Johnny Winter (b. 1944). Ames is also a former federal prison inmate and a man distrusted and denounced by numerous local blues musicians. The extent of that antipathy is best evidenced by the class action lawsuit filed against Ames in August 1994 (with Jerry and Nina Green of Pennsylvania-based Collectables Records named as co-defendants) on behalf of fifteen Houston artists or their descendants. The plaintiffs included Leonard Brown, Roger Collins, Clarence Green, Joe Hughes, Rayfield Jackson, Pete Mayes, Jimmy Nelson, Walter Price, Kinney Abair, Lee Frazier, Al Bottis, Tommy Dardar, Clarence Parker, Lizette Cobb (on behalf of her deceased father, bandleader/saxophonist Arnett Cobb), and Debra Nickerson (on behalf of her deceased father, Weldon "Juke Boy" Bonner). In March of 1997, a federal jury ruled against Ames, with damages awarded in the amount of over a quarter million dollars. But as of the start of 2002, that judgment is still on appeal, and the plaintiffs have yet to receive any monetary settlement from the case.

By the mid-1990s, Ames was already generally perceived as a villain in (and beyond) most Houston blues circles, having been the subject of many angry conversations as well as a 1994 cover-story exposé by Jim Sherman in the *Houston Press* (a piece later reprinted in the internationally circulated magazine *Blues Access,* which also ran a follow-up article by Aaron Howard in 1997). As a result, there was an understandable sense of alienation among some former Semien acquaintances when he elected to be a willing participant in any project coordinated by Ames. In fact, I too was uneasy when I initially talked by telephone to Semien and set a September 26, 1996, appointment for a photo session in the Big Easy office. Given all the bad things I'd heard muttered or seen printed about Ames, plus the implicit (and occasionally explicit) condemnation of Semien I now discovered among other musicians, I wasn't sure what to expect. Yet I knew that Semien had played an important role in postwar Houston blues history, and I was thrilled to have located this previously underground figure (thanks to a chance encounter with his daughter Teresa [aka "Reci," b. 1957], a strong singer herself). So I scheduled the meeting and hoped he would keep the date.

Semien showed up right on time, accompanied by an apparent bodyguard and valet named Earl Sinclair (b. 1927), a large man who identified himself as a Galveston native and a member of the family. Semien also brought along his twenty-something-year-old son and some of his youthful friends, who presumed to set up a huge boombox and PA system in the Big Easy back parking lot and to perform, loudly, a fairly monotonous sequence of rap—to the obvious confusion of early-arriving customers. During the photo shoot, the sharply dressed Semien was cooperative and

Ivory Lee Semien, Big Easy, 1996.

intelligent, even charming, though he seemed a bit suspicious as well as puzzled and intrigued by our motive for wanting to meet with him.

Then, near the conclusion of the session, he suddenly broke into a relieved smile and—looking over my shoulder to an otherwise anonymous white man who had just entered the room behind me—proudly proceeded to introduce his "manager and producer," none other than Ames. I was momentarily stunned. Here, in a side room at the city's most popular blues club, was a man many people (numbers of whom were then standing just beyond that closed office door) had come to despise by reputation. To them, as to me, any reality of Ames was blurred by his almost mythic status as an alleged blues pirate and a recluse, a malicious force complained about but never seen. And now, I realized, he had stepped out of the realm of gossip or accusation and was physically standing there before me, eyes scanning the room.

The fair-haired Ames extended a hand and, in a soft drawl, identified himself. He asked who we were, then immediately inquired about our intentions in photographing and interviewing his artist. After simply telling Ames we had "heard about" him and then summarizing the documentary focus of our fieldwork, Fraher and I mainly just listened. Ames talked at length, rattling off the names (and his assessment of the talents) of various artists he had "worked with" over the years, never mentioning any lawsuits or disagreements. He bragged about unspecified but rare memorabilia he claimed to possess. For some reason, he seemed eager to impress us. Then he abruptly returned to his basic theme, the ironic reason he had paid us this unexpected visit: the need to protect his client, Semien, from being ripped off by unscrupulous people in the music business. After apparently convincing himself that we were no threat to his interests (and seeing that the photo session had concluded), Ames quietly departed, accompanied by two younger male associates he had introduced as his employees.

Ames left that office and passed through the main club, now filled with people awaiting the night's first set of live music. No one seemed to notice him. But that's not surprising, as only his name, not his face, was familiar to most local blues fans. I would not encounter him again, though I continue to hear that name invoked in reference to financial exploitation of blues musicians.

After a few minutes, Semien himself shook my hand and, along with his entourage, departed also. I would see him again, soon, in circumstances considerably different than these.

Several weeks later I tried to contact Semien in order to deliver some recently received complimentary prints from that photo session. Upon calling his home number, I learned from his distraught wife that he had suffered a stroke and was getting medical care at Ben Taub General Hospital, the city's primary charity institution—a place immortalized in an old Juke Boy Bonner song, "It's a Struggle Here in Houston" (on *Life Gave Me a Dirty Deal,* 1992, Arhoolie CD 375). Hoping to visit Semien and deliver the prints, maybe even cheer him up, I spent a confusing afternoon trying unsuccessfully to locate him among the hundreds of indigent cases housed in the

Ben Taub wards. After receiving lots of incorrect information, I was finally told that Semien was being transferred, that very hour, to another institution several miles away.

Following some more detective work by telephone, a few days later I visited the Quentin Mease Community Hospital, a relatively new facility located on the northern bank of Brays Bayou on Third Ward's southeastern edge. However, upon arriving at the double-occupancy room and locating the bed assigned to Lee Semien, I found it empty. Additional inquiries eventually led me to a large and mostly vacant dining area, where about a dozen patients were receiving a midafternoon meal—each one being fed by hand, a spoonful at a time, by a personal attendant. As I walked slowly across the floor toward the group, I could hear the caregivers' occasional verbal encouragement, reminiscent of baby talk, urging the incapacitated patients to eat. Except for some inarticulate groaning, the patients themselves were silent. Most of them dutifully received the offered bites of food; others resisted in an agitated manner; a few just stared blankly, mouths agape. After discreetly surveying the scene, I recognized Semien's now drastically changed face among those in this last group. Unchewed mashed potatoes, placed in his open mouth by a hopeful attendant, were spilling down his chin. As I looked on, I was shocked by the horrible transformation that had occurred in the weeks since meeting the dapper and self-confident Semien at that photo session at the Big Easy. Could this really be the same man?

Finally, I stepped forward, introduced myself to the supervisor, and asked if I could speak to one of the patients at the table. "Sure," she replied, then added, "but it probably won't do any good."

Bending down into his line of vision, I looked Semien directly in the face and said, "You're 'King Ivory,' aren't you?" His expression changed immediately, indicating he had heard me—or at least seen me—and he seemed surprised, maybe even troubled, by the way I addressed him. Then, speaking to all those present in the room, I announced, "Folks, this is 'King' Ivory Lee Semien, the legendary blues artist and entrepreneur." As I presumed to relate a few key facts about the man's life in music, I also opened a folder and produced several eight-by-ten photographic portraits, showing them one at a time to the silent but transfixed Semien and a couple of mildly interested attendants. "We want you to have these photographs, Mr. Semien," I finally said, placing them all back in a large envelope and setting it atop the table near him. He intently gazed at me, as if trying to remember something, then back at the package. For some reason, I reached over and opened it again, extracted one print, and placed it on the surface before him. It was a tight shot: his neatly groomed, smiling face was partially encompassed by the nimbus formed from the underside brim of his Panama hat. He locked it in his focus, studied it, then tears began to stream down his grizzled cheeks.

Though I subsequently would communicate with members of his family and call his case to the attention of the Musician Benevolent Society of Houston, I would not again have the opportunity to visit the man once known by the royal title "King Ivory." So I'm left with these two contrasting images of him: the pitiful stroke victim crying helplessly in a community rehabilitation facility and the cocky bluesman posing suavely during a photo shoot in a nightclub office. In neither case do I feel I ever really knew the man. Looking back and trying to sort through all I'd been told and what I briefly observed before his stroke, one thing seems clear: Semien had recently, maybe even defiantly, been operating outside of the old blues community of his peers—going his own way, for better or worse. As a result, he remains to me an enigmatic figure.

From the start, Semien had been willing to meet at the Big Easy because he was not only curious about our interest in him but also, according to his own admission, eager to visit this particular establishment. "There are black people *and* white people there, right?" he had asked in our initial telephone conversation. Though he said he had never previously been on the premises, he evidently knew the reputation of the club as a highly popular venue for live blues. And, based on some offhand comments he made during the photo session, I believe he was possibly interested in being booked to perform there himself. Of course, his subsequent health crisis changed everything. But Semien's apparent insight about the Big Easy remains valid. Since 1994, no other blues venue has appealed to a sizable and somewhat racially integrated crowd with more consistency than this Kirby Drive club. But it certainly hasn't been the only place to do so in Houston.

Although isolated incidents of racial integration had occurred at least as far back as the final years of the Bronze Peacock, and though ethnically diverse audiences are fairly common in certain Houston establishments today, there wasn't a true blues place that regularly attracted a balanced mix until the advent of the Reddi Room in the early 1980s. Located in the Heights, originally just down the street from the more popular Fitzgerald's (which then featured mostly rock and some blues, and was a favorite performance venue for Stevie Ray Vaughan [1954–1990] before his rise to superstardom), the Reddi Room was unique. Operated by an African American businesswoman, this low-light lounge was a rare place where white college kids, young professionals of all races, and middle-aged working-class blacks congregated comfortably on a weekly basis.

For most of its existence, at both the first location on White Oak Street and the larger spot it moved to (in 1995) on nearby Washington Avenue, the Reddi Room was known in the Bayou City as "Home of the Blues," a slogan propagated on bumper stickers and on its storefront signage. But as was pointed out by guitarist Milton Hopkins, the player with the lengthiest tenure there (from 1984 to 1997), it didn't exactly originate as a blues haven. Hopkins teamed with vocalist and drummer Ardis Turner (b. 1939) and jazz organist Bobby Selby (b. 1936) in some of the earliest Reddi Room gigs—before it assumed its ultimate identity. Though Hopkins had worked for years in the B.B. King band and Turner would later go on to lead popular blues jams at a late-1990s Shepherd Plaza club, they somehow assumed back then that the Reddi Room audience and management desired a more sophisticated repertoire. "It wasn't really jazz, just a line of old standards. And we

The Reddi Room sign, 1996.

did that for about six or eight weeks," Hopkins recalls. But popular demand would eventually redirect their focus. He continues:

> Then one night somebody at the bar kept yelling for a blues tune. And Bobby Selby hated to play blues. And somebody said, "They can't play no blues." So somebody else come up there and put a big tip up on Bobby's organ—for blues.
>
> And the owner say, "Can you guys play the blues?" Well, hell yes, Ardis and I sure could! We grew up on blues, all our lives. And hey man, that was it. It wasn't no more jazz the rest of the night. And we lost Bobby Selby right away.

From that experience, Hopkins went on to assemble and lead a complete blues band, which could range in size from four to eight pieces, often including a powerful horn section featuring venerable saxophonist Robert Phelps (b. 1927). With Turner (who ultimately concentrated on vocals, giving up drumming due to arthritis) and Hopkins as the core, various permutations of this unit played a tasteful, jazz-inflected blues and classic R&B at the Reddi Room every Friday and Saturday for most of the 1980s and 1990s.

Over the years, the club sometimes scheduled live music on additional nights of the week, featuring performances by Big Robert Smith, Joe James, Jerry Lightfoot, and others. However, given his prime-time longevity there, for many people Milt Hopkins—the nattily tailored cousin of the city's most famous guitarist (i.e., Lightnin' Hopkins)—simply *was* the Reddi Room, or vice versa. And through this younger Hopkins and his fellow musicians, this now defunct establishment introduced folks from a variety of cultural backgrounds to the live power of Houston blues.

So, too, did a place appropriately called Local Charm. New Year's Eve of 1994 sadly marked the closing of this southeast-side institution, essentially a neighborhood bar in an old corner grocery building in the multiethnic working-class community along upper Telephone Road. It also was an extraordinarily quaint venue for live music. Founded by native Houstonian Rory Miggins (b. 1955) in 1985, Local Charm featured bands reflecting his love of Gulf Coast blues, zydeco, and roots rock—as well as his close personal friendships with many of the city's longtime practitioners of those idioms. Customers could range from middle-aged and elderly residents of the area to college students from the University of Houston. But most were young professionals who savored the sheer authenticity of this joint—both its aging, memorabilia-packed structure and the down-home music available there. It was there that I (like various other relative newcomers to the city) first directly witnessed some of the undiminished vitality of Houston blues, personified onstage in players such as Texas Johnny Brown, Grady Gaines, Jerry Lightfoot, and Big Walter "the Thunderbird" Price. And it was there that I first realized these musical masters were also—offstage at least—regular people, accessible individuals with stories to tell.

Starting off the year 1995 with the knowledge that Local Charm had closed, I was depressed—and annoyed at myself for not visiting there more frequently (a temptation I had somehow largely resisted while balancing Ph.D. work and a full-time job). Miggins and his partners had done their best, I knew, to pay the musicians what they deserved and keep the place afloat financially. But the white professional clientele's support (on which the business ultimately depended) could be fickle—particularly because this humble club was located in such an out-of-the-way neighborhood beyond the regular entertainment districts. This closure seemed to me yet another example of postmodern Houston insufficiently appreciating certain fascinating elements of its own cultural heritage. It stoked my cynicism, as well as my sense of complicity and regret.

However, coming as it did within a few months of my completion of seven years of doctoral studies, the loss of Local Charm also prompted me to do a couple of things. I vowed to seek out other places to experience the hometown flavors of this music; I was hooked and intensely craved more. Also, without a dissertation demanding my spare time, I began to think more purposefully about pursuing a whole new project: doing deeper research into the city's African American blues people. Where this undertaking might lead I then had no specific idea. But the spirit I had discovered among musicians and clientele at places like Local Charm (which briefly resurfaced at a new location in 2001) made me certain I would be making some wonderful friends.

of course, the Bayou City is an especially spread-out metropolis. Hence, an important factor in the staying power of its homegrown blues scene has been the rise of viable racially mixed venues for the music in certain more distant parts of suburbia. For instance, on the far west side—the area experiencing the greatest population expansion in recent decades—one club in particular emerged in early 1990 as a spot for all types of people to hear authentic live performances. Located well beyond Beltway 8 in a small strip center along the decidedly upper-middle-class thoroughfare called Memorial Drive, the Shakespeare Pub might seem to be an unlikely name, in an even more unlikely place, to find some of the best blues talent in town. But since its inception, this casual joint has consistently highlighted blues and zydeco traditionalists, as well as some of the more established (and generally younger) white artists, such as the harmonica ace and bandleader known as "Sonny Boy Terry" (Terry Jerome, b. 1959), a former sideman for Johnny Copeland, Joe Hughes, and others.

The idea for Shakespeare's (as it's most commonly called) originated with San Jacinto College professor and native Houstonian Eddie Black, whose son Pat now manages the business. Impressed by the quality of roots music readily available in older, centrally located, African American parts of the city, the father-son duo hired and exported some of that talent to the comfortable midsized club they opened approximately twenty miles due west of downtown. Bringing a little bit of Third or Fifth Ward to the culturally sterile suburbs was part of their vision from the start—and that foresight, along with the general friendliness that abounds inside this pub, has been the basis of their continuing success. As a result, for black players such as Hughes, Pete Mayes, Oscar Perry, Don Kesee, Eugene "Sparetime" Murray, Little Joe Washington, and many others, the Shakespeare Pub has become a second home—despite its location in a far-flung area of town they otherwise would rarely have reason to visit. And though the typical audience there is predominantly white, this wood-paneled room with the big U-shaped bar regularly attracts some black clientele too. Whatever their ethnic credentials, people crowd into this laid-back place up to five nights per week to hear locally nurtured live music performed on a raised stage featuring a large Texas state flag as a backdrop.

A sense of interracial community especially pervades this club during its annual "Blues for Food" marathon jam session, an event that takes place each November or December to collect thousands of pounds of canned goods for a local charity. The same spirit holds true as well during the occasional fund-raising concert benefiting a musician in need. Such traditions illustrate a genuine commitment not only to the music but also to the people among whom it originated and developed. Consequently, for players such as Big Roger Collins (who, until his death in October 2001, was a major force in organizing benefit shows there), the Shakespeare's staff and ownership have genuinely been considered to be "like my family" (as he told me one night, demanding they be allowed to join him as he posed for a photograph between sets).

Of course, by the start of the twenty-first century, numerous other clubs have at least occasionally brought some of the city's top African American blues artists to the suburbs. For instance, on the far north side in the community of Humble, there's Cactus Moon; a bit closer in there's Club Hole in the Wall; on the west side there's the Hideaway; and in the really distant southeastern suburbs near NASA headquarters, there's the former Outpost Tavern, a favorite watering hole for astronauts and engineers. These and several other outer-Loop establishments have sporadically offered noteworthy live blues music, including regional touring acts in some cases.

Back inside the 610 Loop, additional establishments, especially just west of downtown, feature prominent local African American blues players on any given weekend night. Several of these can be found along Washington Avenue, including Silky's Blues Bar, Walter's on Washington, the Rhythm Room, and occasionally even the Fabulous Satellite Lounge. In the Heights, the venerable old music hall Fitzgerald's, despite focusing mainly on youth-oriented alternative rock in recent years, still schedules blues shows once in a rare while. For instance, acclaimed Chicago guitarist Hubert Sumlin (b. 1931), a former longtime sideman with the blues icon known as "Howlin' Wolf" (Chester Burnett, 1910–1976), delivered a wonderful performance there in March 2000, backed by Joe Hughes and his band.

Meanwhile, in the gradually rejuvenating downtown entertainment district, a few of the res-

Milton Hopkins, Reddi Room, 1996.

Big Roger Collins Band, Shakespeare Pub, 1995.

taurants (especially Harlon's Bayou Blues, a cafeteria-style barbecue eatery) and upscale night-clubs also occasionally book Houston blues groups. In the Midtown area just south of the central business district, the Continental Club regularly offers free Happy Hour blues performances at least two days a week, which have mainly featured Little Joe Washington, Carol Fran, and I. J. Gosey since the club's opening in 2000.

But none of the mainstream venues mentioned above, suburban or not, can rival the Shakespeare Pub for its comfortable ambience for black musicians, its unwavering booking policy, and its longevity of survival as an institution.

Yet there is another establishment that—given its large size, prominent location, corporate backing, and resultant ability to attract both national touring acts and top local talent—was probably the most publicly noticed blues venue to emerge in the city during the 1990s. It's also a site where people of various races came together to dig the music and, on occasion at least, could establish a broader conception of a Bayou City blues community.

Ask most Houston residents to identify the more popular entertainment districts, and you're likely to hear something about the Richmond Strip on the southwest side. Intersecting the 610 Loop just below the so-called Uptown area (location of many famous shrines to upscale consumerism such as the Galleria and Neiman Marcus), this stretch of the east-west boulevard named Richmond is home to multiple popular restaurants and flashy nightclubs. The latter tend to specialize in youth-oriented dance music, pop rock cover bands, and DJs. Some of the restaurants (such as the Magnolia Bar & Grill) have featured live blues, jazz, or zydeco performances from time to time. But in February 1993, a completely different kind of venue opened there. Like many of the others, it was large, expensively designed and decorated, and reminiscent of a mini theme park, complete with gift shop. But through the turn of the millennium, this combination restaurant and nightclub was devoted almost exclusively to marketing, if not always celebrating, blues. Its focus, unique for the Strip, is suggested not only by its name but also by its primary architectural embellishment: a sixty-two-foot-tall folk-art sculpture depicting a saxophone painted a deep blue. Created from various odds and ends (including the body of an old Volkswagen Beetle, beer barrels, industrial conduits, a surfboard, and other miscellanies), this gigantic icon still looms (though now repainted red) over the 6000 block of Richmond Avenue, signifying the former home of Billy Blues Bar & Grill.

Originally both a full-scale barbecue restaurant and a nightly music performance venue (with a total capacity of nearly 600 customers), until its demise in 2001, Billy Blues hosted concerts by some of the most internationally famous names in late-twentieth-century blues as well as much of the local talent in the genre. Practically every major 1990s-era player in the city has worked that stage at least once—some headlining their own gigs, others hosting or participating in jam sessions. And many have also made appearances at Billy Blues for special events—ranging from

Luvenia Lewis, Ashton Savoy, Faye Robinson, Carolyn Blanchard, Trudy Lynn, Mickie Moseley, Living Blues Bash, Billy Blues, 1997.

Pearl Murray, Big Easy, 1997.

benefit concerts for fellow musicians in need, to postmortem tributes to former colleagues, to large-scale showcases such as the original "Houston Living Blues Bash" in 1997 (which featured over thirty artists profiled in issue 131 of *Living Blues* magazine).

Decorated with artwork and memorabilia commemorating local and regional figures (including some of Benny Joseph's superb 1950s-era photographic portraits of Lightnin' Hopkins, Clarence "Gatemouth" Brown, Albert Collins, Texas Johnny Brown, and others), this venue in its original conception offered the casual tourist a short course in Bayou City blues history. Of course, the main lessons came not from the materials exhibited on the walls but from the performances played on the large stage. People out cruising the Richmond Strip might drop in and unexpectedly discover the vintage swing of a bona fide bluesman such as Jimmy "T-99" Nelson, the melodic pyrotechnics of a guitar slinger such as Joe Hughes, the funky energy of a relatively younger bandleader such as saxophonist Aubrey Dunham (b. 1948), or the versatile grace of a seasoned vocalist such as Pearl Murray. In this way, Billy Blues introduced some of the city's African American musicians to entirely new audiences.

The case of Murray illustrates the point. This Texas native first established herself as a nightclub singer after moving to New York with her husband, Lee, in the early 1960s. Following Murray's success performing in talent competitions at places such as the Apollo Theater, the couple opened a Manhattan club named Pearl's Place, which occupied the corner of 96th and 2nd Avenue for eight years. Working with minimal backing instrumentation (usually just acoustic piano and bass) and performing a repertoire heavily influenced by the classic songs of Bessie Smith (1894–1937), Murray there developed a confident and commanding onstage persona, adept in interpretive vocal artistry and comedic commentary. Then, after returning to Houston for family reasons, in the early 1980s the couple opened a neighborhood lounge called Pearl's Cotton Club, primarily featuring the namesake artist with a band she dubbed the Jewels. Though it soon moved to a different property, this near-northwest-side establishment was home for six years to a small cast of regular customers and some fine musical performances by Murray and friends. Yet given its limited budget and low-profile location, the Cotton Club and its singing proprietress remained largely unnoticed. Her greatest local exposure would come only after she abandoned entrepreneurship and started booking herself for gigs at other venues, which eventually included the city's largest and best known, Billy Blues. For Murray, as well as for others, playing that stage has obviously helped her establish a presence beyond the neighborhood joints, winning her new fans in the process.

Such has also been the case for Houston native Rayfield Jackson, better known to his audiences as "Guitar Slim," the host and raucous showman at a long-running weekly jam session at Billy Blues. Though his personal performance history is rooted in the kind of Third Ward dives once frequented by Lightnin' Hopkins, Jackson worked almost exclusively at the big blues-and-barbecue entertainment complex on Richmond from the mid-1990s through 2000. He first caught people's attention there as the wildly acrobatic, show-stealing featured guitarist in the Rhythmaires, the band led by the late Clarence Green. But when the management of Billy Blues offered him the opportunity to host a popular weekly jam session, he accepted and reformed his own combo. Combining high-voltage theatrics (such as leaping into the audience and romping around the room in the midst of a string-bending guitar solo) with a gospel-drenched vocal style reminiscent of that of his idol, the original "Guitar Slim" (Eddie Jones), the tall, nimble Jackson soon became an over-the-top crowd pleaser. But in assuming the role of jam-session leader, he also became an inspiration and a good-humored mentor to the younger (mostly white) players who had the nerve to accept his invitation to join or follow him onstage at Billy Blues.

Despite various changes in ownership, management, and marketing, from 1993 through the end of 2000 this Richmond Strip institution served as the largest and highest-profile blues club in the city. By coincidence or not, this time period roughly corresponds to a mini-renaissance of interest in local blues heritage. So, for many people—black, white, and other—who would never venture into the old wards in search of venues where the music survives, Billy Blues provided an accessible setting in which they could experience some of the richness of the Bayou City scene. Its relative spaciousness and prominent location also made it the venue of choice for a variety of consciousness-raising special events sponsored by nonprofit organizations such as the Houston Blues Society (founded in 1993) and blues-friendly KPFT Radio (90.1 FM, a Pacifica network affiliate founded in 1970).

Working independently and in tandem, the Houston Blues Society and KPFT have contributed some sense of cohesion to the ever more spread out local blues culture during the last decade of the twentieth century and into the twenty-first. Apart from the numerous special events they sponsor and promote and the recognition they bring to some deserving individuals and bands, these two organizations have facilitated general communication and mutual awareness among various elements of the demographically diverse community of blues players and fans. Through their efforts, people who care to learn about the past and present blues scene have discovered a network (both formal and informal) through which they can exchange information and heighten awareness.

This type of blues grapevine is especially necessary in Houston, a heavily suburban, freeway-crisscrossed metropolis lacking a multifaceted focal point that represents the city's living blues culture. Meanwhile, in some comparable cities, public appreciation of (and financial investment in) local musical heritage has been encouraged and sustained—despite the drawbacks of commercialization and rampant tourism—precisely because these cities offer some easily recognizable, pedestrian-friendly central district that showcases and capitalizes on that heritage. In New Orleans, there's obviously the French Quarter; in Memphis, there's the rejuvenated Beale Street; in Dallas, there's Deep Ellum, and so on. Of course, there's always a danger when corporate profits primarily define what elements of culture are deemed important. But historic entertainment districts such as these do offer visitors the chance to roam charming old streets, observing and absorbing some of the talent, architecture, food, sociology, and geography that have influenced each city's fundamental musical identity. People often go to such areas not necessarily to patronize a particular club or to see a certain performer but instead mainly to wander and discover—to be part of the larger environs and to get a feel for the city's character. For better or for worse, in Houston there's no such centralized consumer magnet pulling folks toward its largely underappreciated blues scene.

No, these days, if you want to experience the undeniable richness of that scene by visiting multiple venues and sampling a variety of performers, you're going to have to know several different addresses—and likely cover many miles getting from one to the other. And in the petroleum capital of the world, which has been notoriously slow to develop an effective mass transit system, that pretty much means you're going to have to fire up an automobile and drive.

personal inconvenience, expense, and environmental impact notwithstanding, a willingness to drive all over and beyond Harris County has its rewards for the Houston blues aficionado wanting to make the rounds. Not only is that travel necessary to access the various widely separated business establishments featuring live performances on a weekly basis, but for those in the know, it's also the key to experiencing some unique presentations of the music—both of which evoke an earlier era. For me, two sporadically occurring events in particular consistently merit a road trip: those holidays and other occasions when Pete Mayes and the Texas Houserockers return to play the old Double Bayou Dance Hall (east of the city, near Anahuac in Chambers County), and those random Sunday afternoons when Earl Gilliam decides to spread the word and plug in the amps in what he calls his "doghouse" up in Tomball (north of the city, near the Montgomery County line). For rural retreats that offer a different perspective on Bayou City blues, either destination is well worth the drive.

"If it wasn't for Double Bayou Dance Hall, no one would know about Pete Mayes," the former T-Bone Walker protégé told me in a 1998 interview. Growing up in Double Bayou—an all-black community of cowboys, rice farmers, oil field roughnecks, and shrimpers near the eastern shore marshes of upper Galveston Bay—Mayes learned early on to appreciate this rustic entertainment establishment, the longtime social center in an enclave originally settled by freed slaves. After all, the dance hall has been owned and operated by his family for over a half century, and it was already an important part of the community well before that. Most of the structure from the first incarnation, whose 1920s-era origin predates Mayes' memory, was destroyed by a hurricane in 1941. Following the conclusion of World War II, Pete's uncle Manuel Rivers Jr. (d. 1976) came home, salvaged the surviving dance hall floor (with its foundation of hand-cut cedar beams), and moved

Pete Mayes, Double Bayou Dance Hall, near Anahuac, Texas, 1997.

it a short distance down the main road to the current location on his own property, a clearing in the midst of densely growing live oaks draped with Spanish moss. By early 1946, Rivers had erected a short containing wall around the perimeter of the floor, strung chicken wire along the upper sections, and opened for business. He eventually added a low-hanging tin roof and replaced the chicken wire with plywood and rough siding (which, Mayes recalls, "made it a little bit better, but boy, it sure didn't make it no cooler!"). Other than the addition of a couple of hopelessly sputtering window-unit air conditioners in recent decades, the physical structure hasn't changed much since then.

In the late 1940s, the hall frequently hosted a double bill featuring two artists managed by Lola Anne Cullum: pianist Amos Milburn (backed by a band that included Texas Johnny Brown) and guitarist Lightnin' Hopkins. Offering the routinely packed house nonstop entertainment, they rotated turns performing behind the barricade of pine two-by-fours that signified the unraised "stage" area at the north end of the approximately forty-by-eighty-foot rectangular room. "When Amos' band would take a break, Lightnin' would play a solo set," Mayes says. "And boy, they'd tear the place down!"

Among other big names to perform at Double Bayou Dance Hall over the ensuing years were T-Bone Walker, Big Joe Turner, Clarence "Gatemouth" Brown, Elmore Nixon, Percy Mayfield, Albert Collins, Johnny Copeland, Barbara Lynn, and Clifton Chenier. By the mid-1950s, Mayes had mastered guitar well enough to form his own band and was regularly gigging there himself also.

In 1983, Mayes—whose legal first name is actually Floyd (he was dubbed Pete as an infant when a relative quipped, "He looks like a little old Peter Rabbit")—inherited ownership of the sagging building. By then its glory days as a rural concert hall had long passed, and it was mainly functioning as an after-work watering hole and jukebox haven for the dwindling population of blacks in the area. But for close to twenty years now, a strong commitment to his community of origin has kept Mayes from closing the badly weathered joint, despite his own bouts with ill health (including a stroke, heart disease, diabetes, and the amputation of both legs). He persists because he feels he owes it to the place. He also realizes that the neighbors he left behind there when he moved into Houston still need some spot where they can gather and socialize. "Yeah, I keep it going—if I didn't, it would be laying flat on the ground," he asserts, adding, "I spend money keeping that place open." Then he smiles and says, "I'm not complaining, just explaining." After a long pause, he offers some additional insight via metaphor: "Any bridge that you walk over, if that bridge keeps you out of the creek or out of the valley, it's worth looking back at, even if you never cross it again."

Luckily for the residents of Double Bayou—and for those informed Houstonians who make the hour-long drive into the alligator-infested swamplands on such occasions—Mayes still crosses that bridge now and then. That is, every Christmas and at various other times of the year, Pete

Mayes and the Texas Houserockers play a homecoming concert at Double Bayou Dance Hall, sometimes accompanied by special guests. The basic five-piece band typically includes three long-time members who've played together since the mid-1950s. In addition to Mayes on guitar and lead vocals, there's always his cousin (and lifetime Double Bayou resident) Bert Lewis on piano and vocals, and usually also the joyful Creole honker Shedrick Cormier on saxophone. Though the drummer and bassist have changed over the years, in the 1990s those duties have most frequently been handled by Johnny Prejean and Eugene "Sparetime" Murray respectively. Together these veterans conjure up a type of visceral but sophisticated blues, mixing in elements of swamp pop, Motown, and lots of swing.

Defining his sound, Mayes says, "Some people just pump it, you know," as he makes a fist and jerks his arm up and down. Then he slyly grins and adds, "I pump it some, but I *swing* it," now slowly rotating the same arm in a cascading motion. That difference between pumping the blues and swinging the blues is, in a sense, the difference between other places (such as Chicago and the Mississippi Delta) and Texas. And the Houston musicians that Mayes sometimes invites to join him at Double Bayou instinctively understand. Among those I've personally witnessed there swinging with the band are Texas Johnny Brown, Joe Hughes, Jimmy "T-99" Nelson, Calvin Owens, Oscar O'Bear, and Kinney Abair. But there have been countless others over the years.

Mayes' depth of feeling for the old family dance hall is implicit in the song "House Party," which has become his signature set-closer wherever he plays. In the studio during sessions for his 1998 CD *For Pete's Sake,* he was inspired to enhance his lyrical vow to "rock this joint" by improvising a spoken segment in which he addresses various friends from Double Bayou, many of whom have now passed away. As the bass walks a smooth groove with the drums and Lewis chimes in on piano and supporting vocal, Mayes envisions the dance hall friends who have meant the most to him, ad-libbing to re-create what he describes as "the way they spoke, just common everyday language that they used." Among those to whom he pays tribute are characters called "Old Heavy," "Little Bit," "Frogman," and "Big Wheel." Aware that some listeners may not comprehend the personal meaning of the odd exclamations (e.g., "By dogs! Hound pup! This stuff is too thin for me!") and nicknames he utters in this sequence, Mayes shrugs and says, "It's just a novelty song." Then he proudly asserts, "It's novelty *and* my history."

A trip to Double Bayou Dance Hall for a Mayes performance is a lot like that too. For first-timers from the big city, it's almost always an essentially unique experience. It's a journey to a mythic juke joint, now vibrantly come to life, in a setting that—at the beginning of the twenty-first century—seems slightly surreal. For instance, I remember one friend telling me, in awe-struck fashion as we caught fresh air together outside the pulsating structure during a soul-stirring July Fourth show there in 1996, that it was "like being in some remote Caribbean jungle." But, remarkably, this lush locale is also a rare piece of common ground previously tread by the primal

Bert Lewis, 1998.

Lightnin' Hopkins as well as his debonair antithesis T-Bone Walker and many capable blues artists who followed after them. Hence, an even more common impression (overheard in conversations during "Double Bayou Blues Run" chartered bus trips from Houston, a series orchestrated by Steve Sucher in the mid-1990s) is the sense that "it's like going back in time."

The same might be said for visits to Troy Street up in Tomball when Earl Gilliam lets friends know—sometimes by calling one of the Sunday blues programs on KPFT Radio to announce the fact—that he's "in the doghouse." That's a code phrase of sorts, indicating that Gilliam has opened up the huge barnlike structure next to his humble residence, purchased a supply of beverages, thrown some meat on the outdoor grill, rigged the PA system and his double-decker electric keyboard, and is ready to receive visitors with a desire to play (or at least hear) some blues.

The spontaneous gatherings that typically ensue are probably similar in spirit to the original "house party" concept of yore, even if they do take place out in the spacious sideyard and oversized garage he refers to as his "doghouse" (i.e., the earthy refuge to which he's banished by his wife whenever he wants to get rowdy). As the party begins, adults and children from all over this quasi-rural, lower-working-class black neighborhood stroll casually down the ditch-lined street toward the amplified music, ignoring the disapproving stares of congregation members departing the tiny Church of God in Christ located a half-block away. Along with other friends, both black and white, who arrive in cars that end up parked haphazardly along narrow lanes, they might mill about the Gilliam property from early afternoon to well after dark. Some sit on lawn chairs and wooden benches beneath the big oak tree, where up among the branches a battered stereo speaker blares. Along with strings of bare light bulbs, this equipment appears to have been permanently mounted there, tenuously powered by patched-together electric extension cords that stretch overhead. Other visitors crowd before the propped-open double doors, gazing in at the performing musicians or squeezing their way inside. As the spirit prompts them, kids, couples, and elders break into dance steps or sway and wiggle to the music. Meanwhile, everyone makes a point to avoid Gilliam's three ferocious dogs, each of which is staked to a separate chain near the rear fence. Their incessant growling signals that they're back there, even if unseen—just beyond that disorderly pile of scrap lumber, that portable outhouse (fully functioning, apparently procured from a construction site), and that overturned flat-bottomed fishing boat.

What Gilliam calls the "doghouse" is actually an approximately forty-by-sixty-foot single-room building with a high-pitched roof supported by seven massive crossbeams. Its exterior is a patchwork of corrugated tin siding. Inside, old pieces of carpet are hung here and there along the walls, presumably to provide some insulation. Several musty sofas, worn-out easy chairs, and wobbly stools are casually arranged on the concrete slab, near a clutter of microphone stands and amps in the front half of the room. To provide a bit of heating, there are also two antique wood-burning stoves, each with a homemade exhaust pipe precariously rigged to vent the smoke outside. Near

Earl Gilliam, at the "doghouse," Tomball, Texas, 2000.

the rear is a battered washing machine. Numerous smudgy mirrors (salvaged from both houses and cars) are nailed to the walls—sharing space with a hodgepodge display of all types of tools, machine parts, rusty bicycle wheels, and wooden ladders. Interspersed among these are faded concert posters, curled-edged snapshots of musicians and friends, old publicity photos, beer signs, and glittery tinfoil streamers from past Christmas or Mardi Gras celebrations. In a cleared space to one side stands a refrigerator filled with cans of beer and soda; two handwritten messages are duct-taped to its door: "PRIVATE" and "KEEP OUT." Not far away is a long wooden table where Mrs. Gilliam is laying out a large spread of soul food and barbecue, along with paper plates and plastic utensils. On a prominently placed gallon-sized jar, another sign is posted: "DONATIONS." Visitors are expected to help themselves to the food or request a beverage (if they don't bring their own). Many of those who do so also deposit dollar bills or spare change in the jar. In most cases, those who cannot afford to contribute any cash are still graciously received by the Gilliams. Typically the *haves* donate enough funds to cover basic expenses for themselves as well as the *have-nots*. Whatever the case, it seems that participation in the music making more than compensates for anyone's consumption of food and drink.

As a supporting keyboard player, Gilliam has worked professionally with a plethora of Bayou City bluesmen, including early stints with Clarence "Gatemouth" Brown, Albert Collins, and Ivory Lee Semien, as well as more recent collaborations with Joe Hughes, with whom he toured in Europe on several occasions in the 1990s. On the side, he's also fronted his own group. As a result, Gilliam is as capable of precision performance with his instrument as any bluesman in town. But here at home he gleefully leads a makeshift band in a sloppy but good-natured jam. In freewheeling fashion, they start and stop, making abrupt segues from standards (made famous by the likes of Big Joe Turner, Bobby Bland, or Ray Charles) to obscure numbers (such as those Gilliam originally recorded in the 1950s for the Sarg label), even to Creole folk songs rendered in the French patois that reflects the ethnic heritage of the host. Whether he's vocalizing or not, Gilliam ferociously pounds those keys, laying down distinctive rhythms with his quick left hand and improvising melodic riffs with his right. For here in the "doghouse"—unlike most stage gigs where he dutifully follows the lead of others—the piano or organ dominates. And Gilliam clearly enjoys these unfettered workouts in which he can pursue any whim. "I love it. I love music," he says. "I get a feeling from it because some things I have, you know, been through. Well, I get that feeling and I go from there."

At moments during these intermittent "doghouse" jams, that feeling seems to transcend Gilliam's fertile musical imagination and possess everyone at once. As the playing intensifies and the volume swells, onlookers stomp, shuffle, and shout—climaxing in a clamor of whistles and applause at song's end. Laughter and chatter immediately follow, a catharsis from the delicious tension created by the music. Then Gilliam hollers through the microphone, "Anybody want some 'Green

Onions'?" And amidst the cheering responses, a little pig-tailed girl on the front line squeals, "You're good, Mr. Earl!" He chuckles, partially rising to lean toward this fan (who's young enough to be his great-granddaughter), and slaps her open palm "high-five" style. Then after some hearty sighs and the lighting of another cigarette, he yells "Okay," and the band begins to build another groove, starting the process anew.

Like an excursion to Double Bayou Dance Hall, heeding Gilliam's summons to the "doghouse" offers an opportunity to experience blues performance as a galvanizing community ritual. For, in contrast to commercial establishments that must ultimately focus on profit margins and such, these places feature the music for sheer joy, for communal rejuvenation, for what seems to be a spiritual necessity. In doing so they evoke an atmosphere and a purity of motivation rarely discovered in postmodern America (where music is often reduced to a mere commodity on which to capitalize).

Certainly the economic survival of Houston's contemporary African American blues culture has been stimulated by the better-paying gigs available at venues far removed from Tomball, Double Bayou, or even Third or Fifth Ward. By their own admission, many of the musicians have come to depend on working regularly at non-black-owned places such as Shakespeare's, the Big Easy, or the now defunct Billy Blues, along with occasional appearances at high-profile downtown night-clubs or restaurants. For the best known among them—especially relatively active recording artists such as Jimmy Nelson, Trudy Lynn, Sherman Robertson, Joe Hughes, Texas Johnny Brown, Calvin Owens, Grady Gaines, Pete Mayes, the late Clarence Hollimon, and his widow, Carol Fran—the opportunity to tour in the United States and abroad has also obviously been a welcome source of some additional income and another incentive to stay active and true to the music.

But on a different level, the spiritual sustenance of the city's indigenous blues culture would likely be far less potent if not for the little joints and impromptu gatherings that are never advertised or promoted beyond tradition and word of mouth. It's in those kinds of places—such as Double Bayou Dance Hall, Earl Gilliam's "doghouse," C. Davis Bar-B-Q, Mr. Gino's, El Nedo Cafe, the Silver Slipper, Miss Ann's Playpen, and others—that Houston blues maintains its vital connection to its black heritage and its primary reason for being.

And, for me, it's mainly been in those kinds of places that I've found an incredible sense of community—something that seemed so unlikely when I moved to this alien metropolis in 1981. Like most people, I could have easily remained oblivious to such out-of-the-way venues, to a totally different Houston that exists beneath the surface realities. So I feel doubly privileged to have witnessed—both within and beyond the wards where it all began—some of the living legacy of Bayou City blues.

blue resonance

Reunion and Reflection

it's a sunny march weekday afternoon in 1998, and I'm driving home via the Southwest Freeway, that massive traffic funnel that influenced so many of my initial impressions of Houston. Because it's not yet the evening rush hour, the lanes are relatively uncongested, and I'm just cruising along, concentrating on an anonymous saxophone solo that fills my Toyota. As usual, the radio is on—tuned now to KTSU, the noncommercial jazz station at Texas Southern University, the region's major historically black institution of higher education. When the music stops, a soft-spoken DJ delivers a couple of public service announcements. Then, without introduction, a taped commentary begins playing—part of a randomly featured and untitled public service series by the deep-voiced Frank Torry, a longtime presence in local black media. I've always enjoyed catching Torry's two-to-three-minute segments, which generally focus on the modern African American history of Houston, so I adjust the volume knob and pay attention to what he's saying.

"A Great Day in Houston," he begins, in his customarily elegant cadence. "It was the third of January 1998, and they all stood on the winding stairway of the Rotunda. . . ."

It is like being blindsided by a speeding pickup truck—that split-second realization of something totally unexpected and suddenly there, jolting the brain. But no physical collision is imminent, and this shock is good. *The Reunion!* I gasp to myself, stunned. Then, frantically and unnecessarily, I fine-tune the knob as I refocus my ears.

. . . in preparation of having their picture taken . . . the cream of the cream of Houston blues performers. I stood there in awe and realized that I was watching a total of over three thousand years of experience on that stair. Some of them I knew; I'd been writing about most of them for over thirty years. Some of them I did not know. There were too many to name, and I'm sure if I tried, there would be someone I would miss. But I will say this: Think of your favorite veteran blues artist, and there's a good chance he or she was there at this historic picture-taking session. . . .

Absorbed in what I'm hearing, I automatically take my regular exit, then negotiate an intersection before pulling into the first available parking lot where I can stop the car. My pulse thumps in double time, and my emotions soar wildly. Torry isn't really saying anything I don't already know. But hearing his mellifluous tones telling of that gathering—and not having anticipated that he might make it the subject of one of his radio spots—I am still surprised, pleased, and transported back to that time and place.

Like every group of friends and associates from the same profession who had not seen each other for years, there were lots of hugs and kisses. And you could feel the joy and happiness. These were the faces of blues people who had worked everything from the little bucket-of-blood joints and small clubs along thousands of miles of highways where they might or might not get paid, to the great concert halls of the world where they were paid thousands of dollars. They had seen it all: The clubs where you could work but couldn't come in the front door or sit at a table to eat a sandwich. And the four or five hundred miles of riding on two-lane highways to get to the next job. They'd heard the cheers of adoring fans and suffered the indignities and disrespect of the businesspeople they'd worked for. But through it all, they had survived. And there was pride and happiness in their eyes.

The idea for this photo session came from a suggestion by Conrad Johnson in a conversation with C. Roger Wood, an instructor in the English Department of the HCC and a blues buff. Johnson made the statement that it would be a great thing to get all the local veteran blues performers together for a picture, and Wood went into action.

There is historical precedence for this event. Some forty years ago this same thing was done in New York, where some of the greatest names in jazz were photographed. It was called "A Great Day in

Harlem." That was the inspiration for this photo shoot that Wood did. Where jazz figures were shot in New York, blues performers were shot in Houston. Wood's handling of the logistics, and the photographic work of James Fraher from Chicago, made it a wonderful process. And it turned a Saturday afternoon with veteran blues performers into "A Great Day in Houston." [Pause] I'm Frank Torry.

The next set of music kicks off and fills the car, now way too loud. It takes a moment before I reach over and switch off the radio, even longer before I shift into gear and drive away.

Entering the house, I head straight upstairs to my desk, toss down the satchel full of books and papers, and reach for a framed black-and-white image mounted on the wall. I hold it in my hands and study the photograph once again. It won't be the last time something prompts me to do so.

the germinating idea for creating a large-scale group portrait followed the events of January 1996, when James Fraher made his second visit to town to visually document Houston people and places. By then the two of us had been commissioned by David Nelson, then the editor of *Living Blues* magazine, to develop material for a possible special issue focusing on the largely unpublicized local blues scene. One of the pieces we had in mind would eventually be titled "Lady Legends of Houston Blues." That concept had originated during Fraher's initial 1995 visit while photographing some of the blues artists I already knew personally at the time: Teddy Reynolds, Grady Gaines, Jimmy "T-99" Nelson, Texas Johnny Brown, I. J. Gosey, and various others—all of whom happened to be males. Throughout those first shoots, Fraher and I had asked lots of questions and developed leads for additional research, especially in regard to one regular inquiry: Who were some of the great female blues singers around Houston? Certain names—all of which were then new to me—had surfaced again and again, among them Jewel Brown, Luvenia Lewis, Martha Turner, Iola Broussard, Gloria Edwards, and Mickie Moseley. Intrigued by this information, and with special assistance from Texas Johnny Brown and Clarence Green, by the end of the following month I had located each of these women and arranged for future interviews, plus a session with the *Living Blues* photographer when he next returned to town.

Instead of following our usual pattern of simply meeting with each artist individually, Fraher thought it might be interesting to get these six women together for a group portrait. So, in advance of his visit, I pursued that goal, facilitated by the kind support of my friend Cheryl Peters, then the Assistant Dean of Instruction at Central College. I had approached her about this project not only because I sought permission to utilize an empty room on campus as the gathering site, but also because I figured she might want to attend. Given our common background in teaching literature, I knew her to be especially interested in women's studies—and to take great joy in meeting strong, colorful, independent females who evoked the spirit of one of her personal heroes, the late

African American writer Zora Neale Hurston (1891–1960). As I had hoped, the dean fully supported my proposal and vowed to be there herself.

When I later casually mentioned the plan to some of the local bluesmen, I was dismayed to discover that a few (who shall go unnamed) thought this little reunion of women singers was doomed to fail. "Those ladies are rivals," one fellow defiantly emphasized to me, adding, "They ain't going to settle for being herded all together for a picture." Another man mentioned two of the women in particular, described an alleged romantic triangle involving some man they both had supposedly loved, and declared with a laugh, "She's going to want to *kill* her if she sees her." Such opinions, coming from persons who had known these women for decades, obviously concerned me. But since the process was already in motion, and Fraher was soon to arrive, I simply reconfirmed (via telephone) each woman's awareness of the invitation and hoped for the best.

On Saturday, January 27, 1996, Fraher and I showed up early at the designated site: a spacious rehearsal room full of folding chairs, music stands, and a baby grand piano. We busied ourselves arranging furniture, unpacking and assembling equipment, and laying out some modest refreshments. Cheryl Peters soon arrived too and began assisting our general efforts—and insisting that we find larger, more comfortable chairs to offer our guests; she even drafted an unsuspecting fellow faculty member (who happened to be walking down the hall) into the role of furniture mover.

As the 2:00 P.M. appointment time came, so too did Martha Turner, soon followed by Iola Broussard, then Mickie Moseley. A bit later, Gloria Edwards made a gleeful entrance, and Jewel Brown showed up too. Rather nervously, I had introduced myself and my colleagues to each new arrival, then had pointed her toward the others with an invitation to join them for cookies and soft drinks while we finalized preparations. To my deep relief, as I skittered around the room checking arrangements, I was also observing what appeared to be a genuinely good-hearted reunion, full of hugs and kisses and other expressions of mutual delight. That spirit was growing more joyous as the size of the group increased. Within minutes, the room was vibrating with laughter and wisecracks, which ebbed only when someone recalled the name of a now deceased colleague or started to tell another nostalgic anecdote. I soon realized those male warnings against assembling these former female "rivals" had been unfair. And I was thrilled to witness the women, some of whom claimed not to have seen each other in decades, clearly enjoying each other's company.

By 2:30 P.M. everyone was there except for Luvenia Lewis, so I left the room to call her. I was disappointed to learn that she would be unable to attend. However, five of the six invitees had shown up, some accompanied by additional family members and friends (including I. J. Gosey). And by the time I returned to the rehearsal hall, a general party was going on. Eventually Fraher began to call on individuals, one at a time, to come sit for solo portraits. Meanwhile, all the others carried on with their reminiscing, storytelling, and jovial exchanges. When it was Broussard's turn

Iola Broussard, Jewel Brown, Mickie Moseley, Gloria Edwards, Martha Turner,
Fine Arts Center at Central College, Houston Community College, Third Ward, 1996.

to be photographed, she naturally sat at the piano, evoking memories of her session work at Duke-Peacock years ago. As she smiled for the camera, Turner called across the room, "Don't just sit there, Iola. Play us something!"

That request triggered a spontaneous musical outpouring that continued on and off for well over an hour. As Broussard played, other women would sing along, sometimes alone and sometimes as a group. Most memorable to me was a remarkably gospelized version of the pop standard "You've Got a Friend," on which Turner and Moseley each improvised a verse, joined in soulful harmony by the others on the chorus. This hand-clapping jam session culminated in an intense remaking of the old spiritual "Amen," interwoven with lines from "This Little Light of Mine." The rehearsal room's superior acoustics highlighted the rich sound of Broussard's piano playing and the distinctive qualities of each woman's voice, as well as the inevitable laughter and exclamations between songs. And I do not believe I could ever enjoy the live performance of music more than I did that afternoon.

In the months that followed, Fraher and I reflected again and again on the events of that day. Not only had it produced some superb group photographs and the basis for a feature article in the magazine, it had also clearly been a life-enriching experience for all the parties involved. My colleague and I were simply amazed at what had transpired as a consequence of our proposal. Over the course of the next year, during Fraher's subsequent photographic field trips in collaboration with my ongoing research, we sometimes told other blues artists about that special day when five women singers had gathered at our request. A few folks had heard about it already from one of the principal participants; almost everyone expressed a desire to have been there for the occasion.

Then in April 1997, on Fraher's sixth excursion to the Bayou City, I took him to meet and photograph the highly esteemed bandleader and music educator Conrad Johnson. As we studied the display of memorabilia in the music studio of Johnson's Third Ward home, he related that his close friend Mickie Moseley had told him about the fine time everyone had experienced during the "lady legends" photo shoot. Somewhat wistfully, he also suggested that someone should create a really large group portrait that included "all" the blues people of Houston. He asked if either of us had seen the film *A Great Day in Harlem,* a documentary re-creating that summer day in 1958 when Art Kane had photographed fifty-seven jazz players in front of a brownstone in Harlem. When I answered in the affirmative, he said, "Like that. Someone around here needs to do that for us."

in november 1997, following Fraher's seventh round of photographing Houston blues people the month before, I prepared and mailed out approximately ninety copies of an advance letter inviting each recipient to come to a unique reunion planned for the Saturday immediately following New Year's Day 1998. I explained our goal and gave directions to the Theater One Rotunda on my campus in Third Ward, requesting folks to arrive by 12:00 noon. That initial announcement would be followed in December by subsequent mail-outs of hand-drawn maps and reminders, as well as numerous last-minute telephone calls to arrange transportation for those who had requested assistance.

Making it all work out required a group effort. I coordinated a couple of car pools and recruited Musician Benevolent Society of Houston cofounder Steve Sucher and Cultural Arts Council of Houston administrator Reg Burns to serve as individual drivers for Teddy Reynolds and Big Walter "the Thunderbird" Price respectively. I also enlisted the aid of Sheryl Liskow and Travis Peoples of the Houston Blues Society to serve as greeters and facilitators on-site. Professional videographer Henry Vojtek promised to be there with his own crew and two digital cameras. My wife, Marla, assumed total control of producing the refreshments, a process that ultimately included rental of two fifty-cup coffeemakers and the preparation of over one hundred sandwiches, as well as procuring various other foods, soft drinks, and serving supplies. Cheryl Peters was invaluable in granting and overseeing our access to the college's Rotunda, an indoor site that provided an ideal layout for staging the shot as well as some protection against the possibility of bad weather. As before, she also helped out with the hosting. From his home base in Chicago, James Fraher did all the technical planning and packing of appropriate gear for shooting the photograph, including arranging the rental of additional equipment in Houston, which I would pick up on New Year's Eve.

Also as before, a few cynical acquaintances dropped comments implying that it would be miraculous if more than a handful of blues people kept an appointment to pose with their presumed rivals, especially on a Saturday morning so soon after a major holiday. Despite the occasional nay-saying, though, I had come to believe in the inevitability of this project's success. Our prior experience with the five female singers had been enlightening. And this new, more ambitious undertaking seemed to have evolved a life of its own. It was clear to me that most of the invitees were taking it seriously. John Green had suggested that I mail an invitation to Frank Torry (whom I had never met), and provided me with his address so that I could do so. Some musicians had made unsolicited telephone calls to confirm again that they'd be there or to inquire if it was okay to bring along friends or family to observe the proceedings. A few had bashfully broached the subject of proper attire. I assured them all that their personal guests were welcome as spectators and that they should wear whatever clothes they pleased.

Finally, the date of the big event was upon us. Fraher's flight had touched down at Intercontinental Airport on schedule on Friday, and we had devoted that evening to double-checking equipment, supplies, supporting personnel assignments, and such. Then there was nothing left to do but get some sleep and show up at the Rotunda early the next day.

William "Candyman" Hollis, 1998.

The two of us were there by 8:30 A.M., along with the on-duty campus custodian who un-locked the doors and admitted us to the darkened Rotunda. As we carted and lugged in load after load of materials, the room gradually began to feel less empty, less full of echoes. But I was still momentarily disturbed by the sense of all that open space with nobody else in it. *What if they don't come?* However, the numerous tasks at hand soon distracted me from most of my pre-event jitters, and as members of our supporting team began to arrive over the next couple of hours, I grew less apprehensive.

Fraher had possessed the foresight to purchase a little Hallmark "Guests" book for the arrivals to autograph. So while he continued rigging tripods, lights, and cables, I found a small table and positioned it near the entrance, along with the signature book plus a couple of pens. Also included was a "Get Well" card for one of Houston's biggest stars, Katie Webster, whose daughter had called the day before to report the sad news that her mother was confined to a Houston hospital and would be unable to attend. Fraher and I had photographed and interviewed Webster (in the living room of her daughter's League City home, southeast of town) just a few months earlier, at which time she had expressed a genuine eagerness to reunite in early January with some of her home-town friends. That memory had inspired me to buy an extra-large card and bring additional sheets of paper so that those who cared to do so could compose personal messages, which I would send all together in a big envelope a few days later.

As I was printing a sign to explain that plan and to encourage our hoped-for guests to write a note to Katie Webster, I was startled to hear a low voice saying, "Happy New Year, my man. Is this the place?" Standing just inside the doorway behind me, more than a half hour ahead of schedule, was the Third Ward singer known as "Candyman," William Hollis. We greeted each other warmly, and I led him into the Rotunda and to the refreshment table. He took a cup of coffee as I—suddenly realizing that the long prelude was finally ending and the actual event would soon be under way—raced off to complete the task of making that sign. Leaving Hollis alone there in the middle of the room, I sensed his awkwardness—like being the first arrival at a dinner party when the host is still getting dressed—but that situation wouldn't last for long.

Within a few minutes, Steve Sucher was there, slowly escorting a beaming but now crippled Teddy Reynolds into the building. Moving awkwardly with his aluminum-framed walker, the old piano player was audibly expressing his gratitude for being able to attend: "Thank you, Jesus. Thank you, Jesus." As I hugged his now shrunken body, I echoed his words. Given our close friend-ship in recent years, I knew well the poor state of his physical health, which had been in steady decline since he had suffered a heart attack on the morning of September 26, 1995 (the same day I had scheduled him to perform in a concert on this very campus as part of the Quality Blues Band backing Texas Johnny Brown). I also realized that today was the first time in many months that Reynolds had been dressed up and out of the nursing home, and he was relishing that temporary liberation. On previous visits there, I had often told him about the other Houston blues people I was meeting and interviewing, and he had consistently found pleasure in hearing such reports. In fact, he had often provided extra background information and additional leads for me to pursue. More so than anyone else, it seemed to me, Teddy Reynolds wanted *everyone* from his native blues community to be recognized and appreciated. Today he would be reunited with many of those very folks we'd been discussing, and his excitement was uncontainable beneath the broad-brimmed hat he wore.

By the time I got Reynolds situated in a chair (which, despite his weakness, he would soon abandon to circulate among the expanding crowd), other invitees were rapidly showing up, in groups of two and three or alone. A spirit of homecoming was rising, along with the joyful noise of greetings, laughter, and the kind of teasing and instantaneous conversation that is possible only when old friends cross paths again. Some of the musicians proudly introduced family members to their peers, such as bassist Donald "Sweet D" Owens (b. 1954), who made the rounds with his wife, Effie. Eventually, the number of onlookers would swell to almost half that of the assembled musicians.

Frank Torry arrived with a small entourage of family members, introduced himself, and asked permission (immediately granted) to videotape the event for his own archives. And there were many other spectators—among them, former KPFT blues DJ and avid memorabilia hound Ertell Jackson (b. 1937). Sporting an African dashiki and his intricately carved walking stick, he milled about, politely requesting autographs from artists whose old publicity photos he had collected and brought with him. One of his successors on community radio, the former KPFT blues and zydeco DJ known to me only by her nickname of "Sweet Pea," was also there as a guest of singer and radio partner Big Roger Collins—who would later slyly (before we realized it) place her in the group pose for the big photograph. Though we hadn't intended for "Sweet Pea" to be in that portrait, her presence is partially validated by her media position as a supporter of the local music scene (even if several other DJs have far more impressive credentials in this regard).

And I had, in fact, deliberately invited two non-musicians and one non-professional musician to participate. Chief among these was the former business manager at Duke-Peacock Records and head of Buffalo Booking Agency, Evelyn Johnson. Her background role in Houston's postwar music history is unsurpassed, as many of the people who enjoyed visiting with her that day would testify. She was accompanied by a fellow insider from the Don Robey entertainment empire, John Green. Having only recently moved back home following over twenty years in Los Angeles (where he had operated a limousine service that regularly transported celebrity guests for "The Tonight Show," among other clientele), Green truly relished this reunion event. In just one afternoon, as he would later tell me, he had reestablished ties with many of his favorite musicians—veterans of long road trips with the Bobby Bland revue, session work in the Fifth Ward studio, or local

Willie "Mo'e" Moore, at home, 1996.

concerts that Green himself had promoted. Standing side by side in the photograph, Johnson and Green provide a direct connection to the inner workings of the most significant black-owned independent enterprise in the American music industry of the 1950s.

I had also deemed it appropriate to request the presence of one other person who wasn't actually a professional musician: Willie "Mo'e" Moore. A serious painter who often re-creates colorful scenes from his rural upbringing, he consistently conveys a blues sensibility in his multi-faceted visual art. In addition to his evocative work on canvas and sketch paper, "Mo'e" (as he prefers to be identified) is also a recognized storyteller and published poet, as well as an amateur country blues singer and old-style guitarist. I had first serendipitously encountered him in 1996, on Holman Street in Third Ward, while I was on my way to see songster Kinney Abair in his cubbyhole apartment in the Midtown Arts Center. After I had smiled, nodded, and passed the bearded stranger on the sidewalk, he had called out: "You got a guitar in that case?" When I had confirmed his assumption, he asked to see it. I handed him my acoustic six-string and quickly fell under his spell while he fingerpicked the kind of raw music Lightnin' Hopkins might have heard as a child. I would later discover that some of the full-time blues musicians also knew about "Mo'e" and considered him a part of their world. So it made sense to invite this man to join in the reunion too. He represents, to me at least, another element of the local blues consciousness.

Thus, with the exception of these four very different individuals—"Sweet Pea," Johnson, Green, and "Mo'e"—everyone else who posed that day on the Rotunda staircase was a musician who had worked, in varying degrees, in the blues idiom on local stages. At the time of the reunion, the majority of the participants were still actively performing, at least occasionally, at venues around the city. However, a few had already essentially retired from much onstage performing, including Big Walter "the Thunderbird" Price, Henry Hayes, Richie Dell Thomas (who continued to play keyboards in church until her death in January 2001), Robert "Skin Man" Murphy, and of course Teddy Reynolds.

In the twenty-five months between Fraher's first photographic field trip to Houston and this staging of the big group portrait, two of the musicians we had collaborated to document had died: Clarence Green and Eugene Carrier. In response to our regrets that they couldn't be part of the reunion, my colleague had another idea: He would enlarge one of his prints of each man, and it could be displayed in the hands of an appropriate fellow musician. Then it dawned on us that we could also utilize this technique to include images of three other Houston people that I had never been able to interview but whom Fraher had previously photographed on his own in Chicago: Albert Collins, Johnny Copeland, and Lightnin' Hopkins. This way, a total of five deceased Bayou City bluesmen could "be there" by proxy, intermingling with surviving friends on the Rotunda stairway.

Finally, after allowing almost an hour for socializing and late arrivals, it was time to stage and shoot the long-planned-for group photograph. As we organized rows of people along the steps, we also introduced the five "proxy" images Fraher had prepared. The shot of Eugene Carrier would be held by his widow and fellow keyboard player Naomi, who had approved of our plan in advance. Sherman Robertson promptly requested the honor of displaying the portrait of Clarence Green, one of his most cherished mentors. Earl Gilliam volunteered to carry the print representing his former bandleader Albert Collins. Clarence Hollimon quietly took the photograph of his respected friend Johnny Copeland. And Kinney Abair insisted on clutching the image of Lightnin' Hopkins, whose songs he still performs and whose likeness he can capably impersonate onstage.

While Fraher cajoled this assemblage of seventy-four individuals to arrange and rearrange themselves to his satisfaction, and while he then followed up with a series of preliminary Polaroid test shots, I scanned the list of invitees and made quick note of the relatively few no-shows, hoping some of them would yet come rushing into the room. Katie Webster's absence, of course, was already accounted for, as was the absence of a few others. The hard-working Trudy Lynn was reported to be in the midst of a road tour, and Lavelle White had a special performance commitment that kept her in Austin for the weekend. Another Duke-Peacock veteran, singer Mildred Jones, was out of town (as she often is, for months at a time) working a series of five-star hotel lounge gigs in the Far East. But where was Jewel Brown, the former featured vocalist with Louis Armstrong? (Her brother, pianist Theodore Brown [b. 1931], had arrived early.) Where was Luvenia Lewis? And her protégée Faye Robinson? It bothered me to think that the city's tradition of strong female vocalists would not be more completely represented in the photo. But then I looked up and spotted Carol Fran, Martha Turner, Carolyn Blanchard, and Gloria Edwards, plus Pearl Murray, Iola Broussard, Mickie Moseley, Donna "Lady D" McIntyre, and Vanessa Gatlin (the last a featured singer with the late Clarence Green's band). *Not bad,* I consoled myself.

On the other hand, I wasn't really surprised that the reclusive Leonard "J.T." Tyson, Third Ward's front porch "guitar man," had not shown up, for I knew this formerly Memphis-based musician had never felt completely accepted by the established Houston players. Similarly, the absence of Ivory Lee Semien, the self-willed affiliate of the notorious Roy Ames, had been anticipated—especially given the medical crisis he had suffered over a year earlier. (I had mailed an invitation to the address I had for the Semien residence, however, just in case his condition had improved and he cared to participate.)

But what about Elbert "Pops" Stewart (b. 1941), the amiable bass player from so many Blue Monday jams? And the proprietor of Miss Ann's Playpen, singer Bobby Lewis? What could have happened to the popular sideman and pianist Robert Louis "Pee Wee" Stephens (b. 1941), who had played with just about everyone, from old-school legends such as T-Bone Walker to younger blues-

Jackie Gray, Silver Slipper, Fifth Ward, 1998.

rockers such as Jerry Lightfoot? And where, oh where, was the journeyman drummer Jackie Gray (b. 1949), whom I knew from experience loved to pose for pictures, especially those taken by James Fraher—several previous copies of which he had gratefully received and proudly framed and displayed on the wall of his apartment?

Yet what was really gnawing at my guts—and had already prompted Fraher and me to stall for extra time, even though a few people said they couldn't stay much longer—was the inexplicable absence of Joe "Guitar" Hughes, one of the highest-profile stalwarts of the local scene. Not only was I certain that Hughes had intended to be present for the reunion (having confirmed as much with his devoted wife and manager, Willie Mae, just days earlier), but Fraher had also arranged to shoot him solo today, on-site, for the cover story in the upcoming (and second) all-Houston issue of *Living Blues*. Graciously appreciative of our interest in his life and music, Hughes had always previously kept appointments with us, and none had ever been as important as this one. Where could he be?

"Still no Joe Hughes," I glumly muttered to Fraher as we stood together on the balcony overlooking the anxious crowd posing on the stairway below.

He winced back at me and whispered, "I know. But it's getting late. We've got to do it." He fiddled briefly with a nearby light stand, spoke a few final directives to individuals whose postures were slightly out of kilter, and then announced to the group, "Okay, this is for real. Everyone, please, look up here at me."

Over the course of the next ten minutes or so, Fraher shot and reshot the photograph that we had worked so long, with the help of numerous others, to make possible. Now and then he made some minor adjustments to equipment, reloaded film, or stopped to request that someone shift the tilt of a head or the turn of a shoulder. But, sooner than I expected, he looked over at me, grinned, and said, "Okay, man. We've got it."

despite a few regretted absentees, the musicians who do appear in Fraher's reunion portrait represent the diversity of styles, experiences, and instrumental identities that collectively define the African American blues culture of Houston at the end of the twentieth century. The group includes alumni of raucous jam sessions from Shady's Playhouse as well as veterans of big blues and jazz orchestras from establishments such as the Eldorado Ballroom. Most are players whose careers have been influenced primarily by postwar urban blues and classic R&B styles, but the group also includes several people who might better be classified as jazz-blues dualists—in the local tradition of Milt Larkin and Arnett Cobb. Among those not previously introduced in this book, for instance, is drummer and scat singer Ben Turner (1927–2000), who once recorded with Lightnin' Hopkins but later disavowed anything but "pure" jazz. So, along with a few pure country

Houston Blues Reunion, Theatre One Rotunda at Central College,
Houston Community College, Third Ward, 1998.

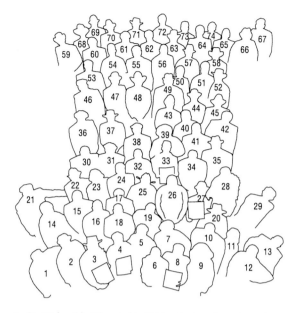

1. Big Walter "the Thunderbird" Price, keyboards and vocals
2. Don "Sweet D" Owens, bass
3. Sherman Robertson, guitar and vocals (with portrait of Clarence Green)
4. Naomi Carrier, keyboards (with portrait of Eugene Carrier)
5. Carolyn Blanchard, vocals
6. Conrad Johnson, saxophone
7. Martha Turner, vocals
8. Clarence Hollimon, guitar (with portrait of Johnny Clyde Copeland)
9. Carol Fran, keyboards and vocals
10. Oscar Perry, guitar and vocals
11. Verta Mae Evans, tambourine
12. Ben Turner, drums and vocals
13. Nathaniel "Pops" Overstreet, guitar and vocals
14. Iola Broussard, keyboards and vocals
15. Morgan Bouldin, keyboards
16. I. J. Gosey, guitar and vocals
17. Curley Cormier, guitar
18. Hamp Simmons, bass
19. Ardis Turner, vocals
20. Joe James, guitar and vocals
21. Jimmy "T-99" Nelson, vocals
22. Lala Wilson, bass
23. Gloria Edwards, vocals
24. Theodore Brown, keyboards
25. D. D. Bret, bass
26. Nelson Mills III, trumpet and keyboards
27. Earl Gilliam, keyboards and vocals (with portrait of Albert Collins)

28. Pearl Murray, vocals
29. Little Joe Washington, guitar and vocals
30. Grady Gaines, saxophone
31. Calvin Owens, trumpet
32. Mickie Moseley, vocals
33. Kinney Abair, guitar and vocals (with portrait of Sam "Lightnin'" Hopkins)
34. Shedrick Cormier, saxophone
35. Bert Lewis, keyboards
36. Willie "Mo'e" Moore, guitar
37. Bobby Alexis, keyboards
38. Robert "Skin Man" Murphy, drums
39. Donna "Lady D" McIntyre, vocals
40. Don Johnson, bass
41. Eugene Moody, guitar and vocals
42. Pete Mayes, guitar and vocals
43. "Sweet Pea," disc jockey
44. Texas Johnny Brown, guitar and vocals
45. Teddy Reynolds, keyboards and vocals
46. Ashton Savoy, guitar and vocals
47. Sonny James, vocals
48. Andy "Too Hard" Williams, guitar and vocals
49. Big Roger Collins, vocals
50. Richie Dell Thomas, keyboards
51. Vanessa Gatlin, vocals
52. Vern Ollison, trumpet
53. Leonard "Low Down" Brown, guitar and vocals
54. Aubrey Dunham, saxophone
55. Eugene "Sparetime" Murray, bass
56. Milton Hopkins, guitar
57. Eugene Hawthorne, bass and organ
58. William Hollis, keyboards
59. Oscar O'Bear, guitar and vocals
60. Robert Phelps, saxophone
61. Big Robert Smith, vocals
62. Joe Halliburton, vocals
63. Ken "Sugar" Hill, drums and bass
64. Jimmy "Louisiana" Dotson, guitar and vocals
65. John Green, road manager, promoter
66. Evelyn Johnson, Duke-Peacock Records
67. Johnny Prejean, drums
68. Charles "C.C." Carlson, keyboards and vocals
69. Rayfield Jackson (Houston's "Guitar Slim"), guitar and vocals
70. Paul David Roberts, trombone and vocals
71. Don Kesee, guitar and vocals
72. Wilbur McFarland, saxophone
73. Henry Hayes, saxophone
74. William "Candyman" Hollis, vocals

Nathaniel "Pops" Overstreet, at home, 1996.

blues throwbacks (such as reclusive guitar picker Nathaniel "Pops" Overstreet, b. 1928) and zydeco-blues utility players (such as keyboardist Bobby Alexis, b. 1941), this assemblage of musicians posing in the Rotunda embodies the key facets of Bayou City blues.

The levels of professional experience range from rudimentary players who'd worked only in small joints to versatile individuals who'd toured the world performing with giants of show business. That latter group includes bassist Lala Wilson (b. 1937), a former sideman for Louis Jordan and a participant in various mainstream Hollywood studio productions (e.g., he played that distinctive bass riff starting the theme music for the old TV show *Hawaii Five-O*). Many had recorded at some point for small independent regional labels, if not as featured performers then as part of a backing band. For instance, guitarist Jimmy "Louisiana" Dotson (b. 1934) had first played drums behind Baton Rouge bluesman Silas Hogan (1911–1994) on some early sides, before later recording on his own. A few (guitarist Sherman Robertson is a good example) had also worked in recent years under the auspices of major record companies. Some had begun recording over half a century ago. The earliest I can document is Texas Johnny Brown, who had backed Houston pianist Amos Milburn on the Los Angeles–based Aladdin imprint in 1946 before cutting his own 78 RPM singles for the New York–based Atlantic label in 1949. A close runner-up, Conrad Johnson, is known to have recorded locally at least as far back as 1947. And, of course, scores of the reunion guests had worked sessions during the rich twenty-four-year history of Duke-Peacock Records.

In addition to the many vocalists represented, both male and female, this gathering of Houston blues people included numerous guitarists, keyboardists, trumpeters, saxophonists, bassists, drummers and percussionists, and one trombonist. A few, such as former Clifton Chenier sideman Robert "Skin Man" Murphy, have also dabbled with the accordion, but—because our invitation had not extended to the city's large number of zydeco bandleaders—there were no serious squeezebox players at the reunion. In short, the range of instrument-defined identities in the photograph mainly encompasses the standard tools for making modern blues—with one glaring exception.

The almost total absence of the harmonica among Houston's African American musicians, at least during the latter decades of the twentieth century, is especially noteworthy. Because it's readily affordable, easily portable, and relatively simple to learn, this instrument has long proven popular with working-class musicians in various genres of American folk music. But its reedy intonation, rendered by both exhaling and inhaling, has been especially well suited for blues, almost since the birth of the idiom. Historically speaking, the great mouth-organ masters—such as Sonny Boy Williamson (Aleck Ford Miller, 1899–1965) or Big Walter Horton (1918–1981)—typically have hailed from the Mississippi Delta region or from Chicago, and in huge numbers. The Bayou City legacy, however, is limited to only a few figures, such as Weldon "Juke Boy" Bonner and former Lightnin' Hopkins sidekick Billy Bizor (1913–1963). A couple of Duke-Peacock stars,

Lala Wilson, 1997.

Jimmy "Louisiana" Dotson, Big Easy, 1995.

Junior Parker and Big Mama Thornton, did sometimes blow harmonica on record and onstage in Houston, but they both originally hailed from east of the Mississippi River. And the Texas sound in general, though often heavily embellished by horns (especially the tenor saxophone), has never really emphasized the harmonica. In contrast, blues performances in the Delta or in Chicago still regularly involve bands featuring a harp master steeped in the African American tradition. But the harmonica players in Houston venues are almost always relatively younger and white.

Nevertheless, for most of the past century, hometown blues has been a potent force within, if not always beyond, the larger black community of Houston. Certain neighborhoods, both past and present, have nurtured a depth and diversity of solid talent. If much of it has gone unrecognized, that's likely because it was often performed in the shadows of stars. As saxophonist Wilbur McFarland once put it:

> You've got more historical musicians in Houston than, I believe, in any other city in the union. Because the blues artists that was real big back in the fifties and sixties—listen at me real good— T-Bone Walker, Lightnin' Hopkins, Amos Milburn, B.B. King, Bobby Bland, Gatemouth Brown, Junior Parker, Albert Collins . . . many of the musicians in town played with those artists.

And even at the start of a new millennium, this city is home to numerous veteran sidemen who played, recorded, or composed in support of such figures. But perhaps because they stood outside the spotlight early in their careers, they seem to realize that good musicianship is not necessarily about acclaim or riches; instead, for some at least, it's mainly a vehicle for self-expression, a source of personal satisfaction, and a way of life.

Because of this, the local blues culture has remained largely self-contained. Guitarist and singer James Bolden (b. 1945) says it best: "Houston is a camouflaged city when it comes to music. There's something there—but away from it, you can't really see it." That distortion is perhaps also a consequence of the city's widely touted self-image and basic values. Choosing to identify itself primarily with the futuristic and the technological—as evidenced by the NASA-inspired slogan "Space City U.S.A."—Houston has historically shown maximum interest in the acquisition of the new and minimal interest in preserving elements of its cultural past, especially its African American legacy. Instead, its urban planners and visionary capitalists have typically banked on the capacity for unmitigated innovation (building the world's first major indoor sports stadium, inventing Astroturf, developing wider freeways, constructing taller hi-tech skyscrapers, and such)—a mentality that often disregards the virtues of older modes of life.

Moreover, Houston's rapid rise from a middle-sized American town to the fourth largest city in the nation has been triggered mainly, of course, by its role as the petrochemical capital of the world. For many residents, that industry is the primary source of jobs and, hence, of civic pride.

James Bolden, 1998.

So any impulse to cultivate some deeper sense of itself—for instance, some pride in its own significant music heritage (which extends well beyond blues)—has been minimal at best.

Consider, for example, that a modest proposal to rename a short part of Montrose Boulevard (the roughly quarter-mile stretch that crosses over the unpopulated Buffalo Bayou floodplain to become Studemont on the other side) as "Lightnin' Hopkins Way" was rejected by local authorities shortly after the master's 1982 death. In Third Ward, similar attempts to name a then newly constructed (and tiny) street-corner park after Hopkins also failed. In sad fact, no public space in this city that Lightnin' Hopkins called home even acknowledges the existence, much less the cultural importance, of its arguably most historically significant musician: no street sign, no marker, no statue, not even a small plaque. Meanwhile, in contrast, in nearby Austin a prominently placed life-sized sculpture of the late Stevie Ray Vaughan has become a shrine visited by devoted fans and casual tourists—and serves as a constant visual reminder to otherwise indifferent passersby that a city's musical heritage really does matter. And in the smaller Texas town of Crockett (located approximately forty-five miles from Hopkins' Centerville birthplace), enthusiasts have raised funds to erect a statue of the legendary musician, unveiled in January of 2002.

Yet, in Houston, community-rooted blues has somehow persisted—its staying power based in part on the tradition of self-reliance originally necessitated by widespread racial segregation. Throughout the population explosion and massive construction that so radically changed the city following World War II (peaking in the early 1980s), predominantly African American communities such as Third Ward remained somewhat isolated. To most outsiders who noticed them at all, such places superficially seemed to be urban wastelands, impoverished and insignificant relics unworthy of investment or appreciation. Today some of that attitude is changing as the city experiences a shift away from rampant suburbanization and toward unprecedented inside-the-Loop urban renewal, albeit almost exclusively for upper-middle-class residential purposes. For the most part, to the developers investing there now, it's just the land (in close proximity to the central business district) that matters—another space ripe for construction. Yet behind those marginal areas where such transformations are taking place, there remains an old Third Ward, a Fifth Ward, and enclaves beyond where the blues is part of a once-glorious past and a culture that still survives.

after the shooting of the big reunion photograph, some of the musicians had to depart at once. But many others stayed behind, extending the socializing and reminiscing for several hours. Fraher had also requested that certain individuals meet him in an adjoining room (where we had already set up another temporary studio) to make some additional solo portraits. Among those who lingered on-site were several people once affiliated with Duke-Peacock Records or the Buffalo Booking Agency. Naturally, many of them clustered around Evelyn Johnson, their

SEATED L–R: *Mickey Moseley, Evelyn Johnson, Teddy Reynolds, Pete Mayes;* STANDING L–R: *Carolyn Blanchard, Iola Broussard, Texas Johnny Brown, Conrad Johnson, Kinney Abair, John Green, Calvin Owens, Oscar Perry, Milton Hopkins, Grady Gaines, Jimmy Nelson, Reunion photo session, 1998.*

Robert Louis "Pee Wee" Stephens, C. Davis Bar-B-Q, 2000.

former employer, swapping stories and cracking jokes. At one point, Fraher coaxed them before his lens for an ensemble photograph. But by then the spirit was so loose and playful that it took some pleading to get folks to pose, and while they did, they just kept right on visiting.

About the time the laughter was beginning to fade and the remaining guests were growing more pensive and subdued, a visibly stressed-out but finely tailored Joe Hughes came rushing down the sidewalk and into the Rotunda—triggering another round of hearty chortles in the process. "Hey, Joe," Pete Mayes teased, "where you been? Out getting that suit pressed?" Hughes good-naturedly related his tale of misadventure: Car trouble had left him stranded on the freeway en route to the site. And though he would soon patiently sit while Fraher secured the cover shot for a future *Living Blues* (issue 140), he repeatedly bemoaned his bad luck in being so late for the reunion. As he said, hearing about the presence of numerous old friends he had missed hurt him almost as much as not being included in the big group portrait.

Months later, when Hughes would view the final print at its public unveiling (at an exhibition and blues show that served as a fund-raiser for the Musicians Benevolent Society), his unfortunate absence would pain him again. "It just ain't right," he said, adding correctly, "I belong in that picture."

So, too, do singer Jewel Brown and pianist Robert Louis "Pee Wee" Stephens, both of whom managed to show up at the Rotunda even later than Hughes. Various other musicians would also express regrets that they had been unable to attend or, in many cases, had not been invited (due to my ignorance or oversight). Since that day, Fraher and I have documented additional local blues players (such as Leo Morris, Melvin Newman (1936–2002), James Bolden, Diunna Greenleaf, and Larry Guy, just to name a few) who would surely have been asked to participate had I only known about them at the time. Yet, even so, the group photograph depicts a fairly thoroughly representative, if not absolutely comprehensive, gathering of Houston's African American blues people in the late 1990s.

Among the positive comments Fraher and I have received, perhaps none has been as unexpected and gratifying as a stationery card that arrived via U.S. mail. Dated July 10, 1998, it was a note of appreciation from New York filmmaker Jean Bach, whose documentary *A Great Day in Harlem* had inspired Conrad Johnson's suggestion. Through the kind efforts of archivist Tad Hershorn (of the Institute of Jazz Studies at Rutgers University), Bach had managed to acquire one of our "Houston Blues Reunion" copy prints (which had been sold in exchange for donations at the previously mentioned fund-raiser), and she was pleased and complimentary. The message also included her personal check in support of the Musicians Benevolent Society of Houston. In retrospect, it made our "great day" seem even better.

However, as might be expected, January 3, 1998, had also been an exhausting day. By 4:00 P.M., Fraher and I were still on-site—tired, hungry, but satisfied with what we'd been able to accom-

Donna "Lady D" McIntyre and Big Walter "the Thunderbird" Price, Reunion photo session, 1998.

plish. There was still a huge load of equipment to dismantle and pack into cars, as well as cleanup chores to perform. So as the number of guests dwindled to only a few, I felt obliged to begin the process of preparing to vacate the premises. Meanwhile, ever since taking the main photograph in the Rotunda, Fraher had been steadily at work in his side-room studio shooting individual portraits. As planned, he had concentrated his efforts on persons who had not previously posed solo. But the last two guests to sit for him that day had in fact already done so—in separate sessions back in November 1995.

Big Walter "the Thunderbird" Price and Donna "Lady D" McIntyre, whom I had introduced to each other at a recent Christmas party, had lingered in the back of the room, talking and apparently waiting until the other musicians were gone. Then they approached Fraher to request that he let them pose together for a duo shot, just for fun. In her typically flamboyant style, McIntyre had even donned a brand new wig for the occasion, only recently retrieved from her car. And Big Walter—now out of the range of colleagues who might have teased him about it—seemed eager to flirt with this relatively younger female vocalist. So Fraher complied and snapped some final images as the two mugged for the camera. It would be his gift for "the Thunderbird," perhaps the oldest surviving headliner from the Duke-Peacock roster.

And Big Walter, a widower, particularly seemed to enjoy all the attention he was getting—both from a professional photographer and from a woman. Though his volunteer driver had waited patiently for hours, "the Thunderbird" would ultimately dismiss him with a smile, having sweet-talked McIntyre into giving him a ride home. As he said upon exiting the room, his arm locked in hers, "I ain't ready for the fun to stop just yet."

Despite my own physical fatigue, I felt the same way. Something beautiful, far bigger and better than any one of us, had transpired that day, and on one level I did not want to see it end. But on another, I knew it must, for the time had simply come.

I get the same mixed feelings when I reflect on my larger experience with Houston blues. Though its role in certain African American communities remains vital, many of its most distinguished practitioners are growing old, retiring, and passing away. As I write these lines, I think of all those who've died, just since posing for that reunion photograph—good friends and music now silenced by the passage of time. They will not be replaced. Some well-intentioned acquaintances decry the fact that few among the younger generation of African Americans seem to value the musical styles and traditions of their elders—that nobody seems poised to carry on their songs, their sound. So they earnestly speak of doing something to "save" old-school Houston blues culture from disappearing. But, in my opinion, one may as well try to stop the sun from setting. It's inevitable, and organic, that what has been, eventually will be no more. And that's not necessarily something to fear or resist.

As with a glorious sunset, the best one can do perhaps is to savor it while it's still here. Appreciate the moment, the perspective, and encourage others to do so too. Document it, if possible, so that the fact of its splendor can be at least partially preserved, recalled, and conveyed to those removed in time or space. Enjoy it. Love it. Mostly, pay attention.

As I helped my colleague break down equipment in that temporary portrait studio, I figured that Big Walter's farewell had been the last of the day. The large Rotunda beyond the door seemed suddenly devoid of all the energy it had so recently contained. No voices now resonated, just a satisfying quietness. "I guess everybody's finally gone," I said.

But I was wrong. For upon gathering a load of materials, I stepped into the main room to find it not yet empty. Teddy Reynolds was still there, seated and silent. He seemed to be basking in the exhilaration of the day. And I believe he probably was wishing, despite knowledge that it must be otherwise, that this fine time together could last forever.

Sherman Robertson, Miss Ann's Playpen, Third Ward, 2000.

APPENDIX A. CATALOGUE OF INTERVIEWS

Abair, Kinney. Interview by author and James Fraher. Tape recording. Houston, TX, November 10, 1995.
———. Interview by author. Tape recording. Houston, TX, January 9, 1997.
Blanchard, Carolyn. Telephone interview by author. Tape recording. October 26, 1996.
Bland, Bobby. Onstage comments between songs, public performance. Notes. Miller Outdoor Theater, Houston, TX, June 6, 1996.
Bolden, James. Interview by author. Tape recording. Houston, TX, May 22, 1998.
———. Telephone conversation with author. Notes. March 16, 2000.
Bouldin, Morgan. Interview by author. Tape recording. Houston, TX, December 5, 1999.
Broussard, Iola. Interview by author. Tape recording. Houston, TX, January 27, 1996.
———. Telephone interview by author. Tape recording. July 1, 1996.
Brown, Clarence "Gatemouth." Interviews by author. Tape recording. Houston, TX, January 26, 1996; June 8, 1996.
Brown, Jewel. Interview by author. Tape recording. Houston, TX, January 27, 1996.
———. Telephone interview by author. Tape recording. August 13, 1996.
Brown, Johnny. Onstage interview by author. Video recording. Heinen Theater, Central College, HCCS, Houston, TX, September 26, 1995.
———. Interview by author and James Fraher. Tape recording. Houston, TX, November 12, 1995.
———. Interview by author. Tape recording. Houston, TX, September 23, 1998.
———. Telephone interviews by author. Tape recording. July 8, 1997; October 9, 1998; November 12, 1998; April 1, 1999; June 14, 1999.
Brown, Leonard. Interview by author and James Fraher. Tape recording. Houston, TX, October 2, 1997.
Caldwell, Booker T. Interview by author and James Fraher. Tape recording. Houston, TX, September 30, 1997.

Campbell, Milton. On-air comments during interview by James Vaughn. KPFT Radio. Notes. Houston, TX, February 15, 1998.
Carlson, Charles. Interview by author. Tape recording. Houston, TX, December 1, 1996.
Carrier, Eugene. Interview by author and James Fraher. Tape recording. Houston, TX, September 28, 1996.
Chevis, Wilfred. Telephone interview by author. Tape recording. January 15, 1998.
Collins, Roger. Interview by author and James Fraher. Tape recording. Houston, TX, November 12, 1995.
———. Interview by author and Edwin Gallaher. Tape recording. Houston, TX, October 20, 1996.
Cormier, Curley. Interview by author and James Fraher. Tape recording. Houston, TX, January 8, 1998.
Dotson, Jimmy. Interview by author and James Fraher. Tape recording. Houston, TX, November 9, 1995.
Earle, Steve. Onstage comments between songs, public performance. Notes. Aerial Theater, Houston, TX, April 5, 1999.
Edwards, Gloria. Interviews by author. Tape recording. Houston, TX, January 27, 1996; June 28, 1996.
Evans, Verta Mae. Interview by author. Notes. Houston, TX, October 4, 1998.
Fisher, Jim. Telephone conversation with author. Notes. September 19, 2000.
Fran, Carol. Interview by author and James Fraher. Tape recording. Houston, TX, October 4, 1997.
———. Onstage interview by author. Video recording. Heinen Theater, Central College, HCCS, Houston, TX, April 9, 1998.
Gaines, Grady. Interview by author and James Fraher. Tape recording. Houston, TX, November 9, 1995.
———. Interview by author. Tape recording. Houston, TX, January 21, 1997.
———. Telephone interviews by author. Tape recording. November 13, 1998; June 16, 1999.
Gaines, Roy. Telephone interviews by author. Tape recording. September 3, 1998; August 4, 1999.

319

———. Interview by author. Tape recording. Houston, TX, November 27, 1998.

Gilliam, Earl. Interview by author and Edwin Gallaher. Tape recording. Houston, TX, September 13, 1996.

Gosey, I. J. Interview by author and James Fraher. Tape recording. Houston, TX, November 12, 1995.

———. Interview by author. Tape recording. Houston, TX, December 5, 1999.

———. Telephone interviews by author. Tape recording. Houston, TX, October 20, 1996; September 24, 1998; October 9, 1998.

Green, Clarence. Interview by author and James Fraher. Tape recording. Houston, TX, January 26, 1996.

Green, John. Interviews by author. Tape recording. Houston, TX, November 14, 1997; July 23, 1998.

———. Interview by author and James Fraher. Tape recording. Houston, TX, January 7, 1998.

———. Telephone interview by author. Tape recording. Houston, TX, January 10, 1998.

Greenleaf, Diunna. Interview by author and James Fraher. Tape recording. Houston, TX, January 8, 1999.

Halliburton, Joe. Interview by author and James Fraher. Tape recording. Houston, TX, September 30, 1997.

Harris, Stephen. Interview by author. Tape recording. Houston, TX, January 7, 1998.

Hayes, Henry. Interview by author. Tape recording. Houston, TX, September 25, 1997.

———. Interview by author and James Fraher. Tape recording. Houston, TX, October 2, 1997.

———. Telephone interview by author. Tape recording. November 12, 1998.

Hickson, Ethel Lee. Telephone interview by author. Tape recording. June 14, 1999.

Hollimon, Clarence. Telephone interview by author. Tape recording. July 7, 1997.

———. Interview by author and James Fraher. Tape recording. Houston, TX, October 4, 1997.

———. Onstage interview by author. Video recording. Heinen Theater, Central College, HCCS, Houston, TX, April 9, 1998.

Hopkins, Milton. Interview by author and James Fraher. Tape recording. Houston, TX, January 26, 1996.

———. Interview by author. Tape recording. Houston, TX, September 15, 1996.

Hughes, Joe. Interviews by author and James Fraher. Tape recording. Houston, TX, November 12, 1995; October 2, 1997.

———. Telephone interviews by author. Tape recording. July 9, 1997; November 14, 1998; May 15, 1999; June 11, 1999; January 13, 2000.

Jackson, Rayfield "Guitar Slim." Interview by Ethel Lee Hickson. Tape recording; transcribed by author. Houston, TX, October 19, 1996.

———. Interview by author and James Fraher. Tape recording. Houston, TX, April 19, 1997.

Jackson, Vernon "Shady." Telephone interview by author. Tape recording. March 3, 1998.

James, Joe. Interview by author and James Fraher. Tape recording. Houston, TX, April 20, 1997.

Johnson, Conrad. Interview by author and James Fraher. Tape recording. Houston, TX, April 18, 1997.

———. Telephone interview by author. Tape recording. November 25, 1997.

Johnson, Evelyn. Interview by author and James Fraher. Tape recording. Houston, TX, January 7, 1998.

———. Telephone interviews by author. Tape recording. April 3, 2000; April 5, 2000.

Jones, Mildred. Telephone interview by author. Tape recording. March 28, 1996.

Kesee. Don. Interview by author and Edwin Gallaher. Tape recording. Houston, TX, October 25, 1997.

Lewis, Bobby. Interview by author and James Fraher. Tape recording. Houston, TX, September 30, 1997.

———. Interview by author. Tape recording. Houston, TX, November 18, 1997.

Lewis, Luvenia. Interview by author and James Fraher. Tape recording. Houston, TX, January 28, 1996.

———. Telephone interview by author. Tape recording. July 17, 1996.

Lightfoot, Jerry. Telephone interview by author. Tape recording. October 26, 1999.

Lynn, Trudy. Interview by author and James Fraher. Tape recording. Chicago, IL, May 31, 1996.

———. Telephone interview by author. Tape recording. March 28, 2001.

Mayes, Pete. Interview by author and James Fraher. Tape recording. Houston, TX, January 26, 1996.

———. Telephone interview by author. Tape recording. July 6, 1997.

———. Interview by author. Tape recording. Houston, TX, August 6, 1998.

McFarland, Wilbur. Interview by author. Tape recording. Houston, TX, November 3, 1997.

Moody, Eugene. Interview by author. Tape recording. Houston, TX, February 5, 1998.

Morris, Leo. Interview by author and James Fraher. Tape recording. Houston, TX, May 21, 1998.

Moseley, Mickie. Interviews by author. Tape recording. Houston, TX, January 27, 1996; August 6, 1996.

Murphy, Robert. Interview by author and James Fraher. Tape recording. Houston, TX, October 3, 1997.

Murray, Pearl. Telephone interview by author. Tape recording. February 17, 1998.

Nelson, Jimmy. Interview by author and James Fraher. Tape recording. Houston, TX, November 10, 1995.

———. Onstage interview by author. Video recording. Fine Arts Center, Central College, HCCS, Houston, TX, November 26, 1996.

———. Interviews by author. Tape recording. Houston, TX, June 26, 1999; June 4, 2000.

———. Telephone interviews by author. Tape recording. August 6, 1999; January 13, 2000.

O'Bear, Oscar. Interview by author. Tape recording. Houston, TX, December 27, 1997.

———. Telephone interview by author. Tape recording. October 10, 1998.

O'Brien, Derek. Telephone interview by author. Tape recording. August 18, 1998.

Overstreet, Nathaniel. Interview by author and James Fraher. Tape recording. Houston, TX, March 9, 1996.

———. Interview by author and Alan Ainsworth. Tape recording. Houston, TX, October 11, 1996.

Owens, Calvin. Interviews by author. Tape recording. Houston, TX, March 11, 1997; March 13, 1997; March 15, 1997; September 18, 1997; December 11, 1997; December 21, 1998; January 3, 2000; June 4, 2000.

———. Interview by author and James Fraher. Tape recording. Houston, TX, April 18, 1997.

———. Telephone interview by author. Tape recording. February 4, 1998.

Perry, Oscar. Interview by author and James Fraher. Tape recording. Houston, TX, January 27, 1996.

———. Telephone interview by author. Tape recording. July 7, 1997.

———. Interview by Alan Ainsworth. Tape recording; transcribed by author. Houston, TX, March 17, 1998.

Prejean, Johnny. Interview by author. Tape recording. Anahuac, TX, July 4, 1997.

———. Telephone interview by author. Tape recording. July 9, 1997.

Price, Walter. Interview by author and James Fraher. Tape recording. Houston, TX, November 11, 1995.

———. Interviews by author. Tape recording. Houston, TX, December 21, 1995; April 13, 1996.

———. Onstage interview by author. Video recording. Fine Arts Center, Central College, HCCS, Houston, TX, February 29, 1996.

———. Telephone interviews by author. Tape recording. December 17, 1995; November 3, 1996; July 9, 1997; May 9, 1999.

Querfurth, Carl. Telephone interview by author. Tape recording. June 28, 1999.

Reynolds, Teddy. Interview by author and James Fraher. Tape recording. Houston, TX, November 9, 1995.

———. Interviews by author. Tape recording. Houston, TX, July 1, 1996; May 16, 1997; May 22, 1997; July 8, 1997; July 10, 1997; December 6, 1997; December 12, 1997.

Robertson, Sherman. Interview by author and James Fraher. Tape recording. Houston, TX, April 17, 1997.

———. Interviews by author. Tape recording. Houston, TX, August 22, 1997; June 10, 1998; January 19, 2000.

———. Telephone interview by author. Tape recording. September 21, 1998.

Robinson, Faye. Interview by author and James Fraher. Tape recording. Houston, TX, September 26, 1996.

Savoy, Ashton. Interview by author. Tape recording. Houston, TX, November 11, 1995.

———. Telephone interview by author. Tape recording. January 14, 1998.

Semien, Ivory Lee. Interview by author. Tape recording. Houston, TX, September 26, 1996.

Simmons, Hamp. Interview by author and James Fraher. Tape recording. Houston, TX, January 8, 1998.

Singleton, Rena. Interview by author. Tape recording. Houston, TX, December 7, 1999.

Smith, Robert. Interview by author and James Fraher. Tape recording. Houston, TX, January 28, 1996.

———. Interview by author and Edwin Gallaher. Tape recording. Houston, TX, October 10, 1996.

———. Interview by author. Tape recording. Houston, TX, November 6, 1997.

Strachwitz, Chris. Interviews by author. Tape recording. Jonesboro, AR, April 16, 1998; April 17, 1998.

Thomas, Richie Dell. Interview by author and James Fraher. Tape recording. Houston, TX, April, 19, 1997.

———. Interview by author. Tape recording. Houston, TX, September 3, 1997.

Turner, Martha. Interviews by author. Tape recording. Houston, TX, January 27, 1996; June 26, 1996; September 15, 1996.

Tyson, Leonard. Interviews by author. Tape recording. Houston, TX, September 12, 1997; September 17, 1997.

Walker, Phillip. Interview by author. Tape recording. Houston, TX, June 4, 2000.

Washington, Marion "Little Joe." Interview by author. Tape recording. Houston, TX, September 12, 1997.

———. Interview by author and Alan Ainsworth. Tape recording. Houston, TX, September 17, 1997.

Webster, Katie. Interview by author and James Fraher. Tape recording. League City, TX, October 4, 1997.

White, Lavelle. Interview by author and James Fraher. Tape recording. Houston, TX, March 9, 1996.

Williams, Andy. Telephone interview by author. Tape recording. February 15, 1998.

Abair, Kinney. *The Row House Sessions*. ttweak / Project Row Houses, 2001. Recorded live, direct to two-track, over two nights in 1996 in a Third Ward shotgun shack.

Bland, Bobby. *Greatest Hits, Vol. 1—The Duke Recordings*. MCA (MCAD-11783), 1998. The vocalist at his best (ca. late 1950s–1960s), backed by Houston players such as Pluma Davis, L. A. Hill, Teddy Reynolds, Joe Scott, Hamp Simmons, et al.

———. *Two Steps from the Blues*. MCA (MCAD-27036). Perhaps the single greatest LP issued by Duke-Peacock, title song written by Texas Johnny Brown.

Bolden, James. *The Legend, Vol. 3*. Global International, 2001. The third self-produced CD by this obscure but valid Houston blues guitarist and singer.

Bonner, Juke Boy. *Life Gave Me a Dirty Deal*. Arhoolie (CD 375), 1992. Includes "Houston, the Action Town" and "Struggle Here in Houston," among other gems.

Brown, Gatemouth. *The Original Peacock Recordings*. Rounder (CD 2034), 1990. Twelve historic tracks, including the classic Texas swing of "Okie Dokie Stomp."

Brown, Texas Johnny. *Blues Defender*. Choctaw Creek (CCR 10002), 2001. Proof from the veteran guitarist that Houston blues lives on in the new millennium.

———. *Nothin' but the Truth*. Choctaw Creek (CCR00012), 1997. Includes the last session work by keyboardist Teddy Reynolds. Handy Award nominee.

Cobb, Arnett. *Arnett Blows for 1300*. Delmark (DD-471), 1994. Recorded in New York City in 1947, this disc highlights the intelligent jazz and soulful blues of one of Houston's greatest tenor saxophonists and bandleaders; highlights include vocals by Cobb's mentor Milt Larkin on "Big League Blues" and "Flower Garden Blues."

———. *Texas Sax*. AIM (1302 CD), 1999. Recorded in Houston (1971), includes guitarist Clarence Hollimon.

Collins, Albert. *Deluxe Edition*. Alligator (ALCD 5601), 1997. Thirteen tracks capturing Third Ward's Iceman at his mature best, including reinterpretations of the Duke Records hit "Blue Monday" and the lively "Get to Gettin'" by his former bossman Big Walter Price.

Copeland, Johnny. *Catch Up with the Blues*. Verve (314 521 239-2), 1993. Mostly original songs, with guest spots by Houston's Joe Hughes and "Sonny Boy" Terry Jerome.

———. *Texas Twister*. Rounder (CD 11504), 1986. A compilation from Copeland's first four Rounder albums; includes the song "Houston," as well as tracks inspired by Copeland's 1982 tour of Africa.

Edwards, Gloria. *The Soul Queen of Texas*. Edsel (EDCD 611), 1999. Recorded in Houston by Huey Meaux (ca. 1960s).

Fran, Carol, and Clarence Hollimon. *See There!* Black Top (BT-1100), 1994.

———. *Soul Sensation*. Black Top (BT-1071), 1992. Debut album for Houston's most talented husband-wife duo.

Gaines, Grady. *Full Gain*. Black Top (BT-1041), 1988. The saxophonist-bandleader features Bayou City stalwarts Clarence Hollimon, Joe Medwick, Teddy Reynolds, Big Robert Smith, et al. and reunites with brother Roy Gaines.

———. *Horn of Plenty*. Black Top (BT-1084), 1992. Features Carol Fran, Clarence Hollimon, Teddy Reynolds, Paul David Roberts, Big Robert Smith, et al.

Gaines, Roy. *Bluesman for Life*. JSP (JSPCD 2110), 1998. A fiery set of Texas-style guitar playing.

———. *I Got the T-Bone Walker Blues*. Groove Note (GRV 2002-2), 1998. A tribute to T-Bone, the primary inspiration for most guitarists of Gaines' generation.

Green, Clarence. *Green's Blues*. Collectables (COL-CD-5229), 1991. Now removed from sale as a result of the lawsuit against Roy Ames and Collectables, this disc compiles fourteen tracks recorded in Houston (between 1958 and 1965) with Green's group The Rhythmaires, featuring backing from Wilbur McFarland, et al.

———. *Guitar Crying the Blues*. Double Trouble (DTCD 3022), 1990. Includes eleven tracks recorded in Houston (in 1987) with Henry Hayes, Teddy Reynolds, et al., as well as five vintage tracks (ca. late 1950s–early 1960s) with backing from Ivory Lee Semien, Ben Turner, Hop Wilson, et al.

Harris, Peppermint. *Penthouse in the Ghetto*. M.I.L. Multimedia (MIL 3033), 1997. A collection of various tracks recorded in Houston (1958, 1960, 1974–1975), including support from Clarence Green, Clarence Hollimon, Teddy Reynolds, et al.

Hopkins, Lightnin'. *The Complete Aladdin Recordings*. EMI (CDP-7-96843-2), 1991. Two-disc set compiles Lightnin's first recordings: thirteen tracks recorded in Los Angeles (1946–1947) and thirty recorded in Houston (1947–1948).

———. *The Gold Star Sessions, Vol. 1*. Arhoolie (CD 330), 1990. All twenty-four tracks were originally recorded by Bill Quinn at Houston's Gold Star studios (1947–1950).

———. *Lightnin' Hopkins: The Complete Prestige/Bluesville Recordings*. Fantasy (7PCD-4406-2), 1991. Seven-disc set covering 1960–1964, including a previously unreleased live concert and an interview by Samuel Charters.

Hughes, Joe. *Down and Depressed: Dangerous*. Munich (NETCD 0044), 1993. Recorded with his Houston road band in a Dutch studio during a European tour; includes the Third Ward–inspired instrumental jam "Dowling and Holman."

———. *Stuff Like That*. Blues Express (BEI-0002-1), 2000. Recorded before a live studio audience in San Francisco, capturing the essence of a Joe Hughes show.

———. *Texas Guitar Slinger*. Bullseye Blues (BB 9568), 1996. A showcase of original tunes, including a witty autobiographical narrative surveying the history of the contemporary Houston blues guitar sound (title track).

Johnson, Conrad, and His Orchestra. *Got What It Takes!* (No label), 2001. A fine document of Johnson's signature "Big Blue Sound," including jazz-blues standards featuring vocalists Carolyn Blanchard, Liz Grey, et al.

Lightfoot, Jerry, and The Essentials. *Burning Desire*. Connor Ray, 1995. Includes keyboards by Robert Lewis "Pee Wee" Stephens, plus guest spots by Grady Gaines, Joe Hughes, Trudy Lynn, and Eugene Moody, and perhaps the last track ever to be recorded by Big Walter "The Thunderbird" Price ("The Preacher Talks and Plays the Blues").

Lipscomb, Mance. *Texas Songster*. Arhoolie (CD 306), 1989. Recorded by Chris Strachwitz (including those initial field recordings made in 1960 in nearby Washington County), these twenty-two tracks document the diverse song styles performed by the most significant rural African American guitar-picker of the region.

———. *You Got to Reap What You Sow: Texas Songster, Vol. 2*. Arhoolie (CD 398), 1993.

Lynn, Trudy. *Twenty-four Hour Woman*. Ichiban (ICH 1172-2), 1994. Good sample of the Fifth Ward native's knack for interpreting soulful ballads and funky shuffles.

———. *U Don't Know What Time It Is*. Ruf (51416 1457 2), 1999. Effective mix of originals and inventive covers.

Mayes, Pete. *For Pete's Sake*. Antone's (10040), 1998. Comprises four tracks recorded in Houston (with his Texas Houserockers band: Bert Lewis, Eugene Murray, Johnny Prejean, et al.) and eight recorded in Austin (with Derek O'Brien et al.). Handy Award nominee.

Milburn, Amos. *The Best of Amos Milburn: Down the Road Apiece*. EMI (7243 8 27229 2), 1993. Early material, recorded mainly in California (1946–1957), by Houston-born pianist and his band the Chicken-Shackers, including guitarist Texas Johnny Brown.

Nelson, Jimmy "T-99." *Rockin' and Shoutin' the Blues*. Bullseye Blues and Jazz (BB 9593), 1999. Comeback recording by the swinging octogenarian vocalist, with Clarence Hollimon on guitar. Handy Award nominee.

———. *Take Your Pick*. Nettie Marie (001), 2002. With Duke Robillard on guitar.

Owens, Calvin. *The Best of Calvin Owens*. Sawdust Alley (SAZ 4232), 2001. The Calvin Owens Blues Orchestra in all its glory; includes guest appearances by Johnny Copeland, B.B. King, Trudy Lynn, David "Fathead" Newman, Norma Zenteno, et al.—compiled from five previous Sawdust Alley CDs by Owens.

Parker, Junior. *Junior's Blues: The Duke Recordings, Vol. 1*. MCA (MCAD-10669), 1992. Eighteen Duke singles (recorded 1954–1964), with backing from Houston players such as Pluma Davis, Joe Scott, Hamp Simmons, et al.

Perry, Oscar. *Brand New Man*. TSOT (5005-2), 1995. Smooth blues from a Duke-Peacock protégé of Joe Scott.

———. *Lonesome Train: The Best of Oscar Perry, Vol. 1*. Edsel (EDCD 614), 1999. Soulful vocalizing on R & B ballads and funky blues (originals and covers); recorded in Houston by Huey Meaux, mid-1970s.

Price, Big Walter. *Git to Gittin'*. Edsel (DIAB 8018), 1999. Includes classic title track, plus "If the Blues Was Money" (co-written with Peppermint Harris) and more.

———. *Vintage Thunderbird*. Collectables (COL-CD-5505), 1994. Now removed from sale as a result of the lawsuit against Roy Ames and Collectables, this disc incorporates three early tracks recorded for the TNT label in San Antonio, as well as additional material produced in Houston (including two songs with Albert Collins on guitar).

Robertson, Sherman. *Going Back Home*. AudioQuest Music (AQ-CD 1050), 1998. Eleven tracks with seven Robertson originals, including autobiographical title song.

———. *Here and Now*. Atlantic (82888-2), 1995.

Semien, Ivory Lee ("King Ivory"). *The Bitch Done Quit Me*. Collectables (COL-5562), 1995. Mid-1990s Houston recording featuring Semien on vocals, piano, and drums, with support from La La Wilson, Shedrick Cormier, et al.

Thornton, Big Mama. *Hound Dog: The Peacock Recordings*. MCA (MCAD-10668), 1992. Eighteen tracks recorded in Houston or Los Angeles (1952–1957), several including the Bill Harvey Band with Roy Gaines on guitar.

Various Artists. *The Best of Duke-Peacock Blues*. MCA (MCAD-10667), 1992. Eighteen tracks, including cuts by Elmore Nixon (backed by Henry Hayes and His Rhythm Kings), plus original versions of "Blue Monday" (with backing from Calvin Owens, Clarence Hollimon, et al.) and "Texas Flood" (later made famous by Stevie Ray Vaughan).

———. *Duke-Peacock's Greatest Hits*. MCA (MCAD-10666), 1992. Sixteen tracks, including "I'm Gonna Play the Honky-Tonks" by Marie Adams, "Pack Fair and Square" by Big Walter Price, the first recording of "Hound Dog" by Big Mama Thornton, and more.

———. *Goin' Down to Louisiana: Goldband Records Blues Anthology*. ACE (CHD 821), 2001. Two-disc set compiled of materials recorded at Louisiana's Goldband Studios, with sixteen of the thirty tracks highlighting three Houston-based performers: Juke Boy Bonner, Ashton Savoy, and Hop Wilson.

———. *Gulf Coast Blues, Vol. 1*. Black Top (BT-1055), 1990. Ten tracks highlighting performances by Carol Fran and Clarence Hollimon, Grady Gaines, Joe Hughes, and Teddy Reynolds.

———. *Men Are Like Street Cars: Women Blues Singers 1928–1969*. MCA (MCAD2-11788), 1999. Two-disc set includes contributions by eight female singers with ties to Houston: Marie Adams, Mildred Jones, Lovey (i.e., Luvenia) Lewis, Esther Phillips, Victoria Spivey, Big Mama Thornton, Katie Webster, and Lavelle White.

———. *Texas Blues Party, Vol. 2*. Wolf (120.631), 1997. Includes four mid-1980s tracks by Pete Mayes (with Bert Lewis, Robert Murphy, Calvin Owens, Lala Wilson, et al.) and one by Joe Hughes (with Wilbur McFarland, Teddy Reynolds, et al.).

———. *Texas Music, Vol. 1: Postwar Blues Combos*. Rhino (R2 71781), 1994. Includes Goree Carter's seminal "Rock Awhile" (with Conrad Johnson, Lonnie Lyons, Nelson Mills Sr., et al.), plus early material by Charles Brown, Gatemouth Brown, Albert Collins (with Henry Hayes et al.), Johnny Copeland (with Johnny Prejean, Teddy Reynolds, et al.), Clarence Green, Amos Milburn (with Texas Johnny Brown et al.), Big Walter and His Thunderbirds (with Grady Gaines et al.), Lester Williams (with I. H. "Ike" Smalley et al.), Bobby Bland (with Pluma Davis, Teddy Reynolds, Hamp Simmons, et al.), Big Mama Thornton, and more.

Vinson, Eddie "Cleanhead." *Cleanhead Blues 1945–1947*. Blues Collection (159462), 1999. Highlights the instincts of the Fifth Ward–born saxophonist and singer for fusing blues with jazz and R&B stylings.

———. *Kidney Stew Is Fine*. Delmark (DD-631), 1993. Recorded in France (1968), with T-Bone Walker on guitar.

Webster, Katie. *Deluxe Edition*. Alligator (ALCD 5606), 1999. A retrospective of the Swamp Boogie Queen's best cuts from her years with the Alligator label.

White, Lavelle. *Miss Lavelle*. Antone's (ANT0031), 1994. A strong set (with Clarence Hollimon) of mostly original songs, including remakes of several classics from the Duke-Peacock era. Handy Award nominee.

Wilkerson, Don. *The Complete Blue Note Sessions*. Blue Note (7243 5 24555 2 2), 2001. On this two-disc set, compiled of material from the saxophonist's three Blue Note albums (1962–1963), the former student of Conrad Johnson mixes straight-ahead jazz with gritty blues; he evokes sonic memories of his early gigs at Third Ward's Eldorado Ballroom on "The Eldorado Shuffle."

Williams, Lester. *I Can't Lose with the Stuff I Use*. Specialty (SPCD-7037-2), 1993. Includes four singles for Specialty, plus seventeen previously unissued tracks, all recorded in Houston's ACA Studios (1952–1953).

Wilson, Hop. *Houston Ghetto Blues*. Bullseye Blues (BB 9538), 1988. Comprises eighteen tracks recorded in Houston in 1960–1961 (with Elmore Nixon, Ivory Lee Semien, et al.).

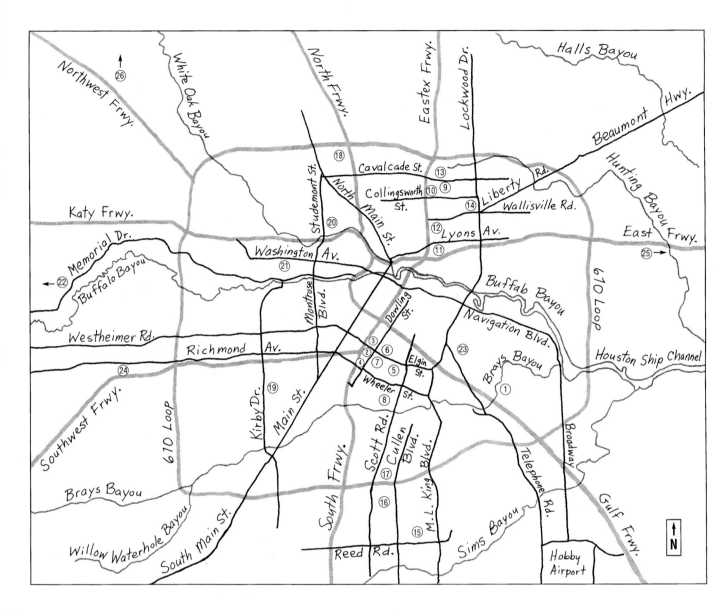

1. Forest Park Cemetery, grave site of Lightnin' Hopkins, 6900 Lawndale Ave. (Section 23, Lot 266, Space 11)
2. Eldorado Building, former home of Eldorado Ballroom, 2300 Elgin St. (Third Ward)
3. Emancipation Park, 3018 Dowling St. (Third Ward)
4. Miss Ann's Playpen, 3710 Dowling St. (Third Ward)
5. Site of the former Shady's Playhouse (original location, demolished), approx. 3339–3341 Simmons St. (Third Ward)
6. Site of the former Shady's Playhouse (second location), 3117 Ennis St. at Elgin St. (Third Ward)
7. El Nedo Cafe, 3401 Ennis St. (Third Ward)
8. Etta's Lounge, 5120 Scott Rd. (Third Ward)
9. The Silver Slipper, 3717 Crane St. (Frenchtown, Fifth Ward)
10. Site of the former Continental Lounge and Zydeco Ballroom, 3101 Collingsworth (Frenchtown, Fifth Ward)
11. Site of the former Club Matinee (demolished, now "Lyons Village"), 3300 Lyons Ave. (Fifth Ward)
12. Neighborhood formerly known as Sawdust Alley, near the intersection of Sumpter St. and Massie St. (Fifth Ward)
13. Mr. A's Club, 3409 Cavalcade St. (Fifth Ward)
14. Site of the former Bronze Peacock Dinner Club and headquarters of Duke-Peacock Records and Buffalo Booking Agency, 2809 Erastus St. (Fifth Ward)
15. Site of the former C. Davis Bar-B-Q, 4833 Reed Rd. (Sunnyside)
16. Ponderosa Club, 4650 Knoxville St. (Sunnyside)
17. Mr. Gino's Lounge, 7318 Cullen Blvd.
18. Dan Electro's Guitar Bar, 1031 E. 24th St. (The Heights)
19. The Big Easy Social and Pleasure Club, 5731 Kirby Dr.
20. Site of the former Reddi Room (original location), 2626 White Oak Dr. (The Heights)
21. Site of the former Reddi Room (second location), 5219 Washington Ave.
22. The Shakespeare Pub, 14129 Memorial Dr. (west, beyond map area)
23. Site of the former Local Charm (original location), 1501 Telephone Rd.
24. Site of the former Billy Blues Bar & Grill, 6025 Richmond Ave.
25. Double Bayou Dance Hall, south of Anahuac, TX (east, beyond map area)
26. Earl Gilliam's "doghouse," Tomball, TX (north, beyond map area)

Map created by Roger Wood, with design assistance by Connie Scanlon.

Bach, Jean, dir. *A Great Day in Harlem*. Castle Hill Productions, 1995. Film.

———. Personal letter to Roger Wood, July 10, 1998.

Beeth, Howard, and Cary D. Wintz, eds. *Black Dixie: Afro-Texan History and Culture in Houston*. College Station: Texas A&M UP, 1992.

Berman, David, dir. *The Strange Demise of Jim Crow: How Houston Desegregated Its Public Accommodations, 1959–1963*. Institute for the Medical Humanities, University of Texas Medical Branch, 1998. Film.

"Black History 24/7/365." Profile of Anna Dupree. *African-American News and Issues* 5, no. 35 (October 4–10, 2000): 1, 7.

Blank, Les, dir. *The Blues According to Lightnin' Hopkins*. Flower Films, 1968. Film.

———. "Obituaries: Lightnin' Hopkins, 1912–1982." *Living Blues* 53 (summer/autumn 1982): 15.

Brown, Clarence "Gatemouth." "Gatemouth Brown: Music That's Right for the World." Interview by Brett J. Bonner and David Nelson. *Living Blues* 107 (January/February 1993): 10–19.

———. "The Way Things Are: All About Me." *Tribe* 7 (April 1996): 38–44.

Bullard, Robert D. *Invisible Houston: The Black Experience in Boom and Bust*. College Station: Texas A&M UP, 1987.

Charters, Samuel. "Po' Lightnin': Some Thoughts about Lightnin' Hopkins." Liner notes. *Lightnin' Hopkins: The Complete Prestige/Bluesville Recordings*. Fantasy (7PCD-4406-2), 1991.

Copeland, Johnny. Interview by Kathleen Hudson and Peter Lee. *Living Blues* 83 (November/December 1988): 12–21.

Dance, Helen Oakley. *Stormy Monday: The T-Bone Walker Story*. Baton Rouge: Louisiana State UP, 1987.

Eagle, Bob. E-mail messages to Roger Wood, May 16, 2002.

Gart, Galen. Liner notes. *Duke-Peacock's Greatest Hits*. MCA (MCAD-10666), 1992.

Gart, Galen, and Roy C. Ames. *Duke/Peacock Records: An Illustrated History with Discography*. Milford, N.H.: Big Nickel Publications, 1990.

George, Nelson. *The Death of Rhythm and Blues*. New York: Plume, 1988.

Govenar, Alan. *The Early Years of Rhythm and Blues: Focus on Houston*. Houston: Rice UP, 1990.

———. *Meeting the Blues: The Rise of the Texas Sound*. Dallas: Taylor, 1988.

Harris, Sheldon. *Blues Who's Who*. New Rochelle, N.Y.: Arlington House, 1979.

Hollimon, Clarence. "You Can't Fire Me and I Ain't Quittin'." Interview, with Carol Fran, by Brett J. Bonner and Brooks Tyler-Bonner. *Living Blues* 116 (July/August 1994): 26–35.

Howard, Aaron. "Texas Rip-Off Revisited." *Blues Access* 30 (summer 1997): 54–57.

Hudson, Kathleen. *Telling Stories, Writing Songs: An Album of Texas Songwriters*. Austin: U of Texas P, 2001.

Humphrey, Mark. Liner notes. *The Complete Capitol/Black and White Recordings* by T-Bone Walker. Capitol Records (D-202856), 1995.

Johnson, Patricia C. "New Art, New Life: Two Community Projects Take Root, Bringing Promise, Style to Third Ward." *Houston Chronicle,* August 6, 2000, 10, 28.

King, B.B. "B.B. King." *Bravo Profiles*. Ian Potts, prod. BBC, 1990.

King, B.B., with David Ritz. *Blues All Around Me: The Autobiography of B.B. King*. New York: Morrow Publishing/Avon Books, 1996.

Kleiner, Diana J. "Fifth Ward, Houston" and "Frenchtown, TX." In *Handbook of Texas Online*. [Accessed February 12, 1999]. Available from Internet: <http://www.tsha.utexas.edu/handbook/online/articles/view/FF/hrfg.html>.

Kolanjian, Steve. Liner notes. *My Blue Heaven: The Best of Fats Domino*. EMI (CDP-7-92808-2), 1990.

Leadbitter, Mike, ed. *Nothing but the Blues*. London: Hanover Books, 1971.

Lichtenstein, Grace, and Laura Dankner. *Musical Gumbo: The Music of New Orleans*. New York: Norton, 1993.

Lightnin' Hopkins: Rare Performances, 1960–1979. Videocassette. Vestapol Productions (13022). Rounder, 1995.

Lomax, John Nova. "Racket." *Houston Press,* August 9–15, 2001, 83, 86.

Lynn, Trudy. "Houston's First Lady of Soul." Interview by Sebastian Danchin. *Living Blues* 131 (January/February 1997): 24–27.

Makeig, John. "Blues Stars Win Verdict from Jury." *Houston Chronicle,* March 8, 1997, sec. A, 33.

Mattieu, Jennifer. "Hitting the Highs and Lows with Little Joe Washington." *Houston Press,* March 22–28, 2001, 26–33.

McComb, David G. *Houston: A History.* Austin: U of Texas P, 1981.

McCormick, Mack. Liner notes. *Country Blues* by Lightnin' Hopkins. Original release on Tradition LP (TLP 1035), 1959. Reissued on CD by Rykodisc, 1996.

———. "Mance Lipscomb." Liner notes. *Texas Songster* by Mance Lipscomb. Original release on the Arhoolie LP 1001 and 1026, 1960. Reissued on CD by Arhoolie, 1989.

Minton, John. "Houston Creoles and Zydeco: The Emergence of an African-American Urban Popular Style." *American Music* 14, no. 4 (winter 1996): 480–526.

Mitchell, Rick. "Ardis Turner Sings Up a Bluesy Storm." *Houston Chronicle,* August 26, 1999, sec. G (*Preview* magazine), 5.

———. "Houston Jazz Legend Larkin Dies at 85." *Houston Chronicle,* August 31, 1996, sec. A, 33.

———. "Houston's Musical Soul." *Houston Chronicle,* June 17, 1990, Texas sec. (Sunday magazine), 6–8, 10–11, 17.

Morthland, John. Liner notes. *The Best of Duke-Peacock Blues.* MCA (MCAD-10667), 1992.

———. "True Blues." *Texas Monthly* (May 1994): 78, 80, 85.

Mowbray, Rebecca. "Signs of Change: The Fifth Ward Is Transforming Itself As New Homes and Businesses Rise." *Houston Chronicle,* May 30, 1999, sec. D, 1, 5.

Murray, Albert. *Stomping the Blues.* New York: Da Capo, 1976.

Nelson, David. "Editorial." *Living Blues* 131 (January/February 1997): 6.

Oliphant, Dave. *Texan Jazz.* Austin: U of Texas P, 1996.

Oliver, Paul. *Conversation with the Blues.* London: Cassell, 1965.

Palmer, Robert. *Deep Blues.* New York: Penguin, 1981.

———. "A Requiem for Hopkins, True Poet of the Blues." *New York Times,* February 17, 1982.

———. *Rock and Roll: An Unruly History.* New York: Harmony Books, 1995.

Racine, Marty. "'He Pulled Songs from the Air'/Houston Loses Rhythm and Blues Songwriter Joe Medwick at Age 59." *Houston Chronicle,* April 16, 1992, Houston sec., 3.

———. "Lightnin' Hopkins: His Music Set Him Free." *Houston Chronicle,* March 31, 2002, Texas sec., 8–13.

———. "What's Happening in the Fifth?" *Houston Chronicle,* September 21, 1997, Texas sec., 8–11, 13.

Reynolds, Teddy. "I Got Somethin' for Everybody." Interview by John Anthony Brisbin. *Living Blues* 138 (March/April 1998): 62–72.

Rust, Carol. "Continental Lounge Owner, Zydeco Promoter Dies after Stroke." *Houston Chronicle,* November 27, 1997, sec. D, 4.

Safire, William. "On Language." *Houston Chronicle,* November 23, 1997, sec. C, 6.

Salem, James M. *The Late Great Johnny Ace and the Transition from R&B to Rock 'n' Roll.* Urbana: U of Illinois P, 1999.

Saxon, Wolfgang. "Sam (Lightnin') Hopkins, 69: Blues Singer and Guitarist." *New York Times,* February 1, 1982.

"Service Set for Country Blues Singer Sam "Lightnin' Hopkins." *Houston Chronicle,* February 1, 1982, sec. 3, 8.

Shadwick, Keith. *The Encyclopedia of Jazz and Blues.* London: New Burlington Books/Quintet, 2001.

Shelton, Beth Ann, et al. *Houston: Growth and Decline in a Sunbelt Boomtown.* Philadelphia: Temple UP, 1989.

Sherman, Jim. "A Hard Case of the Blues." *Houston Press,* April 28, 1994, 6–13.

———. "Texas Rip-Off." *Blues Access* 20 (winter 1995): 10–20.

Smith, Harry. Original liner notes for *Anthology of American Folk Music,* Folkways Records, 1952. Reprinted by Smithsonian Folkways Recordings (FP 251, 252, 253), 1997.

Thomas, Lorenzo. "From Gumbo to Grammys: The Development of Zydeco Music in Houston." In *Juneteenth Texas: Essays in African-American Folklore,* ed. Francis E. Abernethy, Patrick B. Mullen, and Alan B. Govenar, 139–150. Denton: U of North Texas P, 1996.

Tisserand, Michael. *The Kingdom of Zydeco.* New York: Arcade, 1998.

———. "Zydeco Beat." *Living Blues* 131 (January/February 1997): 74–75.

Torry, Frank. "A Great Day in Houston." Radio commentary; transcribed by author. March 1998 (quoted by permission).

Turner, Allan. "History As Close As a Turntable: Music Enthusiast Made Lipscomb, Hopkins Famous and Preserved Black Heritage." *Houston Chronicle,* November 16, 1986, Lifestyle sec., 1.

Tutt, Bob. "Houston's Historic Wards Work to Reverse Fortunes." *Houston Chronicle,* August 4, 1996, sec. A, 37–38.

———. "Prosperity during War Helped Build Up Houston." *Houston Chronicle,* April 13, 1998, sec. A, 19.

Vaughn, Carol. "Preservation Hall: Project Row Houses Will Revive Houston's First Home of Black Music." *Houston Press,* December 16, 1999, 12–14.

Walker, T-Bone. Interview by Jim and Amy O'Neal. *Living Blues* 11 (winter 1972–1973): 20–26.

———. Interview by Jim and Amy O'Neal. *Living Blues* 12 (spring 1973): 24–27.

Welding, Pete. Liner notes. *The Complete Aladdin Recordings: Lightnin' Hopkins.* EMI Records USA (CDP-7-96843-2), 1991.

Wheat, John. "Lightnin' Hopkins: Blues Bard of the Third Ward." In *Juneteenth Texas: Essays in African-American Folklore,* ed. Francis E. Abernethy, Patrick B. Mullen, and Alan B. Govenar, 273–288. Denton: U of North Texas P, 1996.

Wiggins, William H. *O Freedom!: Afro-American Emancipation Celebrations.* Knoxville: U of Tennessee P, 1987.

Wood, Roger. "Behind the Scenes: Evelyn Johnson and the Crucial Link between Houston and Memphis in the Evolution of R&B." *Arkansas Review: A Journal of Delta Studies* 31, no. 3 (December 2000): 206–212.

———. "Big Walter: The Thunderbird Still Flies." Interview. *Living Blues* 131 (January/February 1997): 14–23.

———. "Clarence Hollimon." *Living Blues* 152 (July/August 2000): 114–117.

———. "Consummate Gentleman." *Houston Press,* September 17–23, 1998, 73.

———. "Doris McClendon." *Living Blues* 138 (March/April 1998): 78–79.

———. "Eugene Carrier." *Living Blues* 133 (May/June 1997): 38–39.

———. "Hamp W. Simmons, Jr." *Living Blues* 156 (March/April 2001): 100–101.

———. "Houston Highwayman." *Houston Press,* August 12–18, 1999, 73.

———. "Houston Honker." *Houston Press,* August 5–11, 1999, 85.

———. "Houston's Blues Teachers." *Living Blues* 140 (July/August 1998): 40–45.

———. "The Houston Scene: Ashton Savoy." *Living Blues* 131 (January/February 1997): 46.

———. "Houston Scene: Bobby Lewis." *Living Blues* 140 (July/August 1998): 56.

———. "Houston Scene: Caldwell the Tailor." *Living Blues* 140 (July/August 1998): 52–53.

———. "The Houston Scene: Carolyn Blanchard." *Living Blues* 131 (January/February 1997): 47.

———. "Houston Scene: Curley Cormier." *Living Blues* 140 (July/August 1998): 51.

———. "The Houston Scene: I. J. Gosey." *Living Blues* 131 (January/February 1997): 49.

———. "John Green." *Living Blues* 144 (March/April 1999): 75.

———. "Ladies in Blue." *Houston Press,* December 30, 1999–January 5, 2000, 89.

———. "Lady Legends of Houston Blues." Interviews with Iola Broussard, Jewel Brown, Gloria Edwards, Luvenia Lewis, Mickie Moseley, and Martha Turner. *Living Blues* 131 (January/February 1997): 28–38.

———. "Milton Larkin." *Living Blues* 131 (January/February 1997): 62.

———. "Monday, Monday." *Houston Press,* January 6–12, 2000, 69.

———. "Playbill: Jumping Genres." *Houston Press,* June 17–25, 1999, 95.

———. "Roy Gaines: Entertaining Like 'Bone and Gatemouth." Interview. *Living Blues* 148 (November/December 1999): 24–31.

———. "Sherman Robertson: The In-Between Blues." *Living Blues* 152 (July/August 2000): 21–31.

———. "Southeast Texas: Hot House of Zydeco." *The Journal of Texas Music History* 1, no. 2 (fall 2001): 23–44.

———. "A Tribute to Johnny Clyde Copeland." Interviews with Clarence Hollimon, Joe Hughes, Oscar Perry, Johnny Prejean, Walter Price, and Teddy Reynolds, compiled with additional materials by Brett Bonner. *Living Blues* 135 (September/October 1997): 50–53.

———. "True Blue Texas Trumpet." Interview with Calvin Owens. *Living Blues* 140 (July/August 1998): 30–39.

INDEX

Numbers in italics refer to photographs.

Chavis, Wilson "Boozoo," 139, 149

Chenier, Clifton: at Alfred's Place, 140, 143; and Lightnin' Hopkins, 14, 16, 47; mentioned, 80, 139, 279; and other Houston musicians, 149–150, 152, 154–155, 173, 305; and popularization of zydeco, 48, 143

Chess Records, 47

Chevis, Wilfred, *132,* 139, 140, 143, 147

Chicago (Illinois): as blues center, 10, 28, 42, 47, 139, 280, 305, 308; and James Fraher, 289, 293, 298; and Texas musicians, 33, 34, 35, 100, 212, 215, 218

Choates, Harry, 46

Christian, Charlie, 35

Cinder Club, 237

City Auditorium (Houston), 39

Civil War, 73

Clapton, Eric, 201, 207

Clay, Otis, 170

Clemons, Rev. Harvey, 158

Club Ebony, 29, 43, 86, 129, 237

Club Hey Hey, 258

Club Hole in the Wall, 269

Club Matinee: desegregation of, 29; as popular venue, 31, 80, 86, 138, 158–161, 166, 183, 184, 203; talent shows at, 159–160, 161, 164, 174, 188

Club 90 (Ames, Texas), 37

Club Paradise (Memphis), 203

Club Raven (Beaumont, Texas), 40

Cobb, Arnett: as jazz-blues dualist, 28, 43, 71, 301; mentioned, 261; and Milt Larkin, 82; and other Houston musicians, 167, 169, 217, 237, 239; sound of, 113, 114

Cobb, Lizette, 261

Code Blue Records, 155

Cole, Nat "King," 198

Collectables Records, 129, 260, 261

Collins, Albert: early recordings of, 30, 101–102, 177, 179, 215–216; mentioned, 24, 42, 55, 71, 109, 275, 279, 298, 299, 303; and other Houston musicians, 102, 104, 107, 177, 179, 218, 260, 284, 308; photos of, *103, 302;* profile of, 100–102; and Shady's Playhouse, 59, 62, 87, 92, 93, 95, 100

Collins, Roger: mentioned, 139, 140, 261, 303; photos of, *271, 302;* at reunion, 296; and Shakespeare Pub, 269

Columbia Records, 27

Connie's Combo, 114

Continental Club (Houston), 104, 272

Continental Lounge and Zydeco Ballroom, 139–140

Cooke, Sam, 125

Copasetic Records, 82

Copeland, Johnny: on Joe Hughes, 106; mentioned, 71, 80, 260, 279, 298, 299, 303; and New York, 42–43, 107; and other Houston musicians, 53, 82, 155, 170, 175, 218, 268; photos of, *110, 302;* profile of, 106–107, 109; and Shady's Playhouse (original), 53, 59, 87, 92, 95, 96, 97, 101; and Shady's Playhouse (second), 97, 100

Cormier, Alfred, *135,* 140

Cormier, Curley: mentioned, 303; photos of, *135, 302;* profile of, 140, 143, 146; on Sherman Robertson, 153–154

Cormier, Shedrick, 280, *302,* 303

Cotton, James, 172

Coy, Carlos ("South Park Mexican"), 172

Cozy Corner (nightclub), 100

Cray, Robert, 107

Creoles, black: mentioned, 172, 183, 250, 280, 284; migration to Houston, 29, 47, 134, 139, 153, 166, 177, 188, 197, 260; and zydeco, 29, 47, 138–140, 143, 149–150, 152, 157

Crosstown Blues Band, 154

Crystal Hotel, 31, 80, 158, 159, 160

Cullum, Lola Anne, 21, 42, 270

Cultural Arts Council of Houston, 293

Dallas (Texas), 28, 33, 34, 111, 276

Dal Segno Records, 256

Danchin, Sebastian, 179

Dandridge, Dorothy, 162

Dan Electro's Guitar Bar, 256, 258

Dardar, Tommy, 258, 261

Davis, Clarence, 55, 234

Davis, James, 62

Davis, Larry, 53

Davis, Pluma, 80, 89, 160, 201, 212

Davis, Tyrone, 242

Davis, Wilma, 174

Delafose, John, 139

Delta region (*see* Mississippi Delta)

Deluxe Theater, 158

Fran, Carol: and Clarence Hollimon, 217; mentioned, 272, 285, 299, 303; photo of, *302*

Franklin, Aretha, 24

Frazier, Lee, 261

Freedom Records, 46, 104, 114

Freeman, V. S. "Sonny," 52

French Quarter (New Orleans), 167

Frenchtown: and Club Matinee, 159; concentration of Creoles in, 134, 138–139, 140, 166; as musicians' home, 152, 157, 177; and Silver Slipper, 134, 143, 146; and zydeco, 47, 48, 138–139, 140, 143, 146

Fulson, Lowell, 100, 256

Gaines, Grady: as bandleader, 167; on Club Matinee, 160–161; Duke-Peacock experience of, 201; and Etta's Lounge, 125–126; on Fifth Ward, 158–159; mentioned, 43, 80, 146, 267, 289, 303; photos of, *123, 145, 302, 311;* as recording artist, 43, 125, 285

Gaines, Roy: and Club Matinee, 164; on desegregation, 31, 164, 166; Duke-Peacock experience of, 201; and I. J. Gosey, 53; on Lightnin' Hopkins, 18; photo of, *32;* relocation to California of, 42; rural family roots of, 41; on T-Bone Walker, 39–40

Galveston (Texas), 33, 221, 261

Galveston Bay, 277

Garlow, Clarence "Bon Ton," 46, 48, 150

Gatlin, Vanessa, 177, 299, *302,* 303

George, Nelson, 194

Geto Boys (rap group), 158

Gillespie, Dizzy, 221

Gilliam, Earl: mentioned, 95, 260, 277, 299, 303; photos of, *283, 302;* profile of, 282, 284–285

Gladiators (musical group), 140, 143

Goldband Records, 150, 226

Gold Star Records, 46, 47, 114

Gordon, Roscoe, 100, 116, 195, 201

Gosey, I. J.: and C. Davis Bar-B-Q, 53, 55, 167, 233–234, 239, 242, 245, 247; Duke-Peacock experience of, 53, 212; mentioned, 146, 272, 289, 290, 303; photos of, *54, 186, 230, 235, 251, 302;* on Pressure Cookers, 63

gospel music: and Duke-Peacock empire, 189; and individual musicians, 173–175, 179, 221, 245, 258, 298; and secular music, 28, 29, 30, 292

Govenar, Alan, 82, 194, 195, 197

Grammy Awards, 169, 260

Grateful Dead, 147, 201

Gray, Jackie, *300, 301*

Great Day in Harlem, A (film), 288–289, 292, 313

Green, Buck, 139

Green, Cal, 42, 177, 256

Green, Clarence: Duke-Peacock experience of, 177, 201; mentioned, 80, 146, 152, 261, 298, 299, 303; and other Houston musicians, 161, 173, 175, 177, 179, 180, 183, 218, 239, 276, 289; photos of, *178, 303;* profile of, 177

Green, Jerry and Nina, 261

Green, John: on Bronze Peacock, 199–200; on Club Matinee, 159; on Don Robey, 190, 192, 195, (and songwriters) 209–211; on Eldorado Ballroom, 75–76, 79; on Gatemouth Brown, 192–193; mentioned, 293, 296, 297, 303; photos of, 77, *302, 311*

Greene, Teri, 256

Greenleaf, Diunna, 245, *246,* 313

Grey, Liz, 114

"Guitar Gable" (*see* Gabriel Perrodin)

"Guitar Slim" (the original), (*see* Eddie Jones)

Gulf Freeway, 10, 72

Guy, Larry, 313

Habitat for Humanity, 158

Halliburton, Joe: mentioned, 303; photos of, *26, 241, 302;* profile of, 239, 242

Hampton, Lionel, 43, 188

Handy Awards, 40, 43, 46, 179

Handy, W. C., 116, 172

Harlem Club (Opelousas, Louisiana), 150

Harlem Grill, 192

Harlem Music Makers, 159

"Harlem Slim" (*see* Gary Pisarelli)

Harley, Joe, 155

Harlon's Bayou Blues (restaurant), 272

Harris, Patrick, 125

Harris, Peppermint (b. Harrison Nelson), 42, 46, 154, 253

Harris, Stephen, 139, 140

Hart Hughes Orchestra, 49

Hartney Construction Company, 129

Harvey, Bill: and B. B. King, 52, 160, 169, 203; and Houston-Memphis connection, 52, 114, 116, 160, 203; and other Houston musicians, 88, 203, 212, 217

Hawaii Five-O (television program), 305

Hawthorne, Eugene, *302, 303*

Hayes, Henry: on Club Matinee, 159; on Don Robey, 215–216; mentioned, 298, 303; musical versatility of, 29; photos of, *91, 302;* as record producer, 29, 101–102, 215–216; on "Shady" Jackson, 88; and Shady's Playhouse, 90, 92–93, 95–96, 99

Henderson, Herbert, 106

Henry, Macy Lela, 46

Hershorn, Tad, 313

Hester, Steve, 53

Hiles, Buddy, 161

Hill, Joe, 143

Hill, Ken "Sugar," *302, 303*

Hill, L. A., 87, 107

Hill, Z. Z., 62

Hinton, Joe, 53, 100, 221

Hogan, Silas, 305

Hollimon, Clarence: on Duke-Peacock Records building, 184; mentioned, 153, 164, 201, 221, 223, 285, 299, 303; photos of, *186, 219, 302;* profile of, 216–218

Hollis, William (keyboardist), *302, 303*

Hollis, William "Candyman" (vocalist), 118, *294, 295, 302, 303*

Hollywood Records, 150

Home Cooking Records, 260–261

Hooker, John Lee, 167

Hopkins, Milton: on Lightnin' Hopkins, 13; mentioned, 118, 125, 129, 250, 303; photos of, *12, 270, 302, 311;* and Reddi Room, 265, 267

Hopkins, Sam "Lightnin'": and Blind Lemon Jefferson, 33–34; civic recognition of, 310; and Clifton Chenier, 47; country style of, x, 28, 89, 146, 298; death of, 5, 7, 67; description of filmed performance by, 3–4; at Double Bayou Dance Hall, 279, 282; early recordings of, 46, 49, 260; and Gatemouth Brown, 50; gravestone of (photo), *20;* and Mance Lipscomb, 48; mentioned, 80, 89, 275, 298, 299, 303; and other Houston musicians, 10, 13–14, 16, 18, 21, 92, 101, 117, 150, 260, 267, 275, 301, 305, 308; photos of, *2, 6, 302;* rural family roots of, 41; and T-Bone Walker, 39, 42; and Third Ward, 8, 71, 73, 85–86; and zydeco, 48, 143

Horton, Big Walter, 305

Houston Blues Society, 43, 177, 245, 258, 276, 293

Houston Chronicle, 5, 31, 72, 139, 158, 208

Houston College for Negroes, 113, 197

Houston Community College System, Central College, 7, 288–290, 292–293, 295, 298–299, 305, 313, 315, 316

Houston Police Department, 79, 189

Houston Press, 104, 258, 261

Howard, Aaron, 261

"Howlin' Wolf" (*see* Chester Burnett)

Hudson, Kathleen, 5, 106

Hughes, Joe "Guitar": on Caldwell Tailors, 82; on Eldorado Ballroom, 79, 88; and Johnny Copeland, 106–107; and Lightnin' Hopkins, 10, 13, 39; mentioned, 80, 146, 201, 261, 269, 275, 280; and other Houston musicians, 167, 175, 268, 284; photos of, *11, 51, 98;* as recording artist, 30, 102, 285; at reunion, 301, 313; and "Shady" Jackson, 88, 92; and Shady's Playhouse (original), 53, 59, 87, 88, 95, 99, 100, 101; and Shady's Playhouse (second), 60, 97, 99, 102; on T-Bone Walker, 39, 40, 50; on Teddy Reynolds, 129–130; on Third Ward, 72

Hughes, Willie Mae, 102, 301

Hunter, Long John, 104

Hurston, Zora Neale, 290

Ichiban Records, 179

Ivie's Chicken Shack (nightclub), 162

Ivory Records, 46, 253, 260

J. Geils Band, 201, 226

Jackson, Ertell, 296

Jackson, Rayfield (Houston's "Guitar Slim"): at Billy Blues, 275–276; on Lightnin' Hopkins, 16, 18; mentioned, 100, 218, 261, 303; photos of, *17, 302*

Jackson, Vernon "Shady," 87, 95, 96, 99

Jacquet, Illinois, 82, 158

James, Etta, 76

James, Joe: mentioned, 267, 303; photos of, *148, 302;* profile of, 147, 149

James, Sonny, *302, 303*

jazz: and blues, 86, 90, 92, 111, 113–114, 169, 172, 218, 237, 239, 242; at Bronze Peacock, 188; at Eldorado Ballroom, 75, 79, 86, 301; and gospel, 221; mentioned,

Little Red Rooster (nightclub), 173
"Little Richard" (*see* Richard Penniman)
Living Blues magazine, ix, 34, 41, 139, 217, 275, 289, 301, 313
Lobby Bar (Mexico), 104
Local Charm (nightclub), 267–268
Lomax, John A., 33
Lomax, John Nova, 47
London, Floyd, 146, 152
Long Beach Blues Festival, 256
Los Angeles (California), 21; Hollywood, 35, 42, 212, 296, 305
Lunch Box Diner, 80
Lynn, Barbara, 100, 279
Lynn, Trudy (b. Lee Audrey Nelms): mentioned, 172, 173, 218, 239, 285, 299; photos of, *181, 273*; profile of, 177, 179–180
Lyons, Lonnie, 46, 95
Lyons Avenue: as business center, 157–159, 166; mentioned, 31, 80, 160, 164, 173, 187, 188, 199, 260
Lyons Unity Missionary Baptist Church, 174

Mac & Company (musical group), 239, 242
Macy's Records, 46, 48
Magnolia Bar & Grill, 272
Main Street (Houston), 72
Malaco Records, 62
Mallet Playboys (zydeco group), 155
Malone, Deadric (*see* Don Robey)
Mary Allen Baptist Seminary, 175
Mattieu, Jennifer, 104
Mattis, David, 195, 200–201
Mayes, Pete: as bandleader, 167, 277, 279; and Double Bayou Dance Hall, 277, 279–280, 282; mentioned, 80, 172, 201, 261, 269, 303, 313; photos of, *38, 278, 302, 311*; as recording artist, 40, 280, 285; rural family roots of, 41; on T-Bone Walker, 35, 37, 39, 40
Mayes, Willard, 40
Mayfield, Percy, 42, 279
MCA Records, 169, 207
McBooker, Connie, 52
McClendon, Carolyn Rose, 140
McClendon, Doris, 139–140, *141*

McCool, Brad, 245
McCormick, Mack, 14, 48, 85, 117
McDaniel's Lounge, 10
McFarland, Wilbur: on Houston musicians, 308; mentioned, 303; photos of, *240, 302*; profile of, 239, 242
McIntyre, Donna "Lady D": mentioned, 180, 299, 303; photos of, *302, 314*; at reunion, 315
McLendon, Tom, 258, 260
Meaux, Huey, 173
Medwick, Joe: mentioned, 53, 87, 92, 95, 147, 201; and songwriter's credit controversy, 206–210
Meloncon, Thomas, 172
Melville, Herman, 92
Memorial Hospital (Houston), 197–198
Memphis (Tennessee): mentioned, 28, 114, 129, 245, 276, 299; musical connection to Houston, 52, 116, 195, 200–201, 203–204
Mercury Records, 93, 107
Merritt, Morris, 192
Mesner brothers (Aladdin Records), 49
Mesner, Eddie, 198
Midtown Arts Center, 298
Miggins, Rory, 267, 268
Milburn, Amos: and Aladdin Records, 49, 198, 305; mentioned, 42, 113, 161, 169, 247, 279, 308; and Texas Johnny Brown, 21, 305
Miller, J. D., 150
Miller Outdoor Theater, 85, 154, 190, 203
Mills, Nelson, III, *302, 303*
Minton, John, 139
Miss Ann's Playpen (nightclub): Blue Monday jam sessions at, 23–24, 27, 55–56, 64, 67, 118; mentioned, 75, 104, 285, 299; photos of (exterior), *66*, (interior), *69*
Mississippi Delta region: black immigration from, 28; blues sounds from, 201, 280, 305; as home of musicians, 194, 195, 204, 308; and music history, 47
Mitchell, Andrew "Sunbeam," 116, 203
Mitchell, Frank, 116
Mitchell Hotel (Memphis), 203
Mitchell, Lonnie, 139, 260
Mitchell, Rick, 85, 208
Modern Records, 43, 93, 126
Moody, Eugene: at El Nedo, 122, 125; mentioned, 180, 303; photos of, *70, 121, 302*

Moore, Willie "Mo'e," *297,* 298, *302,* 303

Morris, Leo: mentioned, 260, 313; photo of, *254;* profile of, *250, 253, 255*

Moseley, Mickie: at ladies' reunion, 289, 290, 292; mentioned, 114, 299, 303; photos of, *225, 273, 291, 302, 311;* profile of, 221, 223, 226

Motown Records, 28, 117

Mowbray, Rebecca, 158

Mr. A's (nightclub), 180

Mr. Gino's (nightclub), 52, 55, 67, 250, 285

Murphy, Matt "Guitar," 167

Murphy, Robert "Skin Man": on Lightnin' Hopkins, 14, 16; mentioned, 298, 303, 305; photos of, *15, 302;* on T-Bone Walker, 35

Murray, Albert, 86

Murray, Eugene "Sparetime," 269, 280, *302,* 303

Murray, Pearl: mentioned, 260, 299, 303; photos of, *274, 302;* profile of, 275

Musicians Benevolent Society of Houston, 264, 293, 313

Muth, Ed, 117

Myrl Records, 226

NASA, 4, 269, 308

Nashville (Tennessee), 201, 212

Nelson, David, ix, 289

Nelson, Jimmy "T-99": mentioned, 80, 82, 118, 261, 275, 280, 285, 289, 303; photos of, *45, 127, 302, 311;* profile of, 43, 46, 126, 129

Newborn, Phineas, Sr., 114, 116

Newman, David "Fathead," 170

Newman, Melvin, *22,* 313

New Orleans (Louisiana): and Big Easy (nightclub), 258; and Blue Monday, 58–59; in contrast to Houston, 58–59, 276; mentioned, 28, 111, 138, 167, 190, 205

Newsome, Frank, 96, 107, 109

Nickerson, Debra, 261

Nixon, Elmore: mentioned, 111, 279; as recording artist, 30, 195; and Shady's Playhouse, 87, 93

Nola's (nightclub), 27, 60

North Texas State University, 167

Nuri, Nuri A., 126

O'Bear, Oscar: mentioned, 126, 146, 250, 253, 280, 303; photos of, *65, 302;* on Pressure Cookers, 64

O'Brien, Derek, 40

Old Quarter (nightclub), 48

Ollison, Vern, 239, *302,* 303

O'Neal, Jim and Amy, 34

Oswald, Lee Harvey, 111

Outpost Tavern, 269

Overstreet, Nathaniel "Pops," 301, *302,* 303, *304,* 305

Owens, Calvin: and B. B. King, 52–53, 160, 167; on Don Robey, 211, 216, 227, 229; Duke-Peacock experience of, 201, 203, 218; on Eldorado Ballroom, 75; on Fifth Ward venues, 160, 183–184; on Houston-Memphis connection, 203–204; as jazz-blues dualist, 169, 172; mentioned, 80, 118, 280, 303; and other Houston musicians, 161, 173, 217–218; photos of, *83, 171, 302, 311;* as recording artist, 169, 170, 172, 285; and Sawdust Alley, 169–170, 172–173; on Shady's Playhouse, 90, 92

Owens, Donald, 296, *302,* 303

Palmer, Robert, 4, 46–47

Paradise Records, 107

Paramount Records, 33

Parker, Charlie, 90, 106

Parker, Clarence, 261

Parker, Junior: Duke recordings of, 28, 52, 53, 116, 195, 308; and Houston musicians, 88, 152, 169, 174, 217, 221; mentioned, 80, 153, 201, 308

Pat & Pete's Bonton Room (nightclub), 258

Peacock Records: creation of, 49–50, 157, 188, 190, 193, 198–200; early hit, 88; and Houston musicians, 125, 150, 195, 221, 226–227, 229; success of, 200, 207

Pearl's Cotton Club, 275

Pearl's Place (nightclub), 275

Penn State University, 177

Penniman, Richard ("Little Richard"), 125

Peoples, Travis, 293

Perrodin, Gabriel ("Guitar Gable"), 150

Perry, Oscar: on Johnny Copeland, 109; mentioned, 201, 216, 260, 269, 303; photos of, *214, 302, 311;* profile of, 211, 215

Perry-Tone Records, 215

roger wood has previously written about music in books such as *The Roots of Texas Music* (Texas A&M University Press, forthcoming in 2003) and *The Da Capo Jazz and Blues Lover's Guide to the U.S.* (3rd ed.; Da Capo, 2001), as well as in various periodicals, including *Living Blues, The Journal of Texas Music History* (where he now serves on the Submissions Review Board), *Arkansas Review,* and *Houston Press.* Since 1981, Wood has taught writing and literature at Central College (Houston Community College System) in the city's historic Third Ward. A native of Louisiana, he is a Ph.D. graduate of the University of Houston.

james fraher is a professional photographer who has spent more than fifteen years chronicling the lives of blues musicians through images and interviews. Fraher's photographs have been exhibited in museums and galleries in the United States and Europe; they have also been featured on the covers of *Living Blues* magazine (as well as numerous recordings) and in the *Chicago Tribune, Guitar Player,* and *Downbeat.* He is the author of *The Blues Is a Feeling: Voices and Visions of African-American Blues Musicians* (Face to Face Books, 1998). In 1996, he received the "Keeping the Blues Alive Award" from the Blues Foundation in Memphis.